ART BOOKS

FROM CRESCENT MOON PUBLISHING


*Leonardo da Vinci*
by James Pearson

*Early Netherlandish Painting*
by Rosalind Mutter

*Piero della Francesca*
by Naomi Haskell

*Fra Angelico: Art and Religion in the Renaissance*
by Rosalind Mutter

*Eric Gill: Nuptials of God*
by Anthony Hoyland

*Minimal Art and Artists in the 1960s and After*
by Laura Garrard

*Postwar Art*
by George Knighton

*Vincent van Gogh: Visionary Landscapes*
by Stuart Morris

*Max Beckmann*
by Stuart Morris

*Egon Schiele: Sex and Death in Purple Stockings*
by D. Simon Eade

*Mark Rothko: The Art of Transcendence*
by Julia Davis

*Jasper Johns*
by L.M. Poole

*Brice Marden*
by Laura Garrard

*Frank Stella*
by James Pearson

*The Light Eternal: J.M.W. Turner*
by Jeremy Mark Robinson

# PIERO DELLA FRANCESCA

# PIERO DELLA FRANCESCA

Naomi Haskell

CRESCENT MOON

CRESCENT MOON PUBLISHING
P.O. Box 1312, Maidstone
Kent, ME14 5XU
Great Britain
www.crmoon.com

First published 1994. Second edition 2008. Reprinted with additions 2014
and 2016. © Naomi Haskell 2008, 2014.

Printed and bound in the U.S.A.
Set in Garamond Book 10 on 14pt.
Designed by Radiance Graphics.

The right of Naomi Haskell to be identified as the author of this book has
been asserted generally in accordance with sections 77 and 78 of the
Copyright, Designs and Patents Act 1988.

British Library Cataloguing in Publication data

*Haskell, Naomi*
*Piero della Francesca*
*I. Title*
*759.5*

*ISBN-13 9781861715548*

# Contents

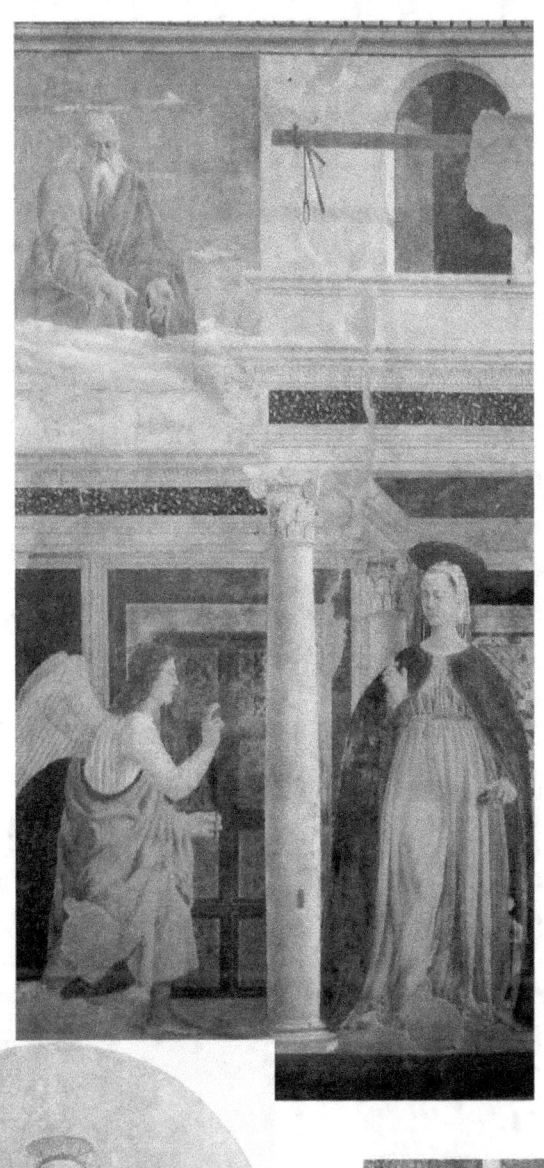

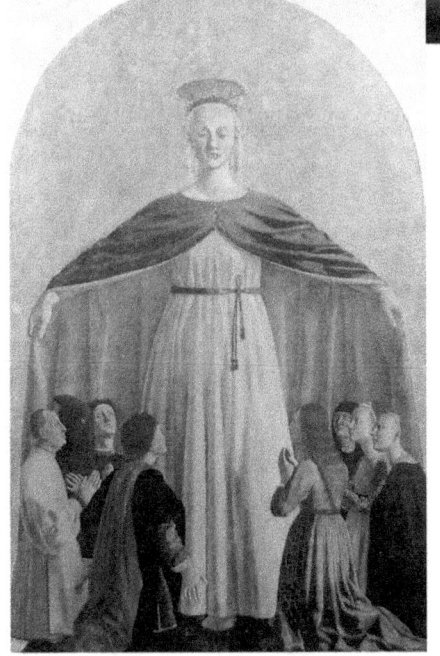

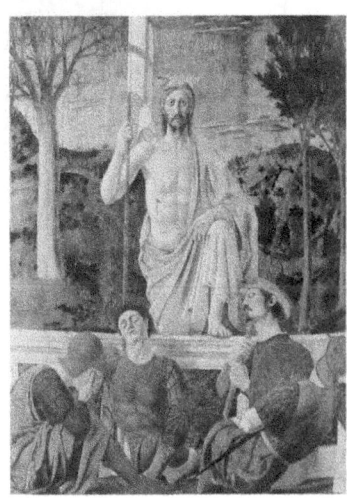

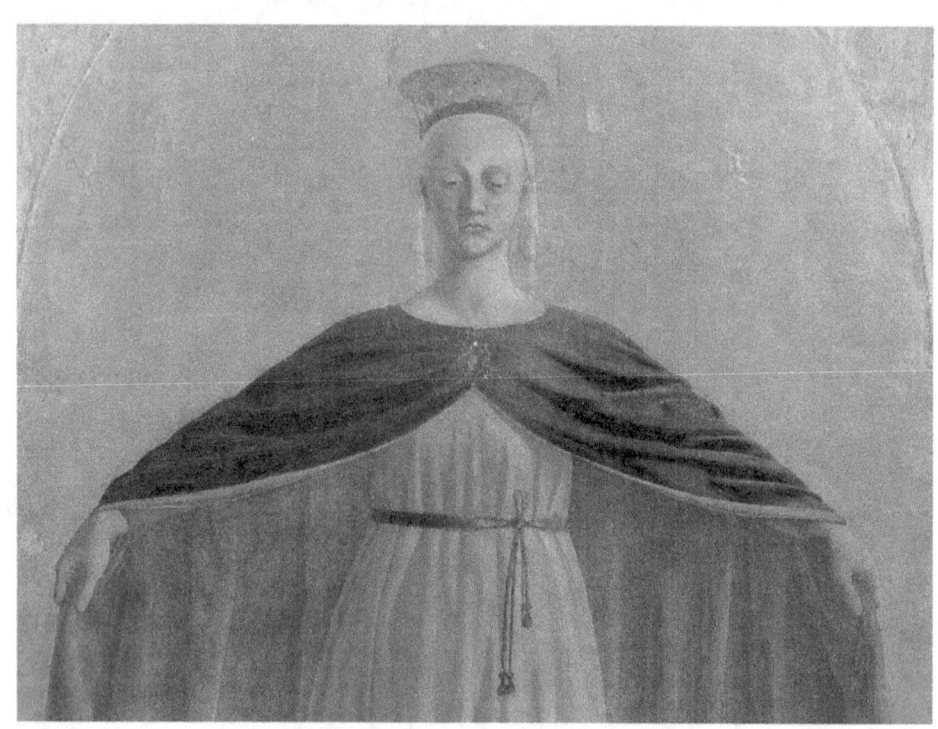

Piero, Madonna della Misericordia, detail

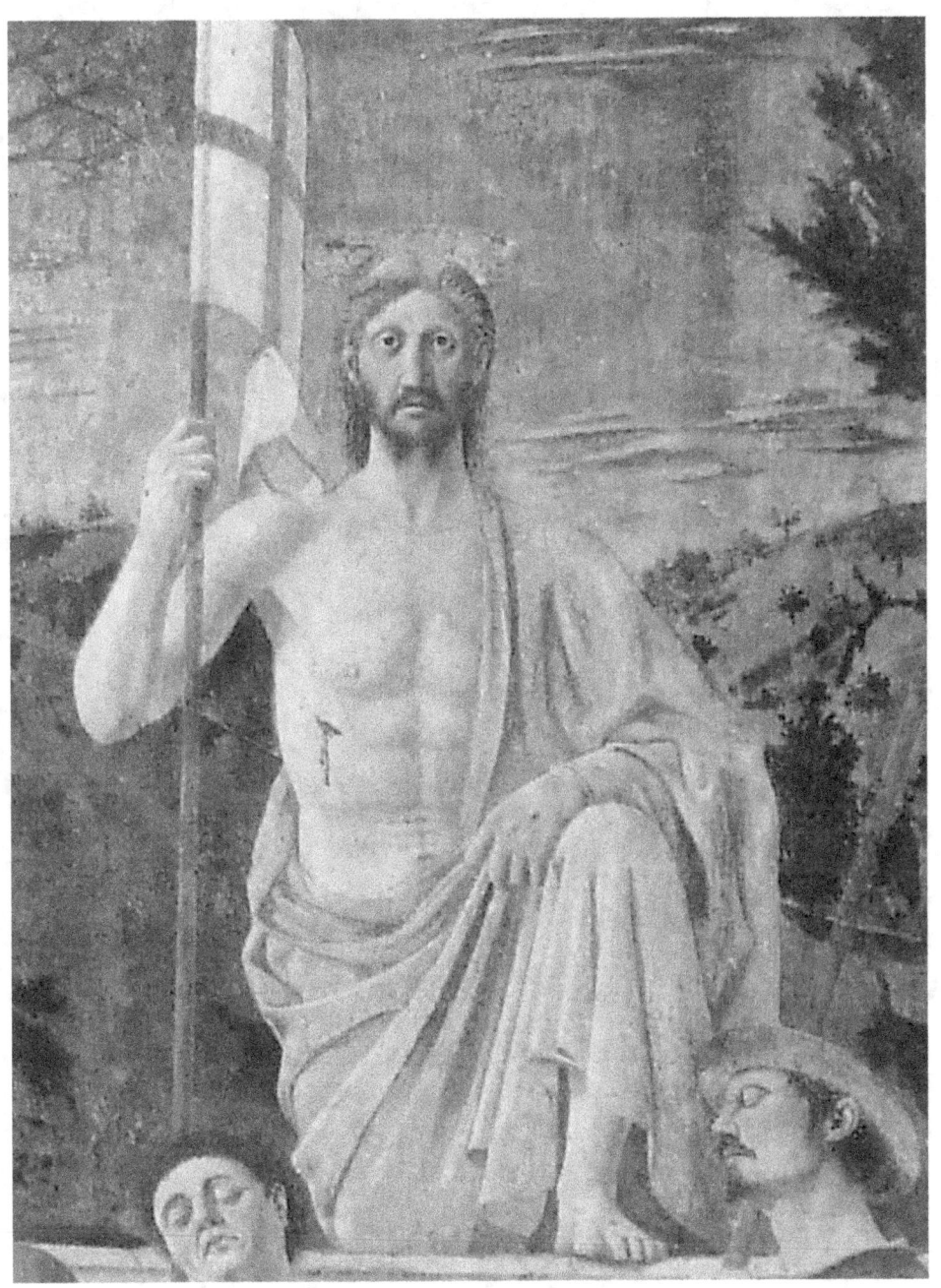

Piero, The Resurrection, detail

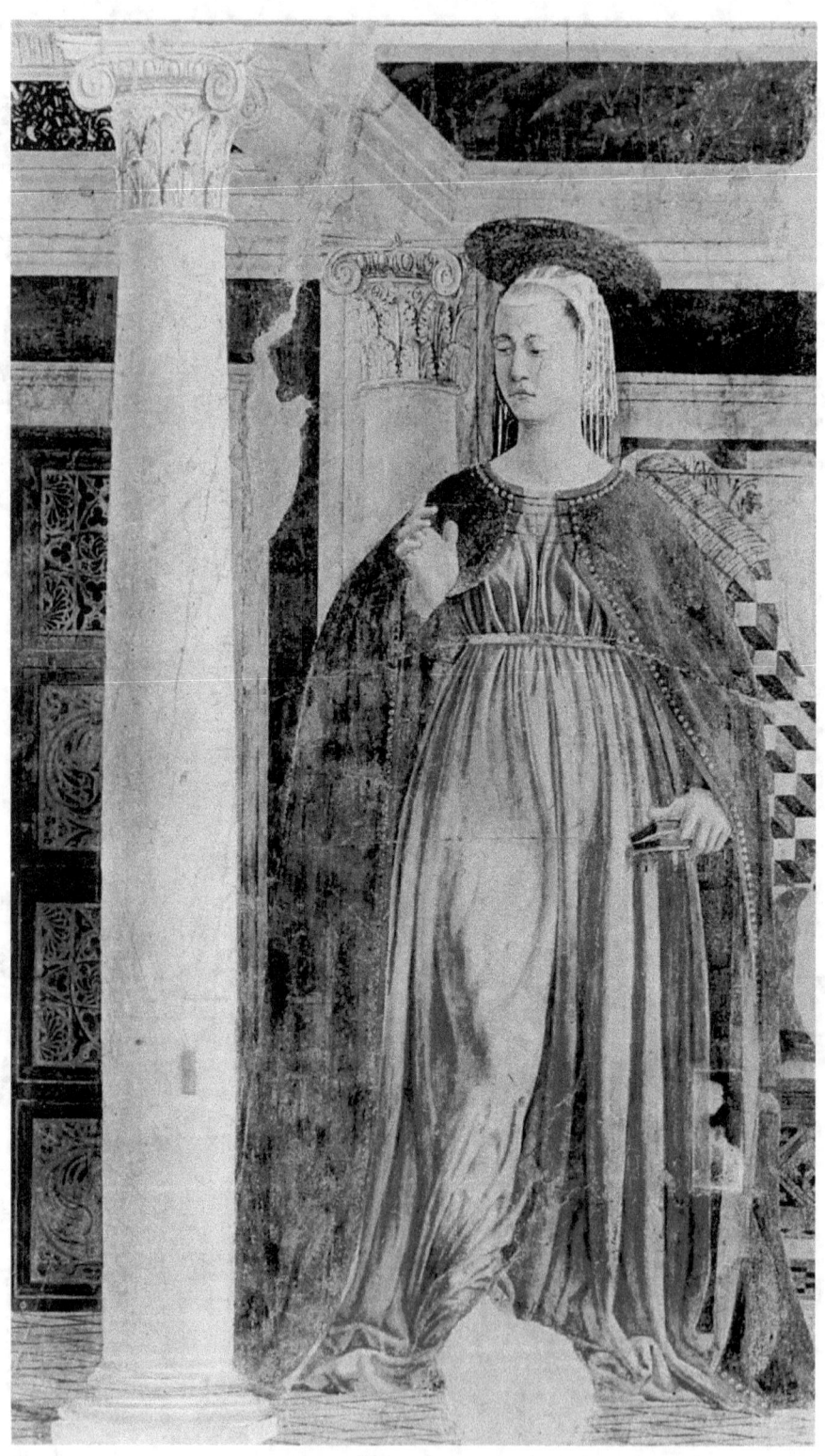

Piero, The Annunciation, detail

# I

# Introduction:
# Piero della Francesca at Arezzo

Arezzo is one of the most beautiful of Italian cities. It is not jam-packed full of Renaissance treasures like, say, Florence. It is not the centre of Catholicism and the Roman Empire, like Rome. It is not a religious shrine, goal of many pilgrims, like Assisi. It is not a cosmopolitan, bustling centre of finance and the arts, like Milan. It is not a romantic city of canals, like Venice. The journey to Arezzo from Florence by train is an epic voyage. You climb higher and higher into the Tuscan hills – over rivers, through tunnels, along valleys. You rattle on a 'Locale' train, stopping everywhere, winding through the central Apennines. It is another country. Florence seems an age away. In the evening sunlight, Tuscany smells beautiful. The colours you see are cream-white walls, red roofs, burnt yellow-white grass, beaten yellow of harvested fields, bright green of the rows of vines and the shutters, pure azure of the sky. This is the landscape in the background of so many Renaissance paintings.

It is the air, perhaps, that makes Tuscany beautiful. For sure the architecture is wondrous, the decaying stone sublime, the flowers and trees delicious, the art incredible, the people fascinating and the colours radiant – but it is the air, scented of hot sun, burnt earth, roses, stone and drifting perfume, that really enchants. There is magic here, real full-blooded magic. .

Arezzo is a small town, nowhere near as bustling as Florence. Yet here lived two towering Renaissance artists, Piero della Francesca and Francesco Petrarch. They are everywhere in Arezzo. You can't imagine even one great artist of the stature of Piero della Francesca or Petrarch coming out of, say, Grimsby or Solihull in Britain. And Renaissance Florence in particular contained some incredible artists, yet how small it was.

It's good to see Petrarch's House, to see a Teatro Petrarca, to see his (albeit rather grim) monument in the Passaggio del Prate. There is the Academia Petrarca, Via Petrarca, viale Piero della Francesca. And, during the 1991 anniversary, to see big banners over the streets announcing a Piero della Francesca exhibition – and to see a della Francesca Gallery.

This is the capital of Piero della Francesca country. As you walk up Corso Italia to the Duomo, you see huge chunks of decayed stone going ocherous in the sunlight. Behind the Cathedral there is a road called Via Madonna Laura. This will seduce you totally, for Laura was Petrarch's beloved. The cicadas echo around the park. Tuscan hills in the distance. Sun, peace, and such quiet. The waxing moon rises over a little garden of roses. Venus rises over the Piazza Grande with its colonnade designed by the chief recorder, the chief source of all writing about Italian Renaissance painters, Vasari. A fountain plays softly.

In the centre of Arezzo is Piero della Francesca's major work, the fresco cycle of *The Legend of the True Cross*. In the Duomo is his fresco of *Mary Magdalene*. Nearby is Piero's *Madonna del*

*Parto*, one of his greatest paintings (at Monterchi). And at his nearby birthplace, Sansepolcro, is his *Resurrection of Christ* and *Madonna della Misericordia* polyptych.

In the morning you'll wake up to the joyous sound of church bells calling the faithful to morning mass. You go out for a saunter around the city. It's the best time to be out and about in Italy – in the cool of the morning. When I was there on a Sunday morning in summer there were no tourists between 7.30 and 9 o'clock, and few locals, too. I had coffee in a cafe opposite San Francesco church, *the* Piero della Francesca church. It was not open, so I walked up to the Cathedral. Mass was being ritualized inside. I found the *Mary Magdalene* fresco by Piero. The bottom of the fresco is worn away, for it is low down on the wall, and people have touched it. I touched Mary Magdalene's feet. I was the first punter in the Municipal Museum. The guards followed me up the staircase. As I looked about the rooms, they walked around the place, opening up all the windows. And then I strolled to San Domenico – another Mass was on. And also to SS Flora e Lucilla in Badia church, and S. Maris della Pieve. And finally, to San Francesco itself, and to the Piero della Francesca frescoes. It's funny to see so many Piero copies: the churches are full of Piero lookalikes.

San Sepolcro is one of the other centres for those following the Piero della Francesca trail. There you can see one of many people's favourite Piero della Francesca paintings – the *Madonna della Misericordia* in the Town Hall. She is as magnificent as you would imagine Her to be: vast, noble, monumental. A Goddess, no less! There are four Pieros in the room in the Civic Museum at Sansepulchro. It's worth that long journey through the Umbrian hills. In Sansepulchro, everything is to do with Piero della Francesca. There's a road, a garden, a house and a foundation named after him, among other things. He dominates the town, culturally. During the 1991 Piero della Francesca 500-year celebrations downstairs in the museum there was an exhibition celebrating Piero and 20th Century art. This exhibition, which should have pointed out many connections between Piero and modern art, was very disappointing. De Chirico, Moriandi and others were there, but it was all figurative. There was no abstract art. Instead of showing images of people standing in Pieroan poses, the exhibition should have been full of abstraction, which was Piero's breakthrough. Colour, space and light and how Piero transformed them with his profound understanding of planar and spatial mysteries. He is the forerunner of Cubism and 60s colourfield painting and Post-Painterly Abstraction, the king of spatial mysticism with his receding planes of delicate colour.

Piero Bianconi is typical of modern critics who regard Piero della Francesca as the forerunner of a certain kind of (European) avant garde art:

> It has been said many times, and rightly so, that the artists rather than the critics contributed to his resurrection, and in fact no other classical painter could have contributed more than Piero to the *avant-garde* tendencies of the end of the last century and the beginning of this one, when rigidly formal, rather than romantic experiences were sought. (7)

It is a common tendency of criticism: to see Piero della Francesca as the master of mathematics and perspective, or as the author of the enigmatic *Flagellation of Christ*, whereas he was an innovator in the realm of colour and light and space. The control of light is one of Piero's specialities (Wudram, 181). Bernhard Berenson was more effusive in his estimation of Piero, as he usually was when he really liked a work, asking whether 'another painter has even presented a world more complete and convincing, has ever had an ideal more majestic, or ever endowed things with more heroic significance.' (B. Berenson, 1960, 135) It is true that Piero's art can approach 'majestic' heights, that is art can appear truly ideal and refined. There are also artists, though, for whom Piero's art is 'cartoon-like', which is how the Abstract Expressionist painter Mark Rothko found Piero's Arezzo frescoes when he visited them.[1]

Other Piero della Francesca centres include Milan, of course, where his influential altarpiece (*The Montefeltro Altarpiece*) is in the Brera; the scholarly city of Perugia, which is on the way to Assisi from Arezzo, where the *St Anthony Polyptych* is; the Uffizi houses the widely reproduced *Diptych of Battista Sforza and Federico da Montfeltro*, the paintings which further connect Piero and Petrarch; Urbino has that Flemish-looking *Senigallia Madonna* and of course the famous *The Flagellation of Christ*, which is now perhaps over-famous (compared to Piero della Francesca's other works); London has two major Piero della Francesca's, in the National Gallery (*The Nativity* and *The Baptism of Christ*); Piero della Francesca's work can also be found in Paris, New York, Rimini and Lisbon, among other places, but Arezzo remains the centre of the Piero della Francesca myth and cult. That is where you go to worship the Piero della Francesca deities, which are the paintings, much as you would travel to Arles for van Gogh, to Paris for Gustave Moreau, to Vienna for Egon Schiele, to Capel-y-Ffin for Eric Gill, to New York for Rothko, to Rome for Caravaggio, to Venice for Titian, to London for Turner, and so on. This study is very much concerned with Piero della Francesca's paintings, as texts, not with his life, which has been discussed at length in other studies. When we speak of Piero della Francesca, then, we mean the 'Piero della Francesca' that emerges from the paintings. That is, the creator of the paintings, but not the 'actual' person. We cannot know the 'actual' Piero della Francesca, we can only know the 'Piero della Francesca' who comes to us through his artworks, and through various testimonies of people who knew him, and of various documents. Our 'Piero della Francesca', then, is built on a response to certain works of art – bits of oil and tempera merely – and bits of paper. This is the basis of our study physically. Culturally, though, there is a vast amount of material written about Piero della Francesca and his works. Like Leonardo da Vinci, Piero della Francesca is one of those painters who fascinates people. His *The Flagellation of Christ* really intrigues people. They have mocked up the architecture in the painting, in three dimensions, so that you can walk around a model of the spaces in the painting. There are many theories as to what is going on in this painting.[2] People have wondered endlessly about the meaning of the work, about the figures in the foreground, about the historical references Piero is making. It is as if Piero's *Flagellation*, like Leonardo's *Mona Lisa*, contains some vast, momentous secret, just waiting to be discovered. Perhaps people believe paintings such as Piero's *Flagellation* and Leonardo's *Mona Lisa* contain some revelation about Italian Renaissance life and politics, or some great sexual mystery, or perhaps the key or map to some buried treasure, as they believe is to be is discovered in Poussin's *Et in Arcadia Ego*. For the art historian, the enigmas of Piero and Leonardo – or Botticelli, Michelangelo and Caravaggio, whoever you care to mention – are of an art historical nature, largely, who painted what when and, importantly, for whom. Art historians spend hours discussing why and how a painting was commissioned; who commissioned it; where it was painted; where it was displayed, and so on. Much time and effort is expended on defining landscapes in the background of paintings, or discovering who is represented in the various donors. In Piero's *Flagellation*, every minute detail has been examined and discussed. For the general public, there must something more than dry history to be uncovered at the end of the search, hence the sensationalizing aspects of hopes for treasure, or the Holy Grail, or a tumultuous revelation. The *Mona Lisa* and *The Flagellation*, though, are supremely unforthcoming. They are very talented works of art, and can sustain whatever reading you wish to give them. The *Mona Lisa* as proof of Leonardo's homosexuality and mother fixation? Done. Or perhaps as the embodiment of misogyny? Done. Or perhaps you'd like it to signify racism? Done. *The Flagellation* as evidence of political conspiracy? You got it. *The Flagellation* as a metaphor of patriarchal violence? You got it. Whatever your favoured reading, Piero's *The Flagellation*, like Leonardo's *Mona Lisa* or Manet's *Olympia* or Monet's *Waterlilies* or van Gogh's *Sunflowers* or Warhol's *Marilyn Monroes* remain enigmatic.

The *Madonna del Parto* also causes controversy. The people of Monterchi do not like it being moved. The women regard the picture of the pregnant Madonna as holy. When the painting was going to be moved in 1954 to Florence for an exhibition, the Mayor of Monterchi 'dared not risk lending it...fearing possible reactions if, during the absence, a woman had a miscarriage.'[3]

---

## II

---

# Space

---

The God-like nature of creation in painting resides in the ability to make a painting that has enough lifelike qualities to keep it alive. In the best moments of sixteenth-century Italian painting, there were always enough of these moments to make it clear that projective reality was the goal of painting and that the job of the artist was to effect successful self-effacement, both of his personality and his craft. This, it seems obvious, is the nature of pictorial illusionism – to make the action surrounded and created by painting seem real, and to make the creator of that action and activity seem remote.

Frank Stella[1]

Piero della Francesca has one of the most special and distinctive forms of space in painting. Piero's sense of space stands out from others painters, as with Cézanne, Rembrandt or Mark Rothko. The bright, timeless spaces of Piero della Francesca are instantly recognizable, and critics sometimes evoke Greek sculpture in connection with Piero's paintings. One might also see in Piero's hermetic, ritualized, timeless paintings the art of Chinese landscape painting, with its evocations of emptiness, which hints at the radical void of Eastern mysticism (in Zen Buddhism and

Taoism). Piero's hypnotic art coolly melds science with art, space with spirit, the personal with the cosmic, and history, myth and religion with time.

Like the art of ancient Greece, Piero della Francesca's paintings rejoice in eternal brilliance, an architectonic precision, a 'Classical' sense of proportion and harmony. In Piero della Fran-cesca's epoch, perspective, proportion and geometry attained a fetishistic quality. 'Seeing was theory-laden' as Michael Baxandall put it (ib.). Piero's sense of mathematics and perspective took in commercial arithemetic on the one hand,[4] and the transcendent purity of the Pythagorean solids on the other. Piero's *De Prospectiva Pingendi* is often cited by critics when dealing with Piero's sense of space:

> La pictura contiene in sé tre parti principali, quali diciamo essere disegno, commensuratio et colorare. Desegno intendiamo essere profili et contorni che nella cosa se contene. Commensuratio diciamo essere essi profili et contorni proportionalment posti nei Inoghi loro. Colorare intendiamo dare i colori commo nelle cose se dimostranno, chiari et uscuri secondo che i lumi li devariano. (Painting comprises three prin-cipal parts, which we say are Drawing, Commensuration, and Colouring. By Drawing we mean profiles and contours which enclose objects. By Commensuration we mean profiles and contours set in their proper places in proportion. By Colouring we mean how colours show them-selves on objects – lights and darks as the lighting changes them.)[5]

For Piero della Francesca, geometry, proportion, perspective and mathematics had a magical quality. His art exalts, on one level, a *jouissance* of mathematics and measurement, in which the 'science' of Renaissance perspective is joyously explored. Piero seemed to learn towards the cool, impersonal, impassive scientific inquiry of Aristotlean philosophy, rather than the more sensuous, more obviously mystical aspects of Platonic philo-sophy: he is regarded by Bernhard Berenson as 'impersonal' (1960, 136). Not a few critics have noted the cool, detached, 'impersonal' approach of Piero's art. R. Vischer calls Piero a 'realist': 'above all he wishes to be a realist, to draw in a realist manner'.[6] A. Stokes regards Piero as the first Cubist, a common view of Piero; while for Kenneth Clark, Piero was a fully 'classic artist'.[7] In his *Tratto della Nabilta della Pittura*, Alberti called Piero 'the greatest geometrician of his age.'[5] F.M. Godfrey was equally breathless, claiming that '[n]ever before has art blended so nobly with a mathematical purity of space-construction' (88). Other art critics, though, have not been so convinced of Piero's talents. Lawrence Wright pointed out that 'his geometry is by our standards involved and laborious.[6]

Roberto Longhi, one of the key Piero della Francesca scholars, describes Piero's art as a poetic transmutation of art into a melody that is choral. The comparison with music is of course apposite, for the connections between music, mathematics and painting are deep, on the metaphysical, symbolic, psychological, social and æsthetic planes.

> How this harmonious interplay of form and colour comes about, in which the art transfers certain elementary forms into the third dimension and then, by the application of his "perspective synthesis", brings them back into the visual plane of colour – this is the essential secret of Piero della Francesca's style.[7]

Piero della Francesca's art does not get stuck on perspective and geometry, though, as if that were all there ever was in painting. His archaic ritual gestures and lightly modelled figures are summations of certain types of humanity, projected onto an extended space of muted colour. His art is harmonic, always aims to harmonize disparate elements (such as the discourses of pain, purity, violence, sin, religion, eroticism, state power, patriarchy, spirituality and death, discourses that are central to Christian and Renaissance art).

Piero della Francesca's sense of space is part of the Renaissance re-ordering of psychology and metaphysics. In the comosmology of Classical Greece, space, the universe, was 'finite and spherical, with no endless stretch of emptiness beyond.'[8] Renaissance science and philosophy, however, destroyed this sense of finite space.[9] Euclidean geometry changed Classic cosmology: after Euclid's *The Elements of Geometry* and *Optics*, space was re-ordered. Renaissance perspective was built on Euclid, with the concept of the 'cone of vision'. With Euclid, space extends infinitely in three dimensions. At the same time, in the midst of this endless space, with its notions of emptiness underneath things so central to post-Renaissance culture, is the individual observer. What sets alight Renaissance space, makes it work, is the homocentric, egocentric, subjective observer.[10] (Piero's art may also be said to explore non-Euclidian space, a geometrical expression that leaps outside of the Newtonian four dimensions. Even as it is grounded in traditional visions of space and perspective, it also extends them.)

Piero della Francesca rejoices in the new monocular Renaissance perspective. Every picture he paints is meticulously worked out in terms of perspective and composition. Not for him the hastily sketched image: mathematics rules supreme, with some might say a clinical clarity, so methodical is he. But in Piero, mathematics is mystical, and it is in this very precision of numbers and subjective viewpoints that Piero's magic as a painter arises.

At the same time, though, Western perspective and sense of space has not changed that much since Euclid, Galileo and Newton. If it had radically altered, we would not recognize Renaissance paintings, or at least, Renaissance paintings would perhaps not be as revered as they are. For Renaissance spaces are so instantly recognizable: despite Picasso, Gabo, Klee, Schwitters, Duchamp, the New York School, Abstract Expressionism, Pop Art, Raushcenberg, Minimalist 'specific objects', Renaissance space remains the basis for all Western art of the past five hundred years. 20th century cosmology, too, has not drastically altered Western conceptions of space:

> The cosmology of modern physics has nevertheless had little impact on the commonly held worldview in the West, which is still predominantly an amalgam of Newton and Aristotleanism - 'places in space', a system of centres of human affairs (homes, workplaces, cities) deployed within a uniformly regular and vaguely endless 'space in itself'.[11]

In Piero della Francesca we find the simultaneous activation of an 'archaic', 'primitive' style with a refined, self-conscious, Early Renaissance approach, where classicism is refined. In Piero, as in Botticelli, Angelico, Lippi, Leonardo and Raphael, we find a 'rebirth' of space, where the notion of a 'renaissance' means a rebirth of illusionism. Each painter in the Renaissance reshaped space to his/ her own liking. Art historians dutifully record the development of illusionistic space from Cimabue and Giotto to Masaccio, Domenico and Masolino, from Fra Filippo Lippi and Fra Angelico through Botticeli and Filippino Lippi, Bellini and Raphael, finding an apotheosis of depth and *sfumato* in Leonardo, but deepening in darkness still further with Cara-vaggio, and, later, Rembrandt.

By the time he came to lay down his bewitching layers of paint, Piero della Francesca had spent a good deal of time working out the geometry, proportion and design of his pictures. His is a very disciplined art. Piero combined mediæval simplicity with an archaic geometry older than Neoplatonism: his art looks back to the monumental architetonics of the ancient Egyptians and the early Greeks. In his paintings he subsumed the teachings of Vitruvius and Alberti to produce a new vision of painterly geometry that took in the circle, the square root of three, and the ancient Golden Proportion (Bouleau, 20-31). Piero usually used division by small numbers - 2, 3 and 4 (ib., 95), though the *Brera Altarpiece* pivots around hexagons (ib., 34-36). With these numbers Piero combined the circle, a device favoured by many architects of the Quattrocento (ib., 117). Piero used the Golden Number many times: it is a constant, irrational ratio, a proportion (derived thus: a:b::b:a+b), and is denoted by the letter ø (Lawlor, 46). The numerical equation is laid out thus:

$$\text{ø} = \frac{(\sqrt{5} + 1)}{2} = 1.6180339...$$

Piero della Francesca's *Baptism of Christ* was based on the number three, as various plans thrown down over the illustrations of the painting have demonstrated.[13] *The Baptism of Christ* may also be based on the Golden Proportion, which symbolizes here the Holy Trinity. Christ's body is contained in the area 1 x 1 / $\text{ø}^3$ and the Holy Spirit is in the area made by the overlapping of 1 / ø with 1 / $\text{ø}^2$, and touches two areas each of 1 / $\text{ø}^2$. Christ's height is 3 x 1 / $\text{ø}^3$. The mystic geometry of *The Baptism* may also relate to Tantric *chakras*, where distances between the 'vital centres' are dictated by proportions such as 1 / $\text{ø}^2$. Piero's love of drawing geometric forms is apparent in all his paintings and drawings. Preliminary sketches by Piero reveal his meticulous scrutiny of solid objects, such as Ionic or Corinthian capitals, or human heads.

Perspective, though, is only one way of seeing the world. Western æstheticians seem to assume that it is the *only* way. For some, relying solely on Western perspective is limiting. For Frank Stella, our sense of space (by 'our' we mean postwar, post-every-thing sense of space) is still firmly caught in the Renaissance. We still see the world through boxes, says Stella.[10] He writes of the space a painting creates, and how this space can envelop the viewer, sensually:

> An effective painting should present its space in such a way as to include both viewer and maker each with his own space intact. It is not that this

experience should be literal; it is simply that the sense of space projected by the painting should seem expansive: expansive enough to include the viewing and the creation of that space. (*Working Space*, 9)

We have seen landscapes before in Early Renaissance art - in the background of Fra Angelico's *Annunciations*, a few flowers, or in Angelico's *Descent From the Cross,* a subject that lends itself to a landscaped treatment, or in Giotto's *Lamentation*, or in Uccello's various *Battle of San Romano* paintings. But in these painters, the landscape is still very much a *background*, flattened spatially, so the action in the foreground is not connected with it. Early Renaissance landscape is full of marvellous passages of detail and light, but it is flat and relatively undynamic. In the background of Giotto's *Lamentation*, where the weeping angels swarm like crazed birds, the landscape is hardly painted in: the suggestions of rocks, a tree, and that's about it. Samuel Beckett used this landscape - the barren, rocky space inhabited by a single, twisted, Giacometti-like tree, in his *Waiting for Godot.*

---

III

---

# Mother of God

---

In Piero della Francesca's paintings, as in all Renaissance
paintings, the Madonna is firmly placed in the centre. In the early
polyptychs of the Renaissance, the Madonna and Child were in
the centre panel (obviously), with various saints in the side
panels, separated by golden pillars, as in Giotto's *Baroncelli
Polyptych* (Giotto and workshop, S. Croce, Florence). The
hierarchy of divine power was also indicated by relative scale, as
in Duccio's marvellous red and gold *Maestà* (in Siena), where
the Virgin dominates the gathering of saints and luminaries by
being twice their size. The polyptych allowed for a compart-
mentalization of power and importance in a painting. With the
*sacra conversazione*, the figures were into a single, unified
architectural space. The golden wooden pillars separating each
panel were left out (Fra Filippo Lippi painted in his *Barbadori
Altarpiece*, in the Louvre, establishing an uneasy relation between
the painterly space of the painting and its relation to the frame).

Domenico Veneziano painted columns in his *St Lucy Altarpiece* (Uffizi) to indicate power relations.

The *sacra conversazione* paintings present an impossible situation: the divine appearing in person, on Earth, in a space at once sacred and secular. There sits the Virgin and Her child, and the mystery remains total to the end, because She is *divine*, yet She appears on Earth, that is, in a profane realm. These Renaissance paintings depict, then, the meeting of the impossible (divinity) with the possible (Earth). It is impossible that the Virgin is there at all; it is impossible that She is a *virgin* yet She has a child. Every *Madonna and Child* painting repeats this mystery. For, there She is, a virgin, but with Her own child on Her knee. In some Renaissance paintings, such as Giovanni Bellini's luminous *Madonna in the Meadow* (in London), the Madonna dominates foreground and background. She is a pyramid, precisely centred, at the apex and core of the world evoked in this painting. Her blue dress spills over the bottom edge of the painting, so it appears She is and is not sitting in the field. Despite the pastoral elements of the *Madonna in the Meadow* – cattle, a farm, peasants – it is a sombre picture. The trees, for instance, have few leaves left on them. Or at least, the trees nearest the Madonna have been stripped of their leaves.

Again and again, we see the tree in Madonna and Child paintings looking forward towards the Cross. The symbolic links between trees and Christ's Cross are well-known. Piero della Francesca's great fresco cycle in Arezzo celebrates the passages of the 'true Cross' from the days of Adam to Jesus. The deeper meaning of the symbolic identification of the Cross and the tree is feminine. The tree is Nature, and Christ is crucified on Nature, on Mother Nature. The Cross is the maternal presence: Christ is crucified on the body of His Mother.

Throughout Renaissance painting, the Mother is primary: the central image is the Mother nursing Her Child. At the Crucifixion, the other most popular Renaissance image, the Mother is present, watching Her son's death. Sometimes the 'three Marys' are depicted. But the Madonna is present in another way: She is the wooden Cross upon which He writhes in agony. The Madonna has always been central to Renaissance religious painting: She is not only central to Renaissance religious painting, She is at the *visual* centre of most Renaissance paintings. She is the focus of the paintings. She sits on a throne, or stands, and is at the centre. The Child sits slightly to one side. The Virgin is central.

It is the same with depictions of the Crucifixion: the Cross is central, and the Cross is the Mother, symbolically (as well as symbolizing other things). Jesus sits on His Mother's lap, just as Horus sits on the lap of the Egyptian Goddess Isis. At His death, too, Jesus rests on the body of His Mother. This mystery - of the present/ absent Mother - is found throughout Piero's paintings.

Although She is at the heart of Renaissance painting, the Madonna is decentred, psychologically and theologically. Although She is the *Mother* of God, His geneatrix, His womb, His birth, She is decentred, sidelined, displaced. The treatment of the Madonna is complex in Renaissance painting and in Western religion. She is eroticized, for a start: most, if not all, Renaissance *Madonna and Child* paintings eroticize the Madonna. Yet, at the same time, She is desexualized; the actualities of motherhood are smoothed over. Breast feeding is shown, but the attitude to it is ambivalent, as it still is today, where people get uptight when they see someone breast feeding 'in public'.

The Madonna is the primal Mother of all, and Her body is the site of so many conflicting feelings. She is both the giver and taker of life, the desired and the loathed object of desire. 'Her replete body, the receptacle and guarantor of demands' writes Julia Kristeva, 'takes the place of all narcissistic, hence imaginary, effects and gratifications; She is, in other words, the phallus.'[1] The Madonna is the Renaissance version of the 'phallic Mother', site of childhood bliss, site of childhood anxiety.

Against science, in the Renaissance, there is religion. The Madonna presides over the religious domain. Julia Kristeva writes:

> There is *Christian theology* (especially canonical theology); but theology defines maternity only as an impossible elsewhere, a sacred beyond, a vessel of divinity, a spiritual tie with the virginal and committed to assumption. (in ib., 237)

Indeed, to be so slavishly worshipped, as the Madonna is throughout Her history and throughout the Catholic world, from South America to St Petersburg, is not simply positive and enriching. It puts Her in a particular position which, understandably, She was probably reluctant to accept. You see this reluctance in the Renaissance paintings of the Annunciation. Andrea Dworkin contends (in her book *Right-Wing Women*) that it is not always honey and milk to be worshipped as a Goddess.[2] Dworkin's ruthless polemic is simplistic: it polarizes notions of masculine and feminine and rides over ambiguities, yet when we apply it to the Virgin Mary, how accurate it seems, in its basic thrust.

Renaissance Madonnas are eroticized through selective parts of the body. We do not see the Virgin naked, ever. We see, in fact, only Her face and hands, sometimes Her neck. Her body is always covered up. And not just loosely covered, but thickly, heavily covered, heaped up with azure and crimson robes, dresses, wimples and hoods.

Every Renaissance painter had to learn how to paint folds in clothes, and Piero della Francesca spends a good deal of time and effort producing deep, shadowy folds, 'the luminous folds and secret depths of the sacred' as Kristeva calls them (260). These folds are themselves part of the overall eroticization of the Virgin, and of motherhood. Unable to paint the *body* of the

Mother of God, Renaissance painters threw themselves into painting Her face and hands, and Her clothes. The Madonna's wardrobe is always rich, always indicative of profusion and luxury. The Blessed Virgin Mary is the mother the painter always wanted: quiet, subdued, passive, nurturing, enfolding the child in swaths of love and connection, symbolized by the arms and hands around the child, and those luxuriant robes.

> ...craftsmen of Western art reveal better than anyone else the artist's debt to the maternal body and/or motherhood's entry into symbolic existence – that is, translibidinal jouissance, eroticism taken over by the language of art. Not only is a considerable portion of pictorial art devoted to motherhood, but within this representation itself, from Byzantine iconography to Renaissance humanism and the worship of the body that it initiates, two attitudes toward the maternal body emerge., prefiguring two destinies within the very economy of Western representation. Leonardo Da Vinci and Giovanni Bellini seem to exemplify in the best fashion the opposition between these two attitudes. On the one hand, there is a tilting toward the body as fetish. On the other, a predominance of luminous, chromatic differences beyond and despite corporeal representation. Florence and Venice. Worship of the figurable, representable man; or integration of the image accomplished in its truth-likeness within the luminous serenity of the unrepresentable.[3]

Not 'feminist', then, Piero della Francesca's paintings in fact uphold every stereotype of 'woman' and 'motherhood' you care to imagine. In fact, Piero does not question stereotypes at all: he maintains them. He depicts the Madonna as the drudge of humanity, the drudge as Goddess. Piero's Madonnas, like those of all Renaissance painters, is really a mask, too, of something that remains always out-of-reach. The Madonna, as Kristeva notes, 'increasingly appears as a *module*, a process' (ib., 264).

Seemingly in the 'bloom of motherhood', to use a typical cliché often applied to pregnant women, the Virgin in Renaissance art looks down, head tilted, eyes open but staring, unfocused, looking at nothing, mouth fixed straight, or, often turning down slightly.[4] There is not much laughter, humour or even joy in Christianity. Instead of emphasizing the Resurrection of Christ, that joyous bursting back into life after the Crucifixion, it is significant that painters concentrate on the Pieta, the dead Christ, looking pathetic and mournful as He is dragged from the Cross and laid in the tomb. This woeful glorification of suffering is at the heart of the Christian religion.

You have to ask the Blessed Virgin Mary: why so sad? Why are you so sad? The answer is that She is a masculine creation, the image of male projections, about patriarchal attitudes towards women and motherhood. In Christianity, it seems you can't be seen to smile or laugh when 'great', 'important' emotions are being portrayed. You can't smile and be serious about motherhood; you can't laugh as you ponder death. There are no smiles at the Crucifixion, even though we all know the Son of God ascends after His 'human' death. Similarly, the Madonna is not shown smiling, except in rare cases.

Present in the painting, the real woman is elsewhere. This is clear when we look at Renaissance Madonnas: the 'real' woman, the flesh and blood, living and breathing woman is elsewhere. She is not in the painting. The painted Madonna is a cipher, a symbol, 'pure figment', as Samuel Beckett says of his Goddess figure in *Ill Seen, Ill Said*. Life is elsewhere said the guru of the Surrealists, André Breton, and in Renaissance paintings, the actual mother is elsewhere. Geoffrey Ashe in his book *The Virgin* calls Mary 'the obscure Jewish wife', remarking that it is amazing that this 'obscure Jewish wife' should become one of the central figures of Western culture, subject of thousands of Renaissance paintings, not to mention mediæval cathedral sculpture.

Any religious painting is an interface between the human the divine, between the secular and the sacred. It is an uneasy, ambiguous relationship. The painting is a mundane object, a bit of wood, canvas and pigment, purchased in the dusty streets, brought back to the studio, and put together by the painter. The painting-as-object is thoroughly secular, thoroughly ordinary. Yet it is also a sacred object, a piece of magic. The painter works with solid, real materials to create something that is illusion, not very solid, really; the painting is something unreal, insubstantial, ethereal, impossible to grasp, something powerful though; in short, something *magical*.

Painters of all eras wrestle with these physical, semantic, psychological, æsthetic and metaphysical tensions. The tensions are between abstraction and representation, between 'illusion' and 'reality', between colour and 'life'. The religious painter has to deal with the ever-impossible task: the depiction of the invisible and the unknown. The artist has to make the ungraspable graspable, as Julia Kristeva notes:

> The artist, as servant of the maternal phallus, displays this always and everywhere unaccomplished art of reproducing bodies and spaces as graspable, masterable *objects*, within reach of his eye and hand.[5]

# The Monumental Madonna:
## *Madonna della Misericordia*

---------------------

The *Madonna della Misericordia* is one of Piero della Francesca's great works, one of the works, like the Arezzo paintings,
that is central to his art. It is an early work, but puts the stamp
forever on how to depict the iconological type of the 'Mother of
Mercy'. The composition derives from the 'mantle Madonnas'
which shelter humanity. A comparison with a *Mother of Mercy*
from the same period, Giovanni di Paolo's *Madonna* of 1437 and
with other interpretations, shows that Piero's picture is clearly
the supreme example. It was a commission from the Con-
fraternity of the Misericordia of Borgo San Sepulcro in February,
1445. The contract stipulated *et deauratam de fino auro et
coloratam de finis coloribus et maxime de azurro ultramarino.*[1]

The city in the background of so many Renaissance landscapes
signifies culture, the presence of culture in Nature. Even in the
countryside, seemingly uncontrolled by people, there are always

people. So, the city is always there, in the background of the Renaissance painting. The city in the landscape occurs in Piero's *Baptism of Christ, Triumph of Federico II da Montefeltro* and Arezzo frescoes, but not in the two *Madonnas* at Monterchi and Sansepolcro. The Madonna in Piero's *Madonna della Miseri-ordia* dominates the foreground; the background is still the gold space of Byzantine icons.

Carlo Bertelli writes of the æsthetic strategy of the *Madonna della Misericordia*:

> The Madonna was supposed to look gigantic compared to the faithful crowding under her mantle. The strategy Piero adopted was of such apparent simplicity as to be almost unobserved. He broke the chromatic unity of the dias which supports the saints, and placed, under the feet of the Madonna and the faithful, a black marble slab, whose left and right edges converge. The central group is placed further back in space than the saints that surround them. By placing the Virgin's head slightly higher than the saints of the lower register, so that her forehead rises above the arches which are placed over the figures to her sides, the image appears incommensurable in respect to all the others. The expansive gesture of the open robe, the authority of the halo in perspective, and the unity which is instantly registered between the curve of the arch and the semicircle of the faithful also gives this panel an architectural authority that is unquestionable. (30)

In a unified space, Piero della Francesca's Madonna presides over a host of Christian saints and worshippers – the 'party faithful' as pundits describe political followers in Western democracies. Scenes from Christianity, scenes that appear in thousands of Renaissance paintings, appear above, below and to the side of the Madonna: the Archangel Gabriel raises his hand to the Virgin in the *Annunciation*; above the Madonna's head, Christianity's primary psycho-drama, the *Crucifixion*, is endlessly played out; below the *Madonna della Misericordia*, are scenes such as the *Flagellation, Burial* and *Resurrection of Christ*. The Goddess in the *Madonna della Misericordia* is the core of this panoply of Christian figures and scenes, a 'serene, generous' figure (Mullins, 165). Kenneth Clark compared the head to a 'negro carving' (23), while Frederick Hartt says the Madonna is like 'an Egyptian statue'. Bertram says that '[s]he is big with mercy.' (1949) Marina Warner writes:

> The Virgin's face is strong and brooding, and her mouth is set in a distant, almost deprecatory expression of gravity, because for Piero, unlike the authors of some of the miracles, there was nothing frivolous in the clemency she accorded... She is monumental, so tall and imposing that the halo above her head is seen in perspective from below. (1985, 327)

Piero della Francesca's Madonna is verily the 'Mother' of all the people underneath Her, the Mother of all people everywhere. She is the centre of the *Misericordia* polyptych, the image upon which the whole structure pivots. She is the largest figure, Her scale is literally monmental. Surrounded by numerous saints and Christian celebrities, the Madonna is the calm centre, just as the Virgin in Leonardo da Vinci's *Adoration* (Uffizi) is utterly tranquil at the centre of the miracle and maelstrom. The Madonna here is one of the most piquant expressions of feminine power. Piero's painting has moved far from mundane forms of representation, towards the creation of an archetypal being, a pancosmic Mother. A universal Mother, in short. Piero's Madonnas always exhibit absolute repose, a sense of inner calm which pervades all his works. Outwards from the centre of the *Madonna della Misericordia* is a radiance of tranquillity. Piero's painting so piquantly captures the primæval yearning for the Mother, the emotional bond that exists between mothers and children.

In her outstanding essay on the Virgin Mary, "Stabat Mater", Julia Kristeva writes:

> Mary's function as guardian of power, later checked when the church became wary of it, nevertheless persisted in popular and pictural

representation, witness Piero dela Francesca's impressive painting,
*Madonna della Misericordia,* which was disavowed by Catholic author-
ities at the time. And yet, not only did the papacy revere more and more
the christly mother as the Vatican's power over cities and municipalities
was strengthened, it also openly identified its own institution with the
Virgin: Mary was officially proclaimed Queen by Pius XII in 1954 and
*Mater Ecclesiae* in 1964.[2]

In Piero della Francesca's image, we are all Her children. There
they are, all the figures of authority in the Christian world, Saints
Andrew, Bernardino of Siena, Sebastian and John the Baptist,
Augustine, etc, looking suitably sombre and masculine, but it is
the Virgin Mary who towers over them. At Her feet kneel
worshippers. Not babies, not children, but grown people, kneeling in front of a woman. This is the double-edged triumph of
Christianity: that, on the one hand, a woman is worshipped, but,
on the other hand, the worshipping sets Her in a stereotypical
role, forever branded the 'virgin' who gave birth. The *Madonna
della Misericordia* is the primal Mother, both feared and desired,
the 'phallic Mother' who takes away as well as gives, who casts
out as well as shelters. The debasement of the people kneeling at
Her feet is also double-edged: though the worshippers are us,
meant to be our representatives in this painting (we look at Her
through them) it is the worshippers in Christianity who have
created Her, who have made Her as they wished.

# V

# The Exaltation of Pregnancy:
## *Madonna del Parto*

The *Madonna del Parto* is in the cemetery chapel at Monterchi, in the Arezzo region. The chapel was originally a part of Santa Maria di Montana church, which was demolished in 1785 to make way for the new cemetery. The Goddess of Childbirth stands in a pavillion or tent which's lined with fur and decorated on the outside with a pomegranate motif.[1] Two angels draw aside the flaps of the pavillion to reveal the Madonna. The Madonna here is a softer, warmer, and more approachable version of Piero's usually severe, monumental Goddess. The Madonna is the archetypal Mother figure, identified with the tent or tabernacle in which She stands (in Latin tabernacle means 'tent'). The Madonna is the tent or house, the body-temple which houses the infant Christ. The analogy links together the child in the womb with the woman in the pavillion/ temple. One inside the other. Child in womb, womb in body, body in tabernacle, tabernacle in world. The Madonna is simultaneously other-worldly and so definitely *there*. Piero's pregnant Madonna is the most powerful example of this type of painting (Clark, 59). There are a few other depictions of a parthenogenic Goddess in Renaissance art, but Piero's is the one that rises above any other. The *Madonna del Parto* exudes a similar magnificence to the *Madonna della Misericordia*. There is the same total authority and self-confidence in Her stance, the same symmetry, the same dominant figure flanked by assistants. Belly forward, with Her hand on Her womb, the Madonna is caught in an archetypal stance of a pregnant woman. Piero's *Birthing Madonna* is quite clearly an image of the Black Goddess, the Goddess as fertile Mother, the deity who 'presides especially over marriage and sex, pregnancy and childbirth' (Warner, 1985, 274). Piero's Goddess openly displays Her sexuality: the *Madonna and Child* paintings of the Renaissance displace and decentre sexuality, repressing and suppressing it. But the pregnant Madonna in *Madonna del Parto* is distinctly sexual. The swollen belly is unmistakable. It is worth noting that pregnant women seen out in public still upset some people even today, even in our hyper-hip super-cynical wordly-wise post-war post-everything age. Even today, the sight of pregnant women, like the sight of women breast feeding their offspring, unnerves people. Why? Perhaps it is because 'the woman's body... reminds men of their own mortality.' (Burgin, op. cit., 116) Women perhaps disturb men partly because they make men aware of the human condition in such a vivid, focused fashion. So when women openly display their sexuality, their procreativity, their fertility, in walking about pregnant, or in breast feeding in public, they are reminding men of their mortality, of the power and vicissitudes of the flesh. Christianity suppresses the body – Christianity quite literally flagellates the body, whips it, cuts it, makes it suffer. But the pregnant Madonna suggests joy and life, a positive well-being. Instead of self-flagellation, as you found in the early Christian and the extraordinary antics of the Gnostics, who sat on top of poles, or who wore hair shirts, or who lived in caves, or holes in the sand,² you find a serenity and fecundity in the Renaissance Madonna, and especially in those Madonnas that acknowledged their sensuality. In Bellini and Giotto, we find a passivity and humility, as in the Virgins of Fra Angelico and Botticeli, where one or two painters like, say, Leonardo and Michelangelo, allowed the Mother of God to be erotic, to be aware of Her eroticism, to allow Her eroticism to be displayed. Piero's Madonnas are generally of the passive, humble type, but his *Madonna del Parto* is given a visible sexuality. It is an eroticism firmly within the confines of Christian authority, to be sure. That is, it is women's sexuality as expressed in procreation: sex for children's sake, not (God forbid!) sex for sex's sake (God, indeed, *did* forbid 'carnal pleasure' for the sake of 'carnal pleasure').

Piero della Francesca's Madonna, though, is a deity operating at the 'intersection of sexuality and spirituality' (Woodman, 121), and it is partly this open admission of sexuality that makes the *Madonna del Parto* so cherished by its admirers. In the Renaissance, and especially in the Byzantine era, an *image* of the Madonna was believed to be, in some way, the Madonna Herself. That is, there was not such a great divide between illusion and 'reality' as there is today. The Renaissance altarpiece, for example, 'played an active, vital role in the central religious ritual' (Cole, 1983, 37). The altarpiece was directly involved with the Catholic mass, where the miracle of the Transubstantiation occurred. The figures depicted in the painting were 'intertwined with this miracle' (Cole, ib., 35). People of mediæval and Renaissance times, it is said, believed in the miraculous properties of paintings: they were magical objects in their own right. This is obvious with famous paintings such as the

*Madonna del Parto*, or the *Mona Lisa*, which was causing a stir in Leonardo's studio way before he had even finished it.

The *Madonna del Parto* is a magical object, which presides over pregnancies: it is regarded as a shrine and altar. The *Madonna del Parto* is one of the most famous of magical paintings. Seemingly humble, Piero della Francesca's *Child-birthing Madonna* presides over the whole matrifocal experience of motherhood, birth and life. Pieros' *Madonna del Parto* looks like a pre-Christian deity, a *diva* or *prima donna*, an austere Goddess dressed in a simply-cut blue dress. The power of Piero's *Madonna del Parto* resides mainly in Her face, in that solemn, authoritative facial expression. The archetypal hooded Piero eyes simultaneously activate humility and divine power: the more humble She is, the more powerful She is. In Piero's painting, sexuality and spirituality are combined: though this woman is clearly pregnant, She is crowned with a halo, a symbol of divinity. The two angels either side of the parthenogenic Virgin are drawn from the same cartoon; the design is simply reversed. (The cartoon process, or *polverello*, transfers a design from the outlines of a shape pricked with a pin – charcoal was dusted through the pinholes to the wall). The simplicity of the design adds to its spiritual power. In the painting, Piero acknowledges that the representation of divine power does not require difficult, complex designs. He knows the power of simple shapes: the Pyramids in Egypt, for example, are supremely 'simple' geometric shapes, yet what power they possess. Piero's art, as critics have noted, has a similar 'monumental' quality, such as found in Oriental statues of the Buddha, or Ancient Egyptian statues of pharaohs.

The magical properties of Piero della Francesca's *Madonna del Parto* were most poetically explored in the Russian filmmaker Andrei Tarkovsky's film *Nostalghia* (1981). Tarkovsky's film follows a Russian exile searching through Italy for notions of homeland. Piero's *Madonna del Parto* presides over the opening of Tarkovsky's film. Gorchakov, the Russian writer, is driven into the misty Tuscan hills by an Italian translator, Eugenia. Eugenia leaves the car and wanders into into a vaulted undercroft or crypt, presided over by Piero della Francesca's magnificent *Madonna del Parto*. This is meant to be the Monterchi chapel (but a different location was used for filming). Tarkovsky builds up a scene of mystery and darkness, where masses of candles glow in front of Piero's painting. Tarkovsky's shots emphasize a sense of awe and worship. A ritual procession of women comes into the crypt. Tarkovsky said the women were meant to be like witches. They carry candles and a large statue of the Virgin Mary (like the Goddess Kali in Indian rituals, or the Madonna in the gypsy festival in Provence, where She is carried into the ocean). The statue is set down in front of the painting. Then – and this is really extraordinary – a kneeling, praying woman, muttering to the Mother of God, opens the clothes over the belly of the statue and hundreds of birds fly out, chirping madly. The birds flutter madly around the church. There are shots of feathers landing on the candles. A shot of Eugenia, in C.U. is followed by a slow track-in to the face of Piero's *Madonna of Childbirth*.

In 1979 Tarkovsky wrote in his *Diary*:

*9 August, Bagno-Vignoni*
Early this morning there was a thunderstorm, very beautiful. Rain. This morning we looked at the hot water baths – St Katherine. It's a fantastic place for a film.
Tivoli showed me the stream, and the room with no windows for the 'Companion' and for the film. M*adonna del Parto.*
We filmed Piero della Francesca's *Madonna of Childbirth* in Monterchi. No reproduction can give any idea of how beautiful it is.
A cemetery on the borders of Tuscany and Umbria.
When they wanted to transfer the *Madonna* to a museum, the local women protested and insisted on her staying. (*Diaries*, 196-7)

Piero della Francesca's *Pregnant Madonna* is a thaumaturgic image, a powerful matriarch, an archaic image of Mediterranean motherhood. In *Nostalghia* She is part of a women's ritual, as the local women gather and kneel and pray before the image of the pregnant Goddess: birds are symbolically released from the statue's womb. Eugenia is identified with the Goddess as Tarkovsky cuts from one to the other in a piquant piece of montage. The scene plays out with a slow tracking shot moving into the face of Piero's austere Earth Mother. On 3 May 1980 Tarkovsky explained the scene:

> The first episode, in the mist. Madonna del Parto. The pregnant women come crowding here like witches, to ask the Madonna to ensure them a safe delivery, and so on. The mist lies in layers around the church. (*Diaries*, 245)

What Tarkovsky's film *Nostalghia* does is to continue the belief in the magical properties of paintings, the notion that paintings have real, physiological effects.

---
VI
---

# Baby Love:
## *The Nativity*

---

Piero della Francesca's *Nativity* (in London's National Gallery) is more of an *Adoration of the Child*. It reveals the influence of Early Netherlandish painting, echoing the kneeling Madonna worshipping and in awe of the God-child in works such as Hans Memling's *Adoration* (Birmingham), or Hugo van der Goes' *Portinari Altarpiece* (Uffizi). The dilapidated cowshed, the singing angels and the detailed vegetation are all common elements in Early Flemish *Adorations*. Piero's *Adoration of the Child* is one of his last works (Longhi and Clark date it to around 1470, and Bottari to 1475). The Virgin's total concentration on the Child looks forward to Italian paintings such as Botticelli's *Mystic Nativity* (also in London). Marina Warner says of Piero's *Nativity* that it is

> a logical development of Franciscan piety that the Virgin should kneel in adoration before her newborn child: one icon of humility before

another… In motherhood Mary was glorified, and through her pros-
tration before her child, became more glorious for her humility. (1985,
183)

Robert Longhi notes how in the open composition of *The
Nativity* the 'scattered elements [are] bound together and
ravished by the sun.' (1955). Whether or not the painting was
finished, it certainly is in a poor state, usually attributed to an
appalling cleaning regime. Fortunately, there is still much in the
painting that survives to delight: the chorus of angels, for
example, which form a row of heads that occurs again in *The
Brera Altarpiece.* Joseph is one of the strangest in Italian
Renaissance art. He is more like an outcast St Jerome than the
husband of the Mother of God. The Virgin, meanwhile, is wholly
rapt in Her mute contemplation of the baby, who kicks His legs
on part of the Virgin's blue robe that extends outwards from Her
to support Him. The painting has a circular geometry (also
concentric circles, a right angle and a diagonal), which is easily
distinguishable by the line of vegetation to the left of the angels,
through the shed, and round to the seated Joseph. One of the
shepherds behind Joseph is pointing upwards, perhaps referring
to the prophetic appearance of the comet. The skyward gesture
also recalls certain gestures in Leonardo da Vinci's art (the
mysterious gesture of St Anne in the *Burlington Cartoon*, for
example). The colouration is dominated by a pale blue. The
other colours (red, sepia, grey, white) harmonize around the
central blueness. The Virgin has a new face in Piero's art: a
delicate oval, quite different from the stern majesty of the
Madonnas in the *Madonna del Parto* or the *Madonna della
Misericordia*.

Julia Kristeva has written thus of the *Nativity*:

The famous nativity of Piero della Francesca in London, in which Simone
de Beauvoir too hastily saw a feminine defeat because the mother
kneeled before her barely born son, in fact consolidates the new cult of

humanistic sensitivity. It replaces the high spirituality that assimilated the Virgin to Christ with an earthly conception of a wholly human mother. (1986, 71)

Indeed, it is quite wrong to see in Piero della Francesca's *Nativity*, or other *Adorations of the Child*, a female subservience before a male master. In the early stages of motherhood the baby often becomes the centre of attention, becomes like a little emperor or king or queen or princess, regardless of their gender. It's true that male babies are treated differently from female babies. In Piero's *Nativity,* though, the baby love is total and beyond gender. It shows how a mother's love for the child is one of the most powerful metaphors or analogies of the love of deities for their creations. Instead of the severe, proud, and repressive love of the Father-God for the mere human, there is the nurturing, reciprocal bond between mother and child. Piero's *Nativity* is one of the few Renaissance paintings in which one could substitute a female baby for the male baby and the overriding expression of the painting would not be altered too much.

# VII

# The Triumph of Architecture:
## *The Madonna of the Egg /*
## *The Brera Altarpiece*

The *Brera Altarpiece*, also known as *The Madonna of the Egg*, depicts the Virgin Mary praying on a throne with Jesus on Her knees, surrounded by six saints, four angels, and the historical human who is most often associated with Piero's art, the Duke of Montefeltro. The saints featured are: John the Baptist, Bernardino of Siena, Jerome, Francis, Peter Martyr and John the Evangelist. The composition is complex, built on the ratios 2 and 3, the intersection of 2 circles, and the forms of the regular solids (most especially the hexagon – in 3 dimensions the icosahedron.[1] The Milan *Madonna* is a glorious painting, made more powerful for its muted colouring. Critics have rightly raved about the painting.[2] Like *The Senigallia Madonna* the figures are so clearly marked in their particular space that one can imagine how the group will look from different angles, as in a 3-D model, or a computer simulation (viewed from above the axis of the Madonna, for example).₃ Combined with the pale blue and vermilion marble panels and the finely decorated architecture, the Madonna and Her retinue form a spectacular display of divinity on Earth. Above the Virgin, on the vertical median axis, hangs an ostrich egg from a scallop shell. The shadow across the pale cream-coloured shell is particularly inventive. (The egg is of course one of those timeless symbols, like the snake or cross, that is loaded with multitudinous associations. In this context it refers to the Virgin Birth and to the Resurrection.)₄

In Piero della Francesca's magnificent vision of an apse, the complex composition is set alight by that single, hanging white egg. Other painters employed the barrel-vaulted apse of a church as the background for their Madonna paintings – Raphael in his *Madonna del Baldacchino* (Uffizi), Ercole de' Roberti in his *Virgin and Child with Saints* (Milan) and Botticelli in his *St Barnabas Altarpiece* (Uffizi). The church apse is a framing device, a symbolic device, but also an opportunity for the painter to show off her/his talent for devising spectacular displays of perspective. Bellini is no exception to this: his apses are certainly spectacular, the most flamboyant being perhaps the *San Zaccharia Altarpiece,* which allows for a slither of landscape on either side, and the familiar Bellini clouds and pale blue sky. Mantegna had exploded the staid monumentality of the apse setting in his *Madonna della Vittoria* (in the Louvre), with its bower of fruit and leaves and birds. The typical Renaissance space reworks the interior of a church. Piero's *Madonna of the Egg* is not as showy or ostentatious as works such as Alvise Vivarini's Berlin altarpiece (*Virgin and Child with Saints*, formerly Kaiser-Friedrich-Museum, Berlin, destroyed 1945). Vivarini's *Virgin and Child* depicts a much grander, more grandiose space than Piero's apse.

The space of the *Madonna of the Egg* is echoed in the

enthroned Madonna in the *Polyptych of St Anthony* in Perugia. These apses are the architectural spaces that Bellini made his own.[5] More than any other painter, Bellini is master of the architectural apse. Piero's seated Madonna recalls Angelico's many altarpieces, but Piero adds some touches of his own. For instance, as with the *Madonna della Misericordia*, Piero draws the Virgin's halo from below, so that it is seen in perspective. The halo becomes a solid object, like the rest of the objects in the painting. Further, the solid halo above the Virgin is detailed that we can see the top of the Virgin's head reflected in it.

# VIII

# Virgin and Whore

## *Mary Magdalene, The Annunciation, The Senigallia Madonna*

Strangely, Piero della Francesca's art seems to move beyond notions of gender and sexism. While most Renaissance painters are sexist, because their culture was thoroughly patriarchal, Piero's art is not really concerned with gender. His female figures are very 'masculine' - the Virgin in the Arezzo *Annunciation*, for instance, is a 'masculine' looking figure, with Her huge columnar body.

In Piero della Francesca's art, for instance, there are few nude figures, other than the Christ child, which is unusual, perhaps, for most artists, it seems, painted nudes at one time or another. Only in the *Mary Magdalene* fresco, and maybe the Queen of Sheba, does Piero della Francesca approach an image of overtly erotic femininity. The common subject of the Renaissance nude was Venus, but Piero did not paint her. One might have expected

Piero to be sympathetic to Venus, or to a portrayal of her, for Venus is the divinity of the underbelly of Renaissance magic, which informs the Neoplatonic philosophy of painters such as Leonardo and Botticelli. As the Goddess of Love in mediæval and courtly love poetry, Venus, with her phallic assistant, Cupid, as the cherub armed with bow and arrow, presided over erotic experiences. Venus was called upon to aid the lover in the pursuit of the Holy Grail, the mystic cauldron of Woman, her womb. Venus is both Holy Whore and chaste Mistress of 'Love'. She is Love personified. A Louvre birth plate, *c.* 1400, shows the Goddess Venus hovering over a Tuscan Garden of Love attended by two angels. Below are six 'famous warriors'. All of them are staring intently at the genitals of the floating Goddess. The lines of sight are marked on the painted salver. The Goddess is depicted in a mandorla, just like the Virgin Mary in *Assumption* images. The centre of the picture is Venus's vulva. Piero was never as obvious as this: for him, eroticism is not really an issue to be dealt with; rather, Piero focuses as much as possible on spirituality.

Many painters of the Renaissance produced works which celebrated the eroticism of looking, and of looking at erotic objects, such as nude women. Giorgione's *Sleeping Venus* makes the looking at the body easier, because she is asleep. Yet this depiction is created very definitely for the pleasures of eroticism, made for the *jouissance* of looking, just like Leonardo's *Madonna and Child* paintings, or his *Last Supper*, which he looked at for hours without moving. He would sit and stare at his painting, clearly enjoying the pleasure of looking. Examples of Renaissance eroticism range from Michaelangelo's deliciously orgasmic Dying *Slave* to Botticelli's *Birth of Venus*, Titian's *Venus of Urbino*, and the Master of Flora's *Birth of Cupid*. These are offered as gorgeous depictions of people, of mythical people painted sublimely, of people who expose their 'looked-at-ness' for all to see. Even in unexpected places, such as in Early Italian Renaissance art, such as Lorenzetti, we find erotic objectifications of women that look towards the 'high art' nude. And otherwise chaste and sober painters, such as Bellini, produced female nudes made to be looked at erotically. Pisanello's drawing of the personification of 'Luxury' undoubtedly depicts a prostitute: his drawing is a form of Renaissance pornography, given 'high art' status because Pisanello was a 'major' artist. Some images of the Renaissance and later nudes contain men in the picture, who modulate the viewer's gaze. The man in the picture stands in for the viewer, and the gaze is distinctly erotic (and male, except in certain cases, such as Simon Vouet's image of Psyche and Amor, where the female contemplates the male body). Piero della Francesca seems curiously apart from these painters of erotic objects. As with Fra Angelico, Piero seems to have kept his works chaste and humble, with only a very few open displays of eroticism (as in *The Baptism of Christ*).

In the representations of Venus, sacred and profane, private and public, fear and desire merge. On the one hand, Venus is depicted often with as much awe and slavish worship as the Virgin Mary. She is a Goddess, with her attendant cherubs, like the Madonna with Her attendant angels. Cupid becomes Christ, echoing the tenet of Catholicism that *deus est caritas* ('God is Love'). But Cupid is often Venus' consort, not simply her messenger, much as Jesus and Mary were depicted as equals, if not lovers, crowned in a spiritual marriage in Heaven. The Goddess alone is not complete, if she is a Goddess of Love. A Goddess must have her consort, according to the male system. Women on their own bemuse and infuriate men. Surely, men think, there must be some companion in the set-up. Thus figures such as Salome, Joan of Arc, many saints (Hildegard of Bingen, Catherine of Siena, St Theresa, etc), Elizabeth I, and others are objects of fascination and ridicule for patriarchal people. Thus, the ancient deities, such as Ishtar, Isis and Venus had their male lovers; the same emphasis on heterosexual pairings occurs in Renaissance art. Thus, the Madonna is seen as Christ's lover in some Renaissance paintings, His equal, sitting beside Him in Heaven. Christ crowns the Virgin, after Her Assumption into heaven, as His consort. Mother and Son become lovers. Piero della Francesca's art, again, seems to be shy depictions of erotic love between heterosexual partners. His Madonnas, for example, are not secretly paired with Jesuses: they are aloof and alone. There is no masculine counterpart to Piero's parthenogenic *Madonna del Parto* or *Madonna della Misericordia*. These are images of self-contained motherhood and femininity. Most of Piero's female personas – *The Madonna of Senigallia, Madonna del Parto, Madonna of the Egg, Madonna della Misericordia, Mary Magdalene* – do not require males to make them whole, to 'complete' them.

Renaissance religious anthropomorphism, then, is supremely patriarchal, for it is always 'man' who is the measure of everything, not woman. This is true in Renaissance geometry and architecture as well as painting and sculpture: men are very definitely at the centre of the Renaissance (and hence the modern) conceptions of art and artistic philosophy. You see this everywhere in Renaissance, and throughout Piero della Francesca's art, but most powerfully perhaps in Leonardo's famous depiction of universal or Renaissance 'man' (*The Proportions of the Human Body*). Here, as Lynda Nead writes, 'the male body is fantasized as pure form.' It would be too subversive if a woman was at the centre of the universe; Leonardo's 'cosmic man' would not work; for 'woman' lacks the 'transcendent signifier', the phallus.

## MARY MAGDALENE

The fresco (*c.* 1460) is near the Sacristy door in Arezzo Cathedral. The figure is unmistakably by Piero della Francesca (art historians are just about unanimous in their attriubtion of the painting to Piero). She stands in a niche, seen from below, and towers over the spectator, just like the monumental, columnar figures of the Virgins in the Arezzo *Annunciation, The Madonna del Parto* and *The Madonna della Misericordia.* Piero's massive Magdalene is of course robed in red – one of Piero's most strident scarlets, which contrasts so vividly with the bright emerald dress. She also has, as usual, long hair, which Piero meticulously paints cascading over her shoulders. The Magdalene's humility is indicated by her gesture of pulling the outer red robe in front of her green dress. What one keeps returning to in this picture, though, as so often in Piero's paintings, is the power of the face and the eyes. Piero has a magic ability to portray a look that is simultaneously demure and direct, humble and proud, sorrowful and contented. It is a look of quietness and thoughtfulness, yet quite self-confident. In his *St Mary Magdalene*, as in other works, Piero strips away all extraneous material, so that his subject can shine through. He is one of the least fussy of all Renaissance painters. He does not let the eye become dazzled or distracted by too much detail. He keeps his compositions clear and bright, quite unlike, say, Leonardo da Vinci or Fra Filippo Lippi. *Mary Magdalene* is so obviously a Piero della Francesca painting no one else – before or after his time – paints quite like him.

## THE ANNUNCIATION

Even such seemingly gentle occasions such as the Annunciation
are not free of sexist, patriarchal and erotic/ pornographic
connotations. In Leonardo's *Annunciation*, as in *all* Renaissance
*Annunciations,* from Simone Martini's exquisite Uffizi *Annunciation* to Konrad Witz's bizarre *Annunciation* in that misshapen
room, and Piero della Francesca's own statuesque version, it is
the male angel who orchestrates the event. The Virgin simply
bows down before him and his master, murmuring *Behold the
handmaiden of the Lord.* This is the emotional event Piero
portrays in his Perugia *Annunciation* of *c.* 1470. The Virgin looks
down in humility, arms crossed protectively over Her chest, as in
Fra Angelico's depictions of the Annunciation in San Marco. The
angel is clad in cool turquoise colours, his wings not peacock-
coloured, but white. The haloes on each participant are like
golden platters. What is striking about this painting, however, is
its elaborate architectural composition. As with *The Brera
Madonna* and *The True Cross Cycle*, the architectonics of the
work dominates the painting. The artist seems much more
concerned with the meticulous evocation of the white
colonnade, as in *The Flagellation*, than with the emotional
interplay that is usually the prime subject of the Annunciation.

The Arezzo *Annunciation* is one of Piero della Francesca's
more famous images. It is one of the most distinctive of Italian
Renaissance *Annunciations*. It is dominated by Piero's
architectural design – the colonade, the door, the structure of the
building. Unusually, God the Father appears prominently in the
painting, in the upper left quarter, releasing the dove. The
Archangel is half-bowing or kneeling before the Virgin, hands
upraised in a gesture of salutation. Gabriel is not unusual, but the
Virgin Mary is. Art historians have noted how 'column-like' the

Madonna is, how much She appears more like a piece of architecture than a flesh-and-blood woman. Certainly the Virgin in the Arezzo *Annunciation* is no demure and humble and frail teenage virgin, as She is in *Annunciations* by painters such as Fra Angelico or Sandro Botticelli. Piero's Annuciate Madonna is a very strong figure, Her cloak opened to reveal the statuesque and sturdy body in the red dress. She is as if carved in stone, as if She has been standing in this pose for millennia. The Virgin Mary is not arrogant – she is humble, as Annunciate Virgins must be. But the humility, the downcast eyes, the delicate gesture with the right hand, do not hide the immense inner strength the Virgin Mary exudes. When one looks at the Virgin's face in close-up, She appears as another of Piero's monumental Madonnas: oval-shape face, hair drawn back tightly over the skull, smooth skin and features, mouth slightly turned down, expression solemn, introspective, humble yet proud.

## THE SENIGALLIA MADONNA

*The Madonna of Senigallia* in Urbino (c.1470) is another Piero della Francesca painting whose authenticity is doubted by some art historians. Like the Perugia *Annunciation*, the Urbino *Madonna* has many of the characteristics of a Piero della Francesca painting: spatial flatness, Flemish influences,[1] soft oval eyes, statuesque figures, precise architectural forms and a limpid, all-over light. It certainly looks like a Piero della Francesca painting. The colours are those of Piero della Francesca: the pinky-red of the Virgin's dress, the white-cream of the angel's robes, the turquoise-azure of the Madonna's wrap. There is that familiar Pieroan geometry and symmetry, which seems so obvious: the Virgin is flanked by two angels, as in *The Madonna del Parto*. The Madonna here is 'profoundly still', as Meiss put it.[2]

# IX

# The Life of Christ:

## *The Baptism of Christ, The Resurrection, The Flagellation, The Arezzo Cycle*

Man is a projection of our awe at the spectacle of the "holy," the uncannily numinous, the *mysterium tremendum et alienum*, the unreachable other. Subjectively experienced, the numinous is taken for an external epiphany of mana.

Weston La Barre,1972, 368

## VISUALIZING DIVINITY

Piero della Francesca's art is deeply concerned, as with most Renaissance painters, with divine power. How is divinity manifested? How can it be represented? What devices can the artist use to show divinity? The halo is one way of indicating holiness, but it is not enough: Renaissance painters used every device they could think of, working within traditional systems and æsthetic conventions.

Through the mediation of artistic expression the attributes of a religious abstraction are revealed, so to speak, for it is presented in a visible form. hence, it may be said that sacred art seeks to represent the invisible by means of the visible.[1]

The question of Christ's divinity was always a problem for painters: if He was just like us, an ordinary human, how could He also be God? How could God let Himself die to Himself? Christ is simultaneously the messiah who has to be slaughtered, the divine king who has to be cut down each year, like Osiris and Dionysius; yet He is also the triumphant Lord, the eternally resurrecting/ resurrected One. He is the 'culture hero' who dies but does not die, who creates endless problematic states of charisma, *mana*, anima and *soma*. The faithful eat the body of their God: in Christianity, the archaic, 'primitive' rituals of god-eating are set against the visionary notions of a 'new' religion, a New Jerusalem, a Second Coming. Christ is simultaneously the all-powerful shaman who travels into the Underworld, like Orpheus and Isis, and returns, triumphant, and He is the 'magic god-baby', simultaneously a baby and a dead man, simultaneously a mother's boy and divine Father who impregnates His mother invisibly and magically. Jesus is the son of Himself, the Father of Himself. Christ represents both a regression to an infantile subjectivity and a transcendence into a higher divine power. Christ is both the childish narcissist, and the Saviour of the whole world. Christianity is at once founded on the 'crass subjectivity of epiphanies of feeling' *and* a sophisticated, materialist 'objectivity.' (La Barre, 1972, 367)

On the one hand in Christianity is Pauline blasphemous self-identification with God ('Christ in me'); on the other, ascetic self-denial and psycho-physical self-abasement before the deity. What Renaissance painters had to contend with were conflicting views of Christ: for the Neoplatonic, magical, neo-pagan view of the world sees humans at the centre, and humans are the microcosm reflecting the make-up of the macrocosm, the 'as above, so below' philosophy of Hermes Tristmegistus and alchemists. On the other hand, in the view of Christianity, God is at the centre (as in Dante's extraordinary vision of a mechanical universe in which God is at the centre of the nine hierarchies of angels, and the rest of humanity). In the Renaissance we see so clearly the crumbling of the hegemony of mediæval culture, where there was an unambiguous system of good and evil, God and 'man', us and them. In the Renaissance, this worldview falls apart, moving towards an emphasis on the individual, on the existential sense of beingness and being alone in the universe.

> Because his body exists in space, any man orients himself by the four horizons and stands between, above and below. He is naturally the center. Any culture is always built on existential experience. (M. Eliade, 1984, 136)

One sees this new existential self-awareness so vividly in Michelangelo, who is distinctly 'modern' in his neuroses and desires, whereas Giotto or Duccio, for instance, are embedded in a God-intoxicated mediævalism. In the Renaissance, God becomes unstable, begins to be 'elsewhere'. The influx of Classical, 'pagan' philosophy and mythology is far superior to Christianity as providing subjects for a painter. In Christianity, every image and gesture has to be subsumed to God and Christ, to the monotheic sense of divinity. In Greek and Roman mythological painting, artists could subvert gestures and genres, they could allow themselves to go wild with personalities and meanings. Christianity put a straight jacket onto painting: every artwork had to conform to accepted notions of 'the sacred'. In mythological painting, artists could explore much looser forms and gestures. At the same time, the Church and religious organizations were important patrons of art: indeed, most of the 'great art' of any era has been made for religious purposes or institutions.

> For the Christian artist the problem of representing divinity has been and still is practically insoluble for no means has yet been found to demonstrate in convincing pictorial form that Christ is God, other than introducing some symbolic element such as the halo. It is for this reason that the masterpieces of Christian art almost never show Christ preaching his messages...but show instead the crucified or resurrected Christ, Christ in majesty, or Christ as judge and ruler of the Universe, since all these epiphanies of Christ could be expressed in comprehensible form. Such restriction of subject matter reflects the difficulty of expressing by artistic means the mystery of the Incarnation, the simple fact that God concealed Himself in human flesh and thereby made Himself no longer recognizable as God.[2]

If the depiction of Christ is unsolvable every painter – and all Renaissance painters painted Him – has to come up with his/ her own solutions. The painter has to bring together death and glory in one image: Christ is going to die, we all know that, and the audience must continually be reminded of it; yet Christ is also going to become God again, He is going to resurrect Himself to Himself. Every image of Christ in the Renaissance thus conjures up the death and rebirth of Christ, the human mortality of Him, and His specialness, His divinity. Every Renaissance painting of Jesus looks towards the *Crucifixion*, the most acute moment where the childish narcissist receives the final blow to His self-esteem. 'In a long series of insults that began at birth, death is the final insult to narcissism.' (La Barre, 1972, 370) Death is verily the final insult to narcissism, to a consciousness (a person) that regards itself as the centre of everything. Christianity is the religion of the triumph over death, and every Renaissance painting of Christ alludes to this enigma.

PIERO'S LIGHT

Piero della Francesca's way of representing divinity was to employ a bright, timeless light. It is the light of Midsummer, in Mediterranean lands. It is an all-over light, hardly creating shadows. The sort of light that painters love; soft and diffuse, the kind of light painters have tried to create by placing parachute material over a skylight (Mark Rothko did this). The sense of shadowless and timeless light makes Piero's paintings look like Oriental art, like the art of ancient Egyptian friezes, like Roman painting and Greek sculpture. Piero's light takes us back to the sacred, because light itself is one of the primary, if not *the* primary manifestations of the sacred. Mircea Eliade believes that the sky is the first object of transcendence and the sacred:

> I believe, personally, that it is through consideration of the sky's immensity that man [*sic*] is led to a revelation of transcendence, of the sacred. (1984, 162)

*THE RESURRECTION*

It is significant in Piero della Francesca's art, with its ambivalent attitudes towards masculinity and femininity, that he should choose in his picture of Christ's life after the Crucifixion to portray the moment of resurrection, not the moment where Mary Magdalene sees Christ walking alone, in the *Noli me tangere* images. Piero's *Resurrection* is not witnessed by the 'three Marys', who came to Christ's tomb. Women are not the witnesses: significantly too, in Piero's *Resurrection*, that the witnesses of Christ's rebirth are all male – and also, of course, that they are asleep. Christ's resurrection from the tomb/ womb is a feminine mystery: His first birth was out of the Mother's body; His second birth is out of the body of Mother Earth. The feminine element here in *The Resurrection* is laid out behind Christ and underneath Him: the tress and the landscape behind Him, and the Earth under His feet. Piero's Jesus does not look like He's spent hours on a Cross and three days buried underground. He looks like He could take on anybody: He looks very strong, and self-confident. The composition of the painting is pyramidal – the apex is Christ's head, and the sides of the pyramid are his arms and the soldiers below. Piero's resurrected Christ affirms by His expression and stance – the macho stance of the aggressive man, one foot on the ledge of the tomb – the transcendence of human mortality. The delicacy of the landscape, with its Tuscan trees and that soft blue sky contrasts with the ultra-sombre fixed stare of the Risen Lord. Resurrection is a deadly serious matter for Piero, and there is nothing in this painting of the exuberance of, say, Grünewald's *Resurrection* (*The Isenheim Altarpiece*, Colmar). Piero's God stands high above, aloof even, from humanity below, which remains dejected or somnolent, unaware of the rebirthing deity rising above. Piero's Risen Christ is aligned with the Gnostic messiah, as found in the Jesus of early Gnostic texts: '[r]aise the stone and there thou shalt find me',[3] and in the Egyptian Hermetic text *Poimandres*, from the *Corpus Hermeticum*, the god Hermes/ Thoth says: 'I have passed out of myself and entered into an immortal body... I have been born again in spirit'.[4]

Piero della Francesca's *Resurrection* does not celebrate the happier side of Easter, traditionally a time of the 'joys of Spring', of eggs, rebirth, the reawakening of Nature after the sleep of Winter. Of the many thinkers who have written of the significance of Easter – not only many Christian theoligians, but commentators on religion such as Eliade, Jung, Freud, Jung,

Neumann – here is French poet Jacqueline Risset (b. 1933) who speaks of this March/ April time:

> Easter for me is a privileged space… it's also the idea of birth, and for me the poem is always something coming to be born. Thus, the idea of Easter is essential – not simply the *day* of Easter but the general period. It's an idea connected to the arrival of Easter, the arrival of birth, if you will. [5]

Piero della Francesca chooses to depict the weight and serious-ness of the rebirth of Nature and the world through Christ. The fact that it is also a time of massive relief for humankind (to have survived another Winter) is not shown. Piero's image is as far from the Springtime festivities of the pagan world as is possible: no dancing on May greens, no music and wine, no flower festivals here.

## THE BAPTISM OF CHRIST

*The Baptism of Christ* is one of those Piero della Francesca paintings that occur in a bright, timeless space. Piero paints rituals that eternally recur. In *The Baptism Of Christ*, the participants are caught, frozen, in hieratic gestures. The gestures are very simple yet Piero renders them mysterious again. What are these people doing in Piero's *Baptism of Christ*? They are surrounding the baptism of Jesus: this is one of the moments of epiphany,[6] like the scene of the Adoration of the Magi, which Leonardo and Botticelli so memorably painted. In Leonardo's *Adoration of the Magi* in the Uffizi, what Leonardo paints is the actual moment of the realization of Christ's divinity. The moment of glory, when the people realize they are beholding the Son of God, or God Himself, creates in Leonardo's painting a fury of movement and consternation. In Piero's *Baptism of Christ*, as in his London *Adoration*, all is quiet and calm. Jesus's pose is humble, for John the Baptist is the active one here. Piero's Jesus appears full of humility.[7] One of the priests behind raises his arm; another initiate takes off his shirt; the angels interlace and the Baptist anoints Christ, but despite all this movement of the other participants, it is Jesus who is the central figure. The Baptist and the angels are flanking Jesus: as in Madonna paintings, Jesus is the core of the image. The geometry of *The Baptism of Christ*, as always in Piero, is extremely meticulously planned. The parts of Jesus's body - hands, navel, head, etc - intersect at key points in the painting's geometric layout. The picture is full of symbols - angels, Byzantine priests, dove, river of life, tree of life - which art historians have interpreted in various ways (the three angels symbolizing the Trinity, or the Three Graces, or schisms in the church,[8] or the Three Baptisms,[9] etc). The light is particularly beautiful: it is an all-over brightness, an illumination that leaves no part of the painting in gloom. The light is 'ethereal',[10] a distinct energy in the painting, not merely a force of light and dark. Piero's light bathes every plane and object in the painting. This is the light that Lawrence Durrell found in Greece: an electric, blue light that bounces around the landscape, that emanates from rocks and trees. It is a magical light, a light that makes Piero della Francesca so different from any other Renaissance painter.

Piero della Francesca's *Baptism of Christ* powerfully mixes the static and the spontaneous, as the placid nature of the angels and of Christ is offset by the movement of the neophyte behind the Baptist taking off his clothes, and the priest raising his arm. The three figures of movement on the right of Jesus - Baptist, initiate and priest - are balanced by the calm of the three angels. The colours play their part in defining the sense of the divine in *The Baptism of Christ*, for the angels are very brightly coloured. The angel near the tree wears a purple dress and a pink cloak over her/ his shoulder; the angel on the left wears bright crimson and bright blue clothes. The central angel is in pale grey, with a floral headdress. Here the colour is functional and decorative: the angels' opulence is contrasted with the deep reds and oranges of the priests, while the landscape consists of dark browns, olives and sepia hues. The darker tones of the landscape frame the lighter figures in the foreground, whereas the opposite might be true in a 'naturalistic' depiction (that is, figures might be dark in tone against a bright landscape).

A contemporary comparison with Piero della Francesca's *Baptism of Christ* is Giovanni Bellini's *Baptism of Christ* (S. Corona, Vicenza). Bellini's picture, like Piero's *Baptism*, is pervaded by a silence of divinity. The figures on the left make shy gestures of wonder. Yet, like so many of Bellini's paintings, in *The Baptism of Christ* what one notices is the warm colouration, the exquisite detail, the simplicity of the design, and that yellowing sky, as of late evening. It is a masterful depiction of the Baptism, but lacks the authority and mystery of Piero's painting.

Piero della Francesca's *Baptism of Christ* is one of his few paintings that contain an erotic element that is built into the design. Christ's nakedness sends conflicting signals. Clearly, nudity has a religious or mythic aspect, connoting nature/ naturalness, purity, birth, creation, renunciation, unveiled reality, truth. In art, however, nudity is ambiguous: in religious contexts it is both spiritual and sexual, a duality which Leonardo exploits in his *Madonnas*, which are both erotic and mystical. Christ's body in Renaissance painting is often sexless, or androgynous, or feminized. Christianity is an ambivalent cult; it has a clothed, virginal woman as the object of worship on the one hand, and a naked, equally virginal and chaste man on the other. In the most holy of churches, nudity is sanctified by the statues, icons and paintings of Christ on the Cross.

The dying or dead Christ, naked but for a slip of cloth and sometimes depicted entirely naked but with his legs bent to one side, hiding the 'transcendent signifier', the phallus, is an image of homoeroticism. Theologians and art historians down the ages did not or would not admit that Christ was or could have been an object of lust. Yet this is clearly the case in some depictions of the naked Saviour, such as paintings by Giovanni Battista Rosso, Caravaggio, or da Messina. These nude figures send a mass of signals, from the pathetic to the narcissistic, from the erotic to the spiritual.

Patriarchal people (mostly male) protect their own interests. So homosexual art is OK, because many male critics and artists appreciate homosexual representations or issues. The reality of lesbian art becoming part of the establishment in the arts is far off. Two of the greatest artists of the High Renaissance (and therefore of all Western culture, according to patriarchal critics) were homosexual (Leonardo da Vinci and Michelangelo Buon-arroti). Leonardo's homosexuality, like Michelangelo's, does not tarnish his image, standing, status or 'genius' at all. What most Christian thinkers would not acknowledge is the eroticism of the Saviour's naked body. Everyone else in the Crucifixion is clothed, but Christ is nearly nude. If we accept that *any* nude has erotic elements, as more commentators than Kenneth Clark have noted, then the eroticism of Christ's naked body must be addressed. Few art critics have acknowledged the eroticism of the naked Christ, yet it is certainly a significant element in the 'great' depictions of Christ on the Cross: by Rubens, Velasquez, Raphael, Rembrandt, Rogier van der Weyden, Mantegna. Piero della Francesca did not make a full-blown near-naked Christ Crucified. More typical of Piero are the depictions of Christ with His Mother, a young Christ not yet embarked upon the hell of His time on Earth. Piero's Christ is essentially either an innocent, a deity for sure, but more of a baby, a young child, happy to be with His Mother in childhood bliss, or He is the victim, being whipped, or the solemn resurrected God. It is curious that there is no major *Crucifixion* in Piero della Francesca's *œuvre*: true, there is the early *Crucifixion* which's part of the *Misericordia Polyptych*, but after this no monumental *Christ Crucified*. Certainly nothing as major as the *Crucifixions* of Mantegna, Angelico, Giotto or Quentin Massys.

## THE FLAGELLATION OF CHRIST

Few paintings have so obsessed art historians as Piero della Francesca's *Flagellation*. Something about this picture drives art critics mad with desire.[11] As with Leonardo's *Mona Lisa* and Botticelli's *Primavera*, Piero's *Flagellation* is regarded as holding some secret which the questing art critic must find.[12] What is interesting about *The Flagellation*, then, is not so much the painting itself, but the way critics have discussed it, *ad infinitum*, in paper after paper, in book after book, in television programmes, and so on. We have had all sorts of interpretations of the painting. We have had articles and books featuring diagrams of the space in the painting,[13] and three dimensional models have been built, to show the relation between the figures and the architecture. Every aspect of the painting seems to have been scrutinized: the personalities of the figures, the political significance of the people, the relation between foreground figures and Christ in the background, the temporal distinctions of foreground and background, the iconology of the colours, and so on. *The Flagellation* is one of those paintings which become a pretext for any number of interpretations and socio-political theses. In *The Flagellation*, æsthetics and ideology mix in an intriguing fashion. Whatever Piero may have 'intended' in making the painting has been superceded by the enormous critical discourse that has grown up around the painting. It is no longer possible to see the painting afresh without also being aware of the meta-art surrounding the painting, the talk about talk about the painting.

Viewed æsthetically, in terms of form, gesture, light and painterliness, Piero della Francesca's *Flagellation* is not particularly exceptional. That is, compared to the *Madonna della Misericordia, The Baptism of Christ* or the *Arezzo Cycle*, the *Flagellation* does not stand out particularly. Yet, like the *Mona Lisa* or Michaelangelo's *Sistine Chapel Ceiling*, Piero's *Flagellation* collects controversy and speculation around it. Some paintings are like this – like magnets, like whirlpools, like black holes, they suck up criticism and speculation.

THE AREZZO FRESCOES

Piero della Francesca's major work, though, is the *Arezzo Cycle*, the frescoes in that smallish church in Arezzo which for so long, it seems, has been half hidden by scaffolding (like so much of Italy's 'art treasures'). The *Arezzo Cycle* of frescoes deals with one of Piero's main themes: the authenticity of divinity, and how divinity comes to be manifested on Earth. The theme is purity and holiness, here symbolized by the search for the 'true Cross', the Cross on which Our Saviour was crucified. The search for the

True Cross is another mystical quest, similar to that of the Holy Grail. For, the True Cross has miraculous qualities, like other relics of Christianity, the sort of relics one finds in churches, those religious establishments that claim to have saint's bones, the Virgin's ring, Jesus's shroud, and so on. By touching the True Cross, one might attain salvation. The prototype of Piero's *Arezzo Cycle* was Agnolo Gaddi's *True Cross Cycle* (c. 1390) which combined two sections of *The Golden Legend*, *The Invention of the True Cross* and *The Exaltation of the True Cross*.[14] For Piero, the cycle was an opportunity for a complex creation of interlocking shapes, colours, gestures, patterns, symbols and meanings. The Arezzo frescoes are Piero's most accomplished works, even if viewing them, as when any fresco cycle, is problematic: some of the frescoes are very high off the ground, and at awkward angles. There are many beautiful passages in the frescoes: *The Adoration of the True Cross and King Solomon's Meeting With the Queen of Sheba* is one of the large works (7.47 metres wide). The right hand half of the painting portrays one of Piero's spacious, airy interiors, dominated by 'a line of Corinthian columns divinely measured', as Vasari described them. This painting reveals, like all of the Arezzo frescoes, Piero's dextrousness in portraying groups of people. The *True Cross Cycle* allows for a variety of group scenes, including battles. Piero's solution is to treat each figure separately, but layered, traced from cartoons, which are, as with the *Madonna del Parto*, sometimes reversed (one can see the *spolveri*, the dots of charcoal which were used to form the outlines of the cartoon shapes).[15] The result is a panoply of figures based on the Pieroan 'types', those figures instantly Piero, and instantly recognizable.

It doesn't matter one bit that Piero della Francesca often used cartoons over and over to draw his figures. It doesn't matter that Piero may have assigned certain parts of the frescoes to assistants.

It doesn't matter that there is hardly any tone darker than a middle tone. It doesn't matter that some of Piero's figures hardly seem to have any sculptural volume at all (such as the groom in *The Adoration of the True Cross*). It doesn't matter that many of Piero's faces are 'types': the same profiles are seen, the same three-quarter views, the same faces facing the viewer (as in Queen Sheba's retinue in *The Adoration of the True Cross*). When Piero is required to portray someone unique, he can do so (as in the Queen of Sheba meeting King Solomon). Solomon's costume is particularly splendorous, despite being faded with age.

*The Dream of Constantine* is one of the most celebrated of Piero della Francesca's paintings, and one of the most frequently reproduced in art books. Rightly so: *The Dream of Constantine* has a marvellous lighting scheme, seldom seen in the Italian painting before the arrival of painters such as Caravaggio. In the big battle and group scenes (*The Battle between Heraclius and Chosroes, The Discovery of the Three Crosses and The Proving of the True Cross, The Adoration of the True Cross and King Solomon's Meeting with the Queen of Sheba,* and *The Exaltation of the Cross*) Piero demonstrates how deft he is at handling complicated scenes requiring intermingled figures and gestures. The compositions are very fine: Piero communicates the solemnity of the dignitaries, and the chaos and pain of battle superbly. The colouration is exquisite: there are pale greens, blues and pinks which occur nowhere else in Renaissance painting. In amongst the sometimes ravishing colours in the *True Cross* frescoes, there are some wonderful details. Piero is not overwhelmed by the whole enterprise, and manages some idiosyncratic passages, such as the helmets and armour in *The Battle Between Heraclius and Chosroes*, or the splendid depiction of Jerusalem in *The Discovery of the Three Crosses*.

# Illustrations

The art of Piero della Francesca, and some of his contemporaries

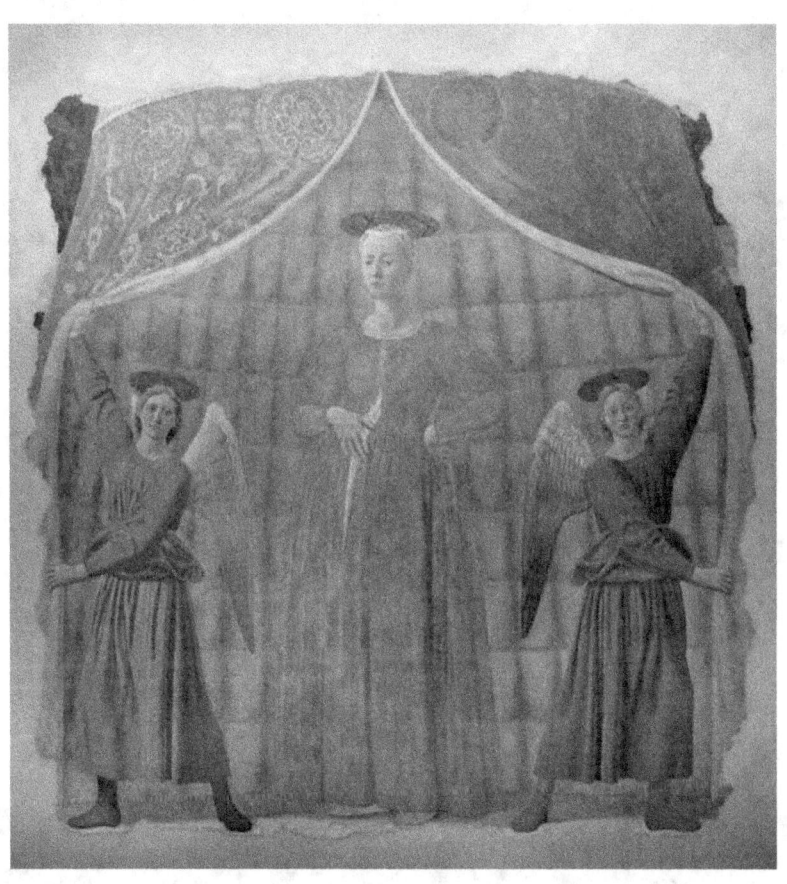

Piero, Madonna del Parto

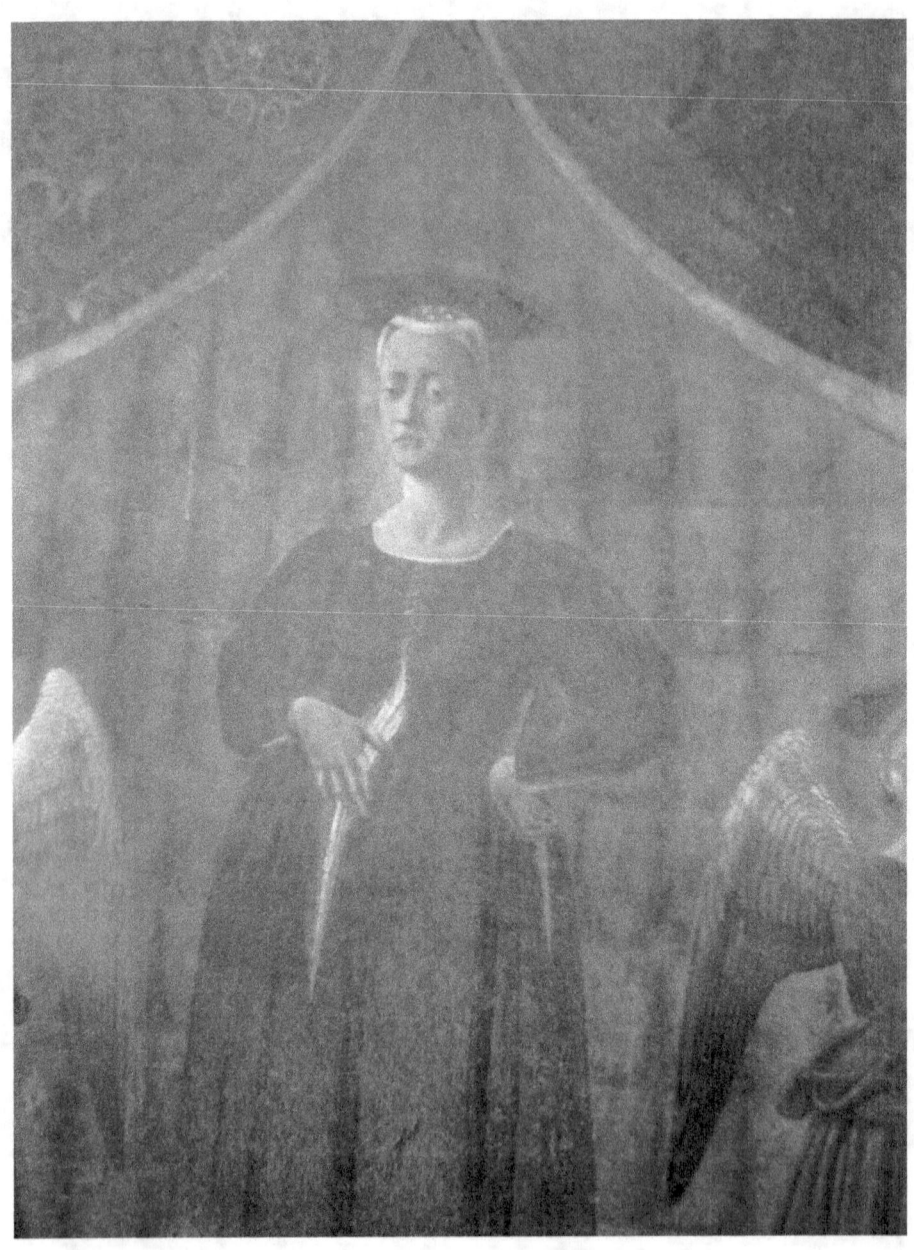

Piero, Madonna del Parto

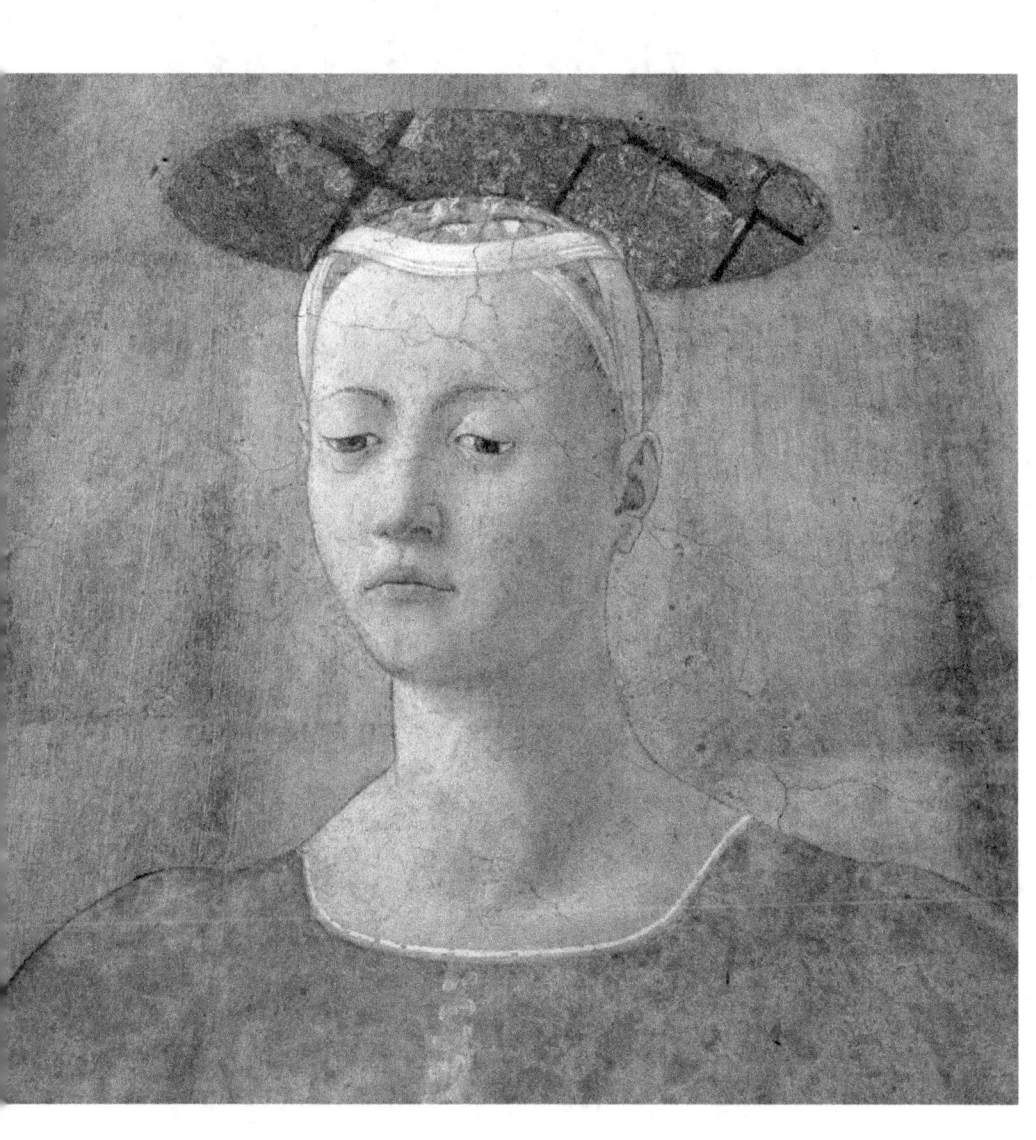

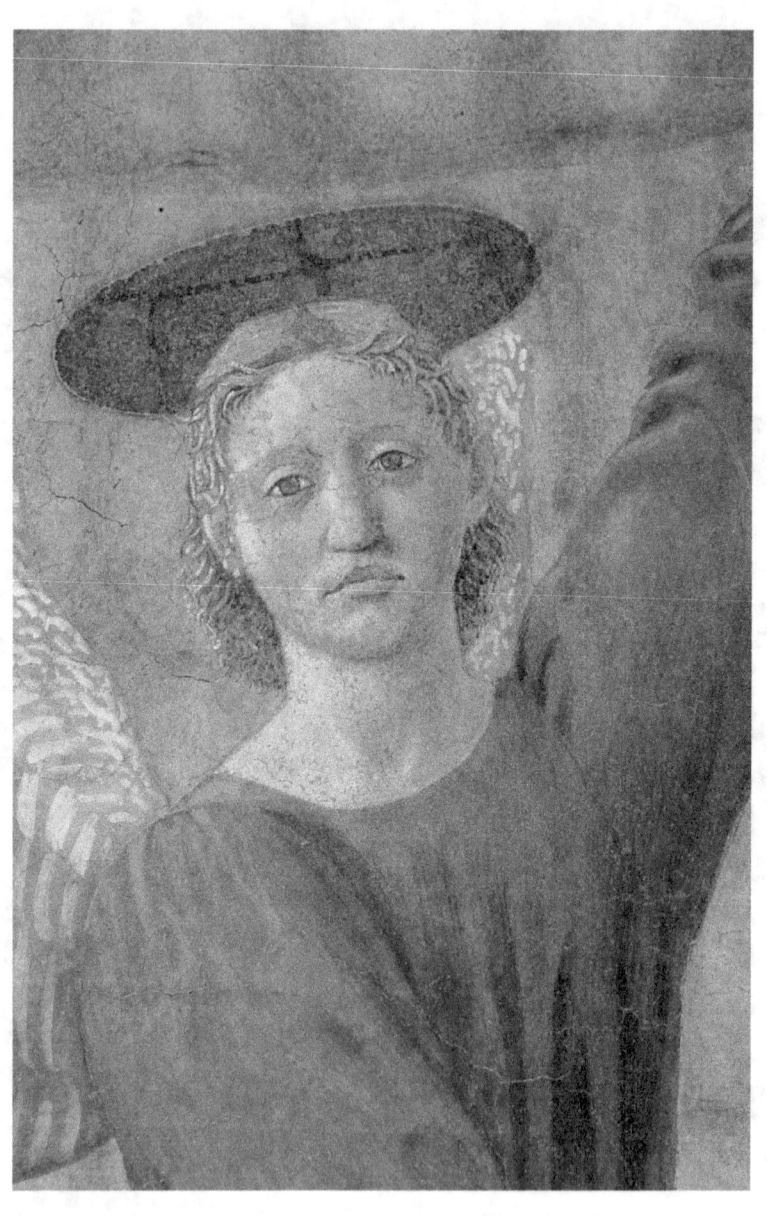

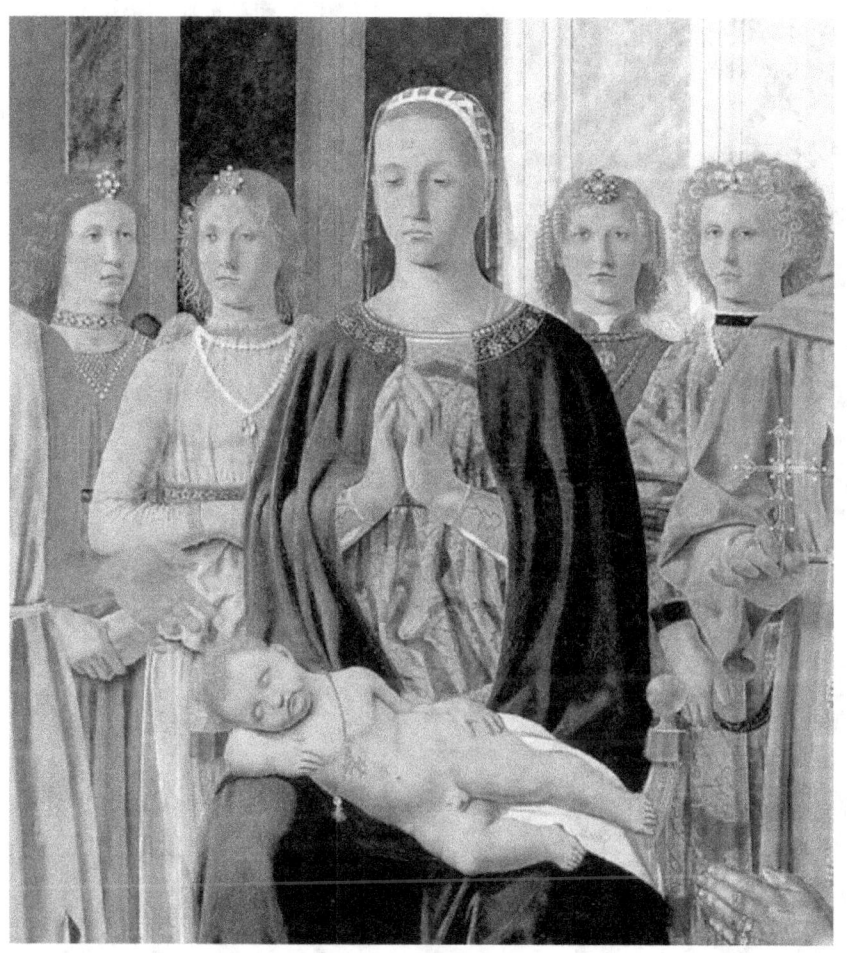

Piero della Francesca, details of The Brera Madonna,
this page and over.

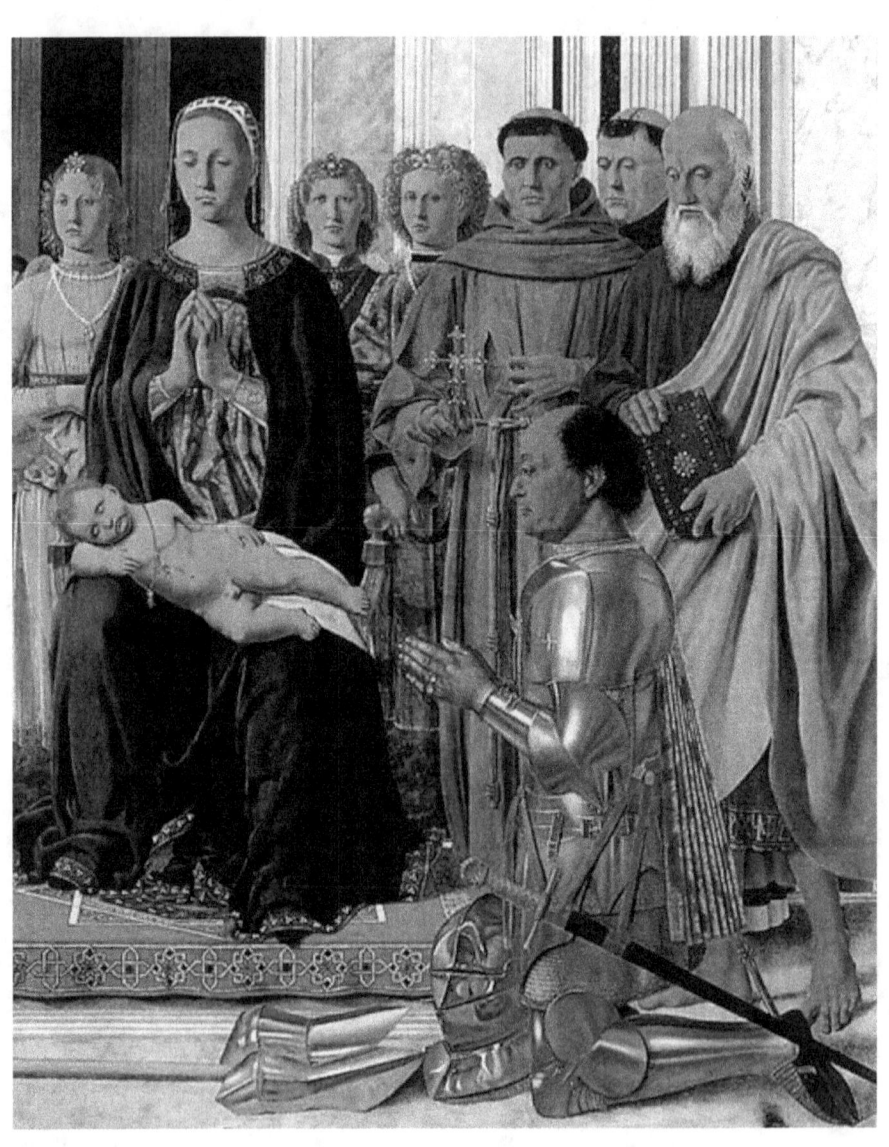

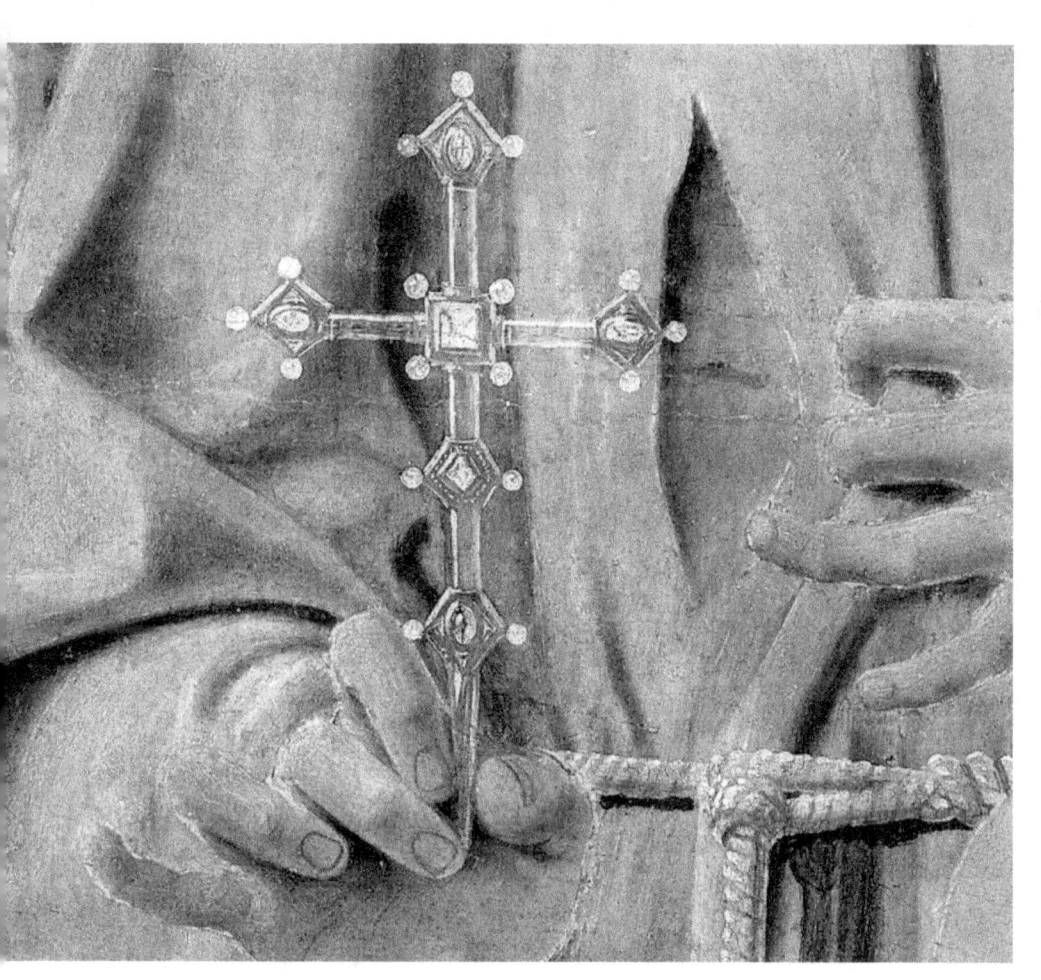

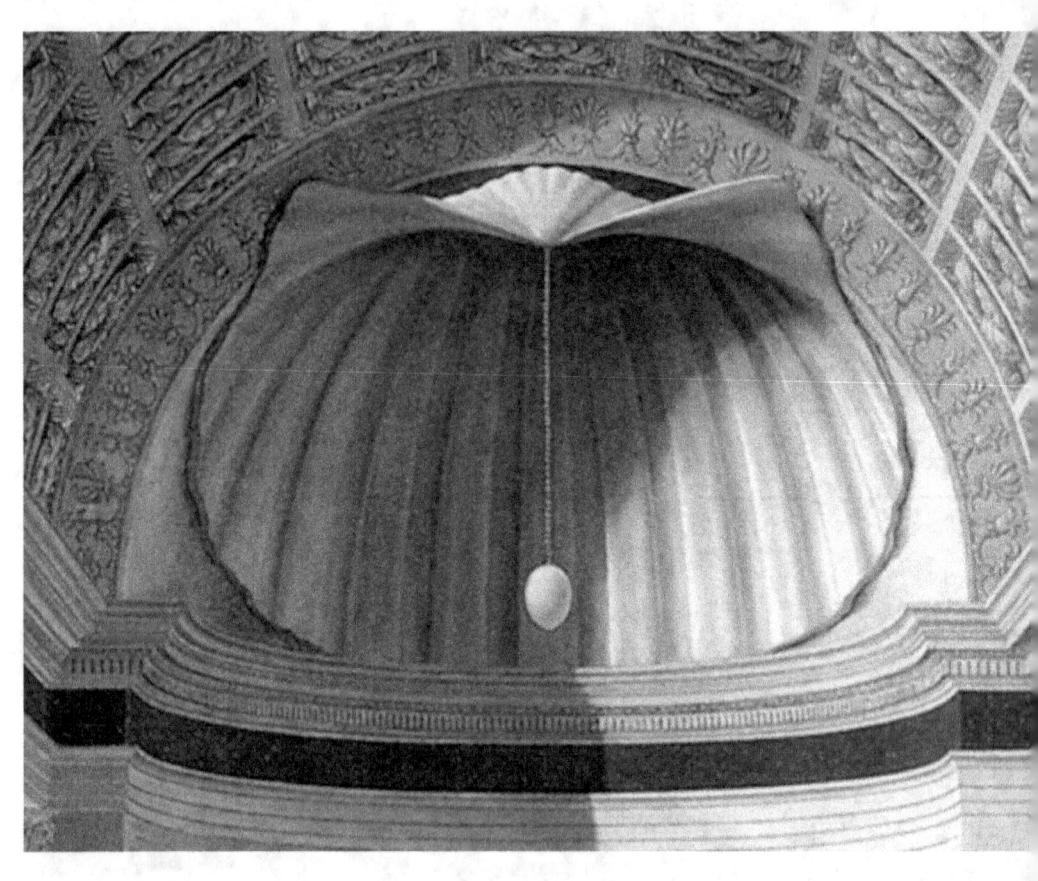

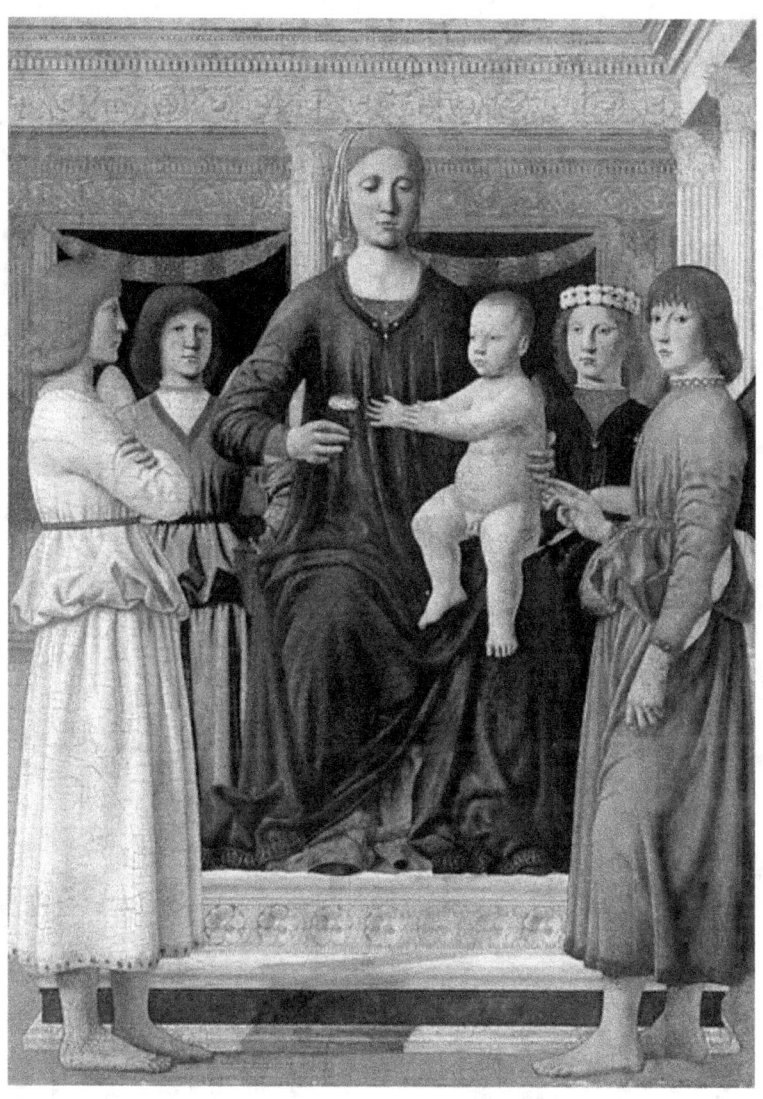

Piero della Francesca, Madonna and Child Attended By Angels,
Clark Art Institute

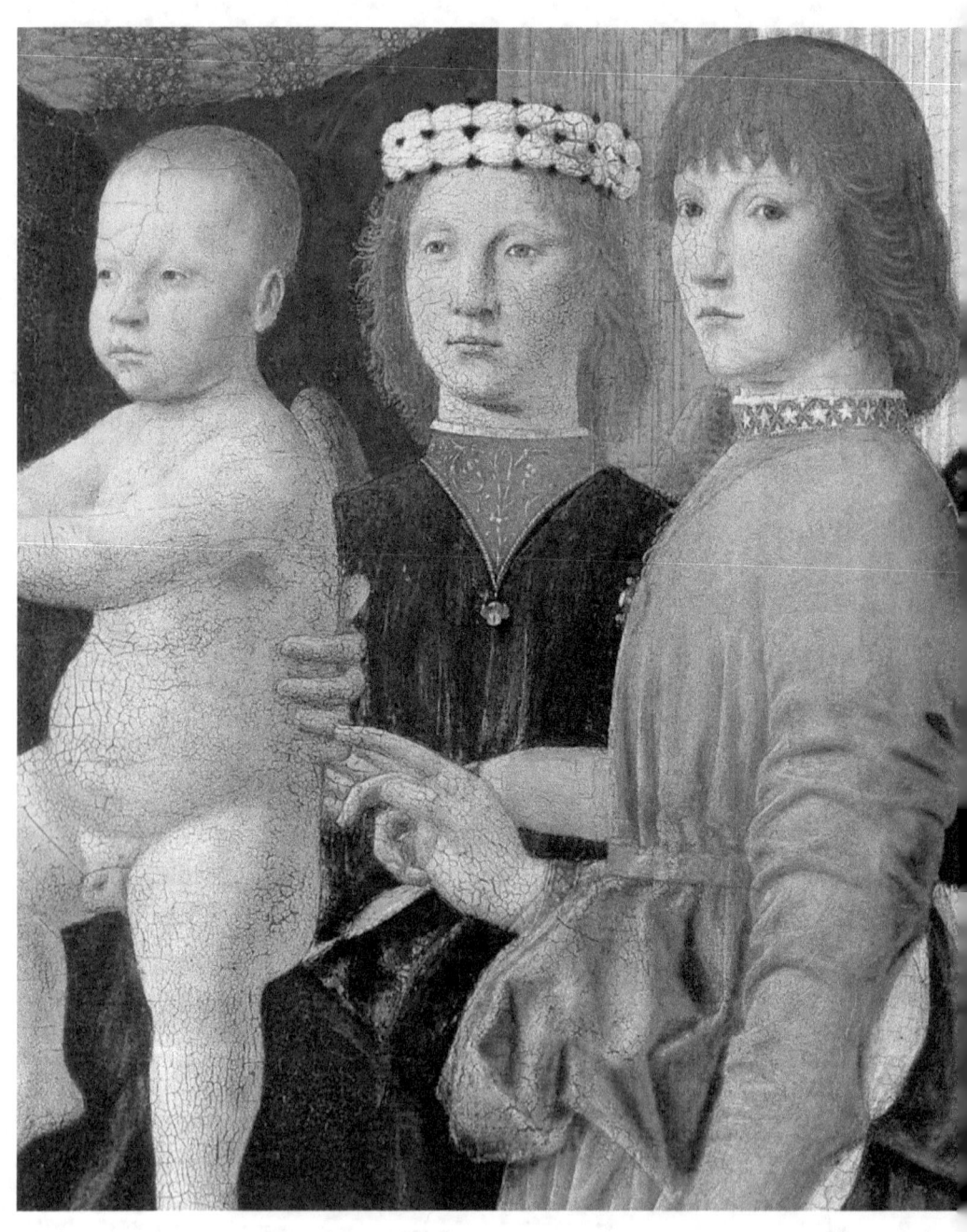

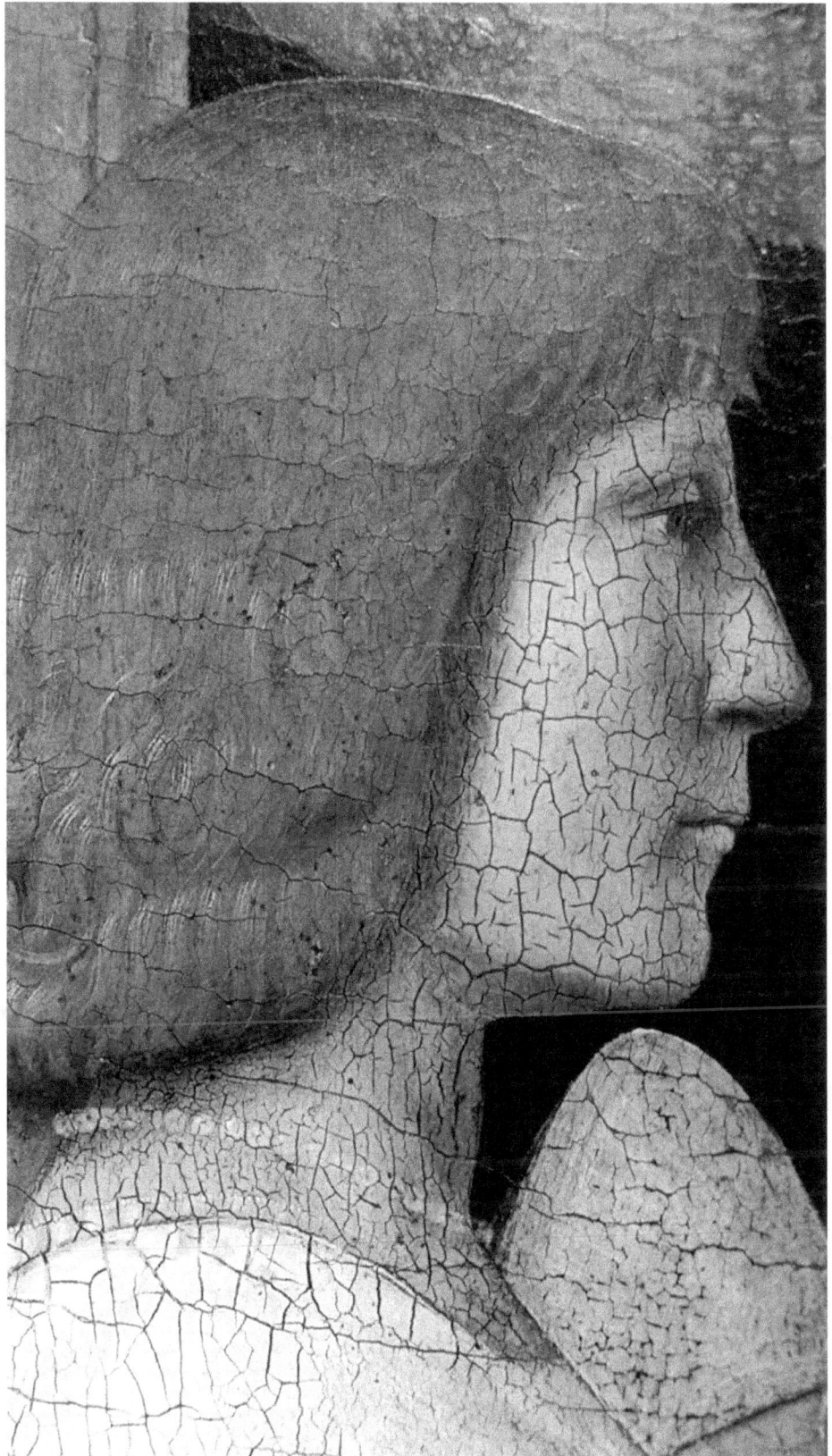

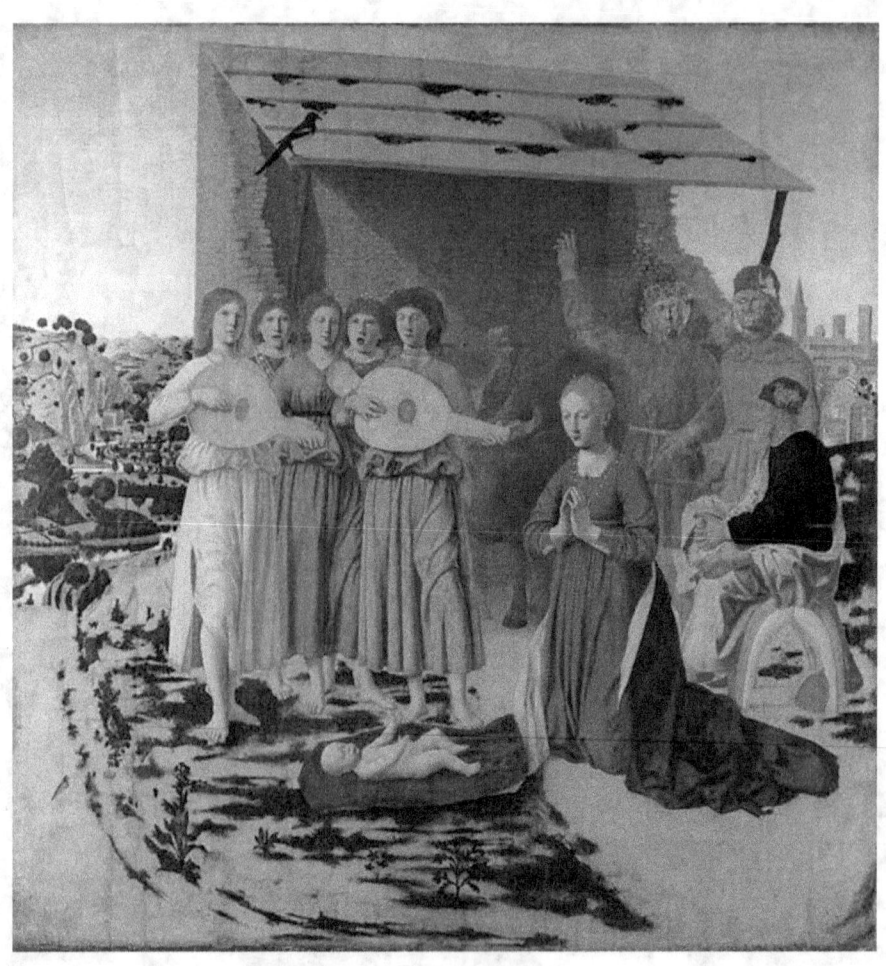

Piero della Francesca, The Nativity,
National Gallery, London

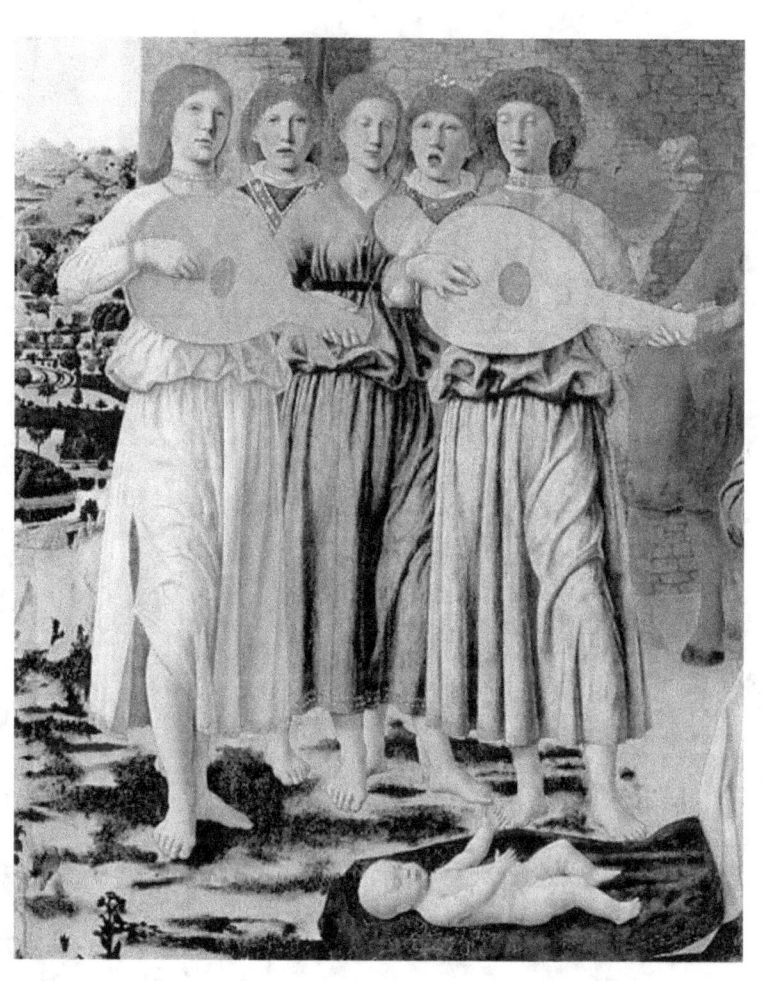

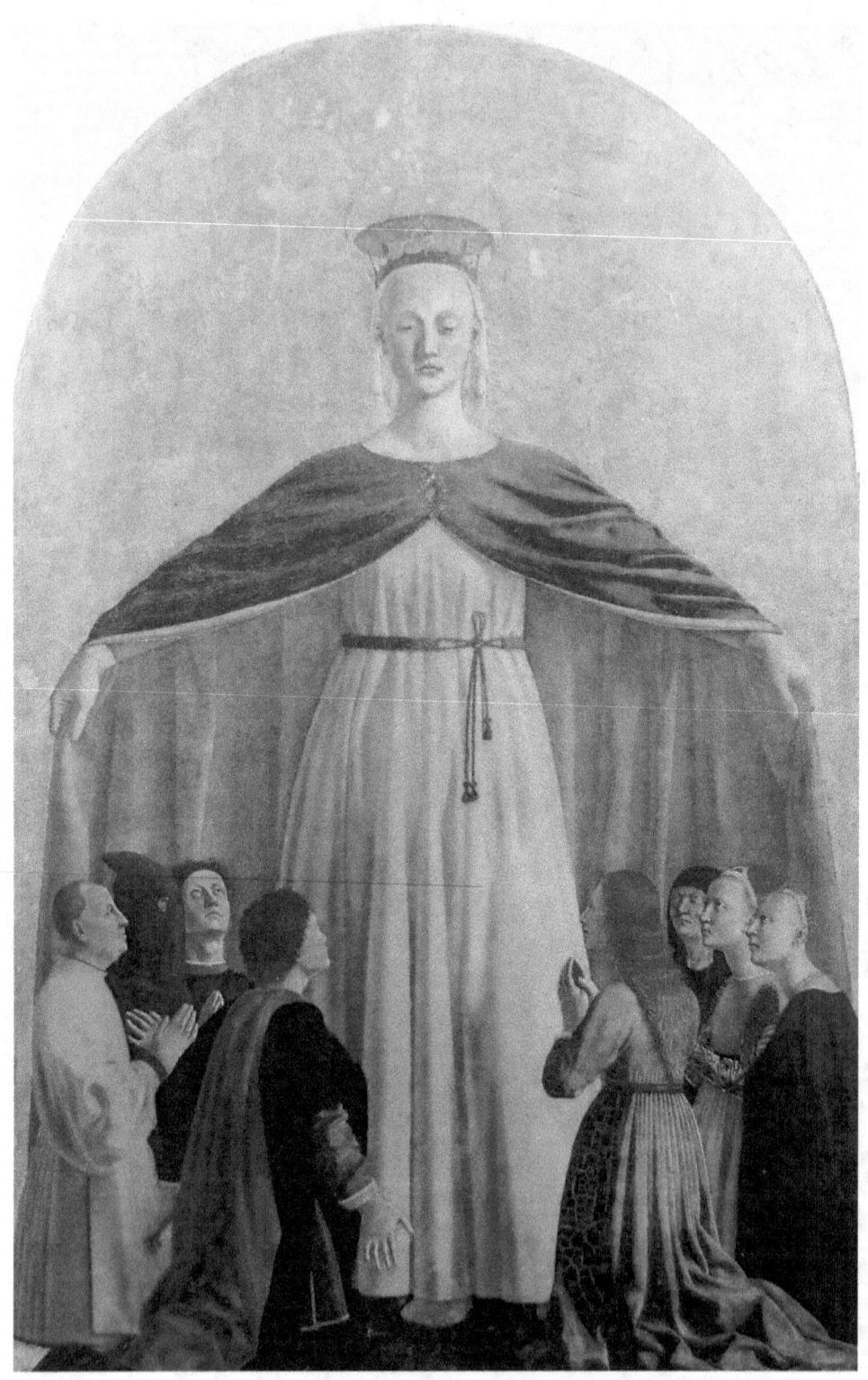

Piero, Madonna della Misericordia, Sanepulchro

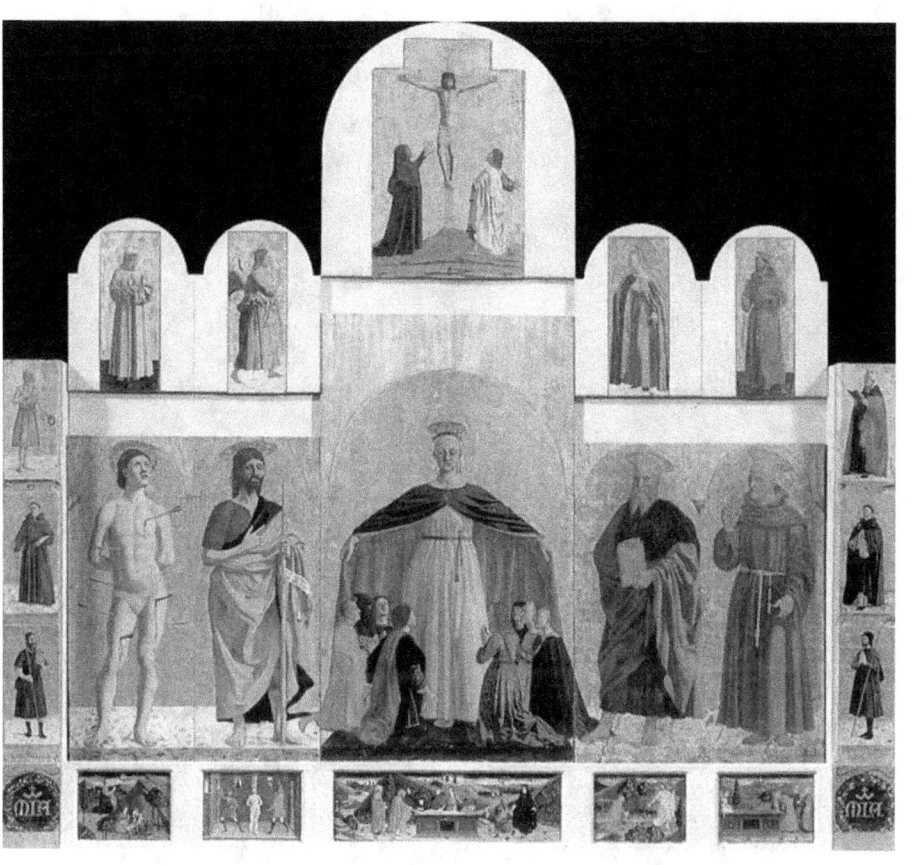

Piero della Francesca, Misericordia Altarpiece, San Sepulcro.
Details from the altarpiece on the following pages.

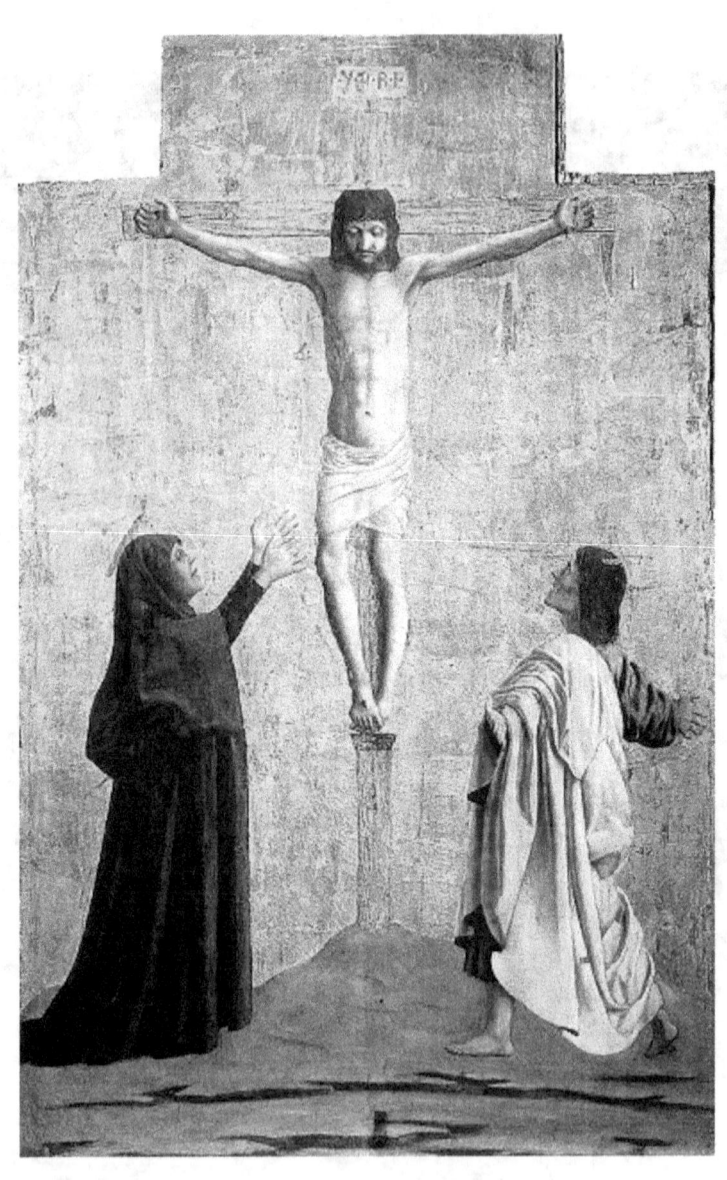

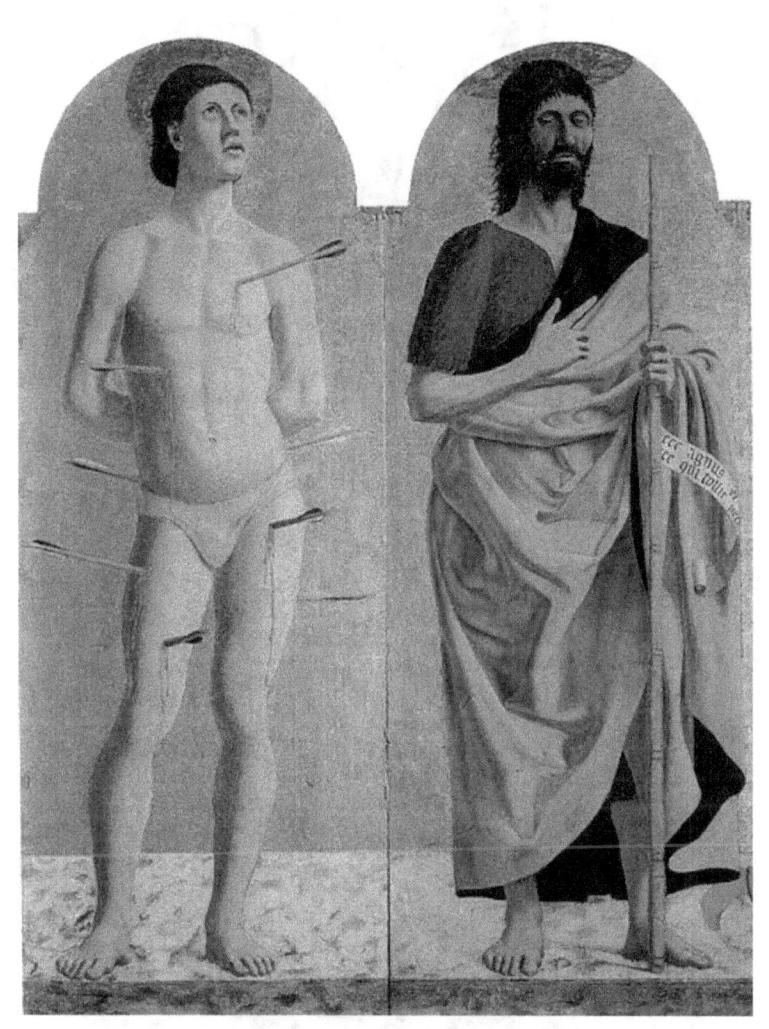

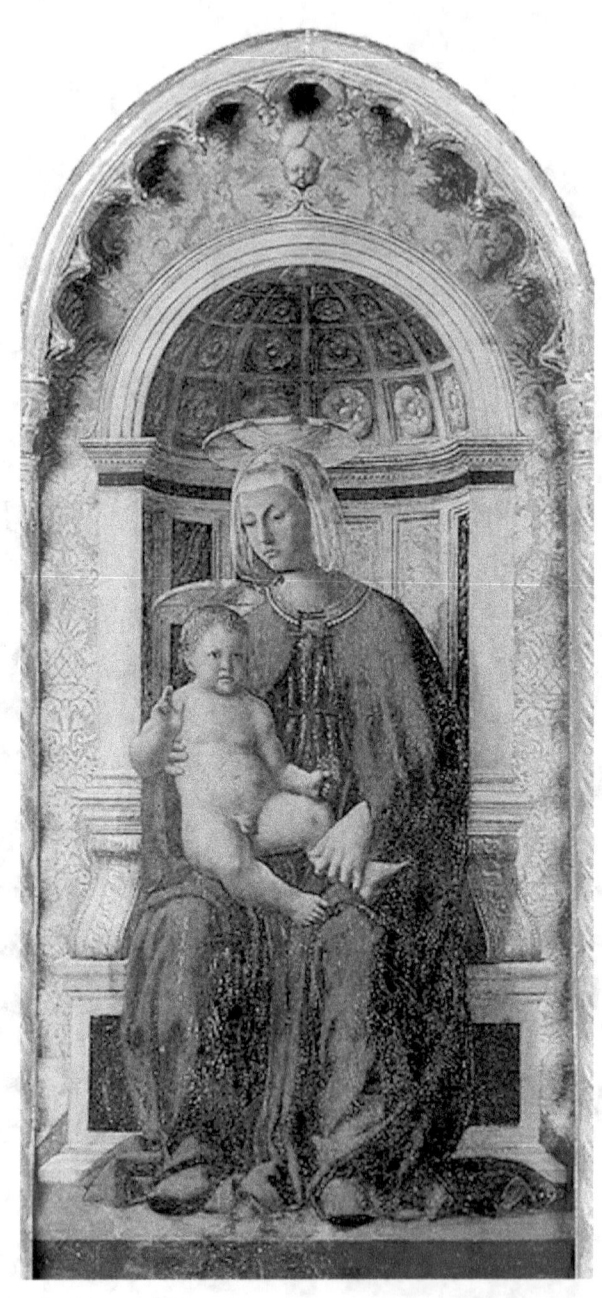

Piero della Francesca, Polittico di Sant'Antonio,
1460-70, Perugia

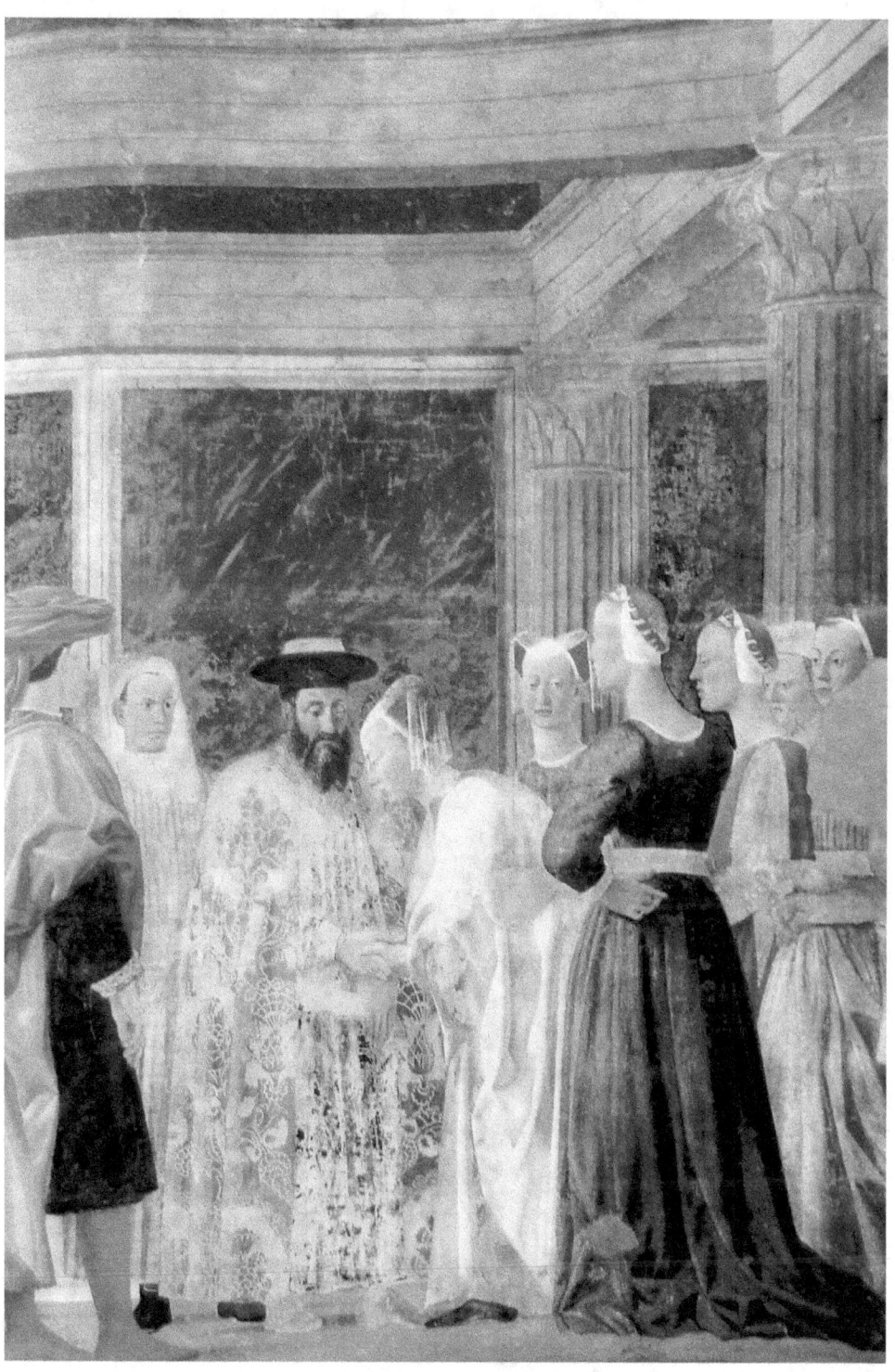

This page and over: Piero's Arezzo frescoes

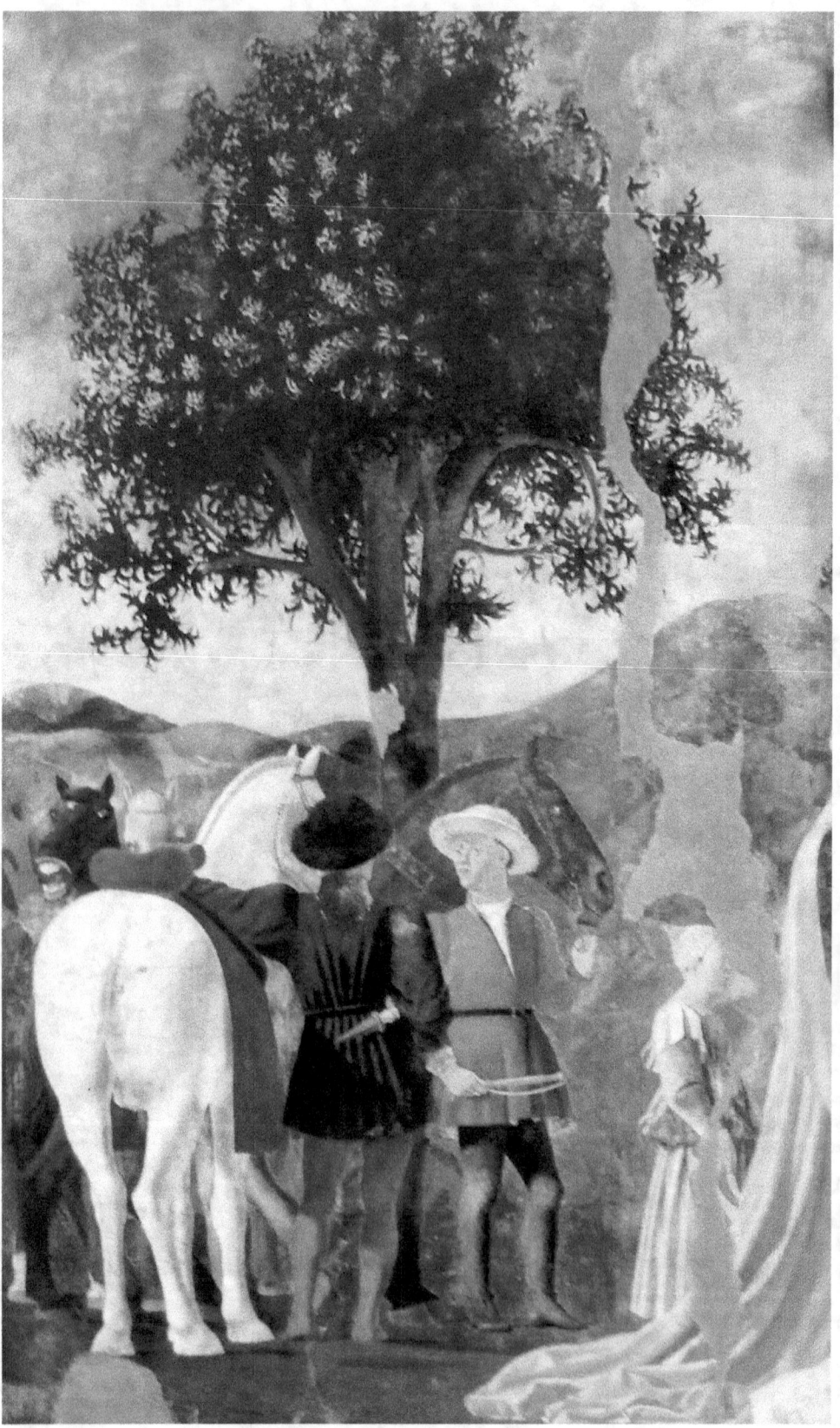

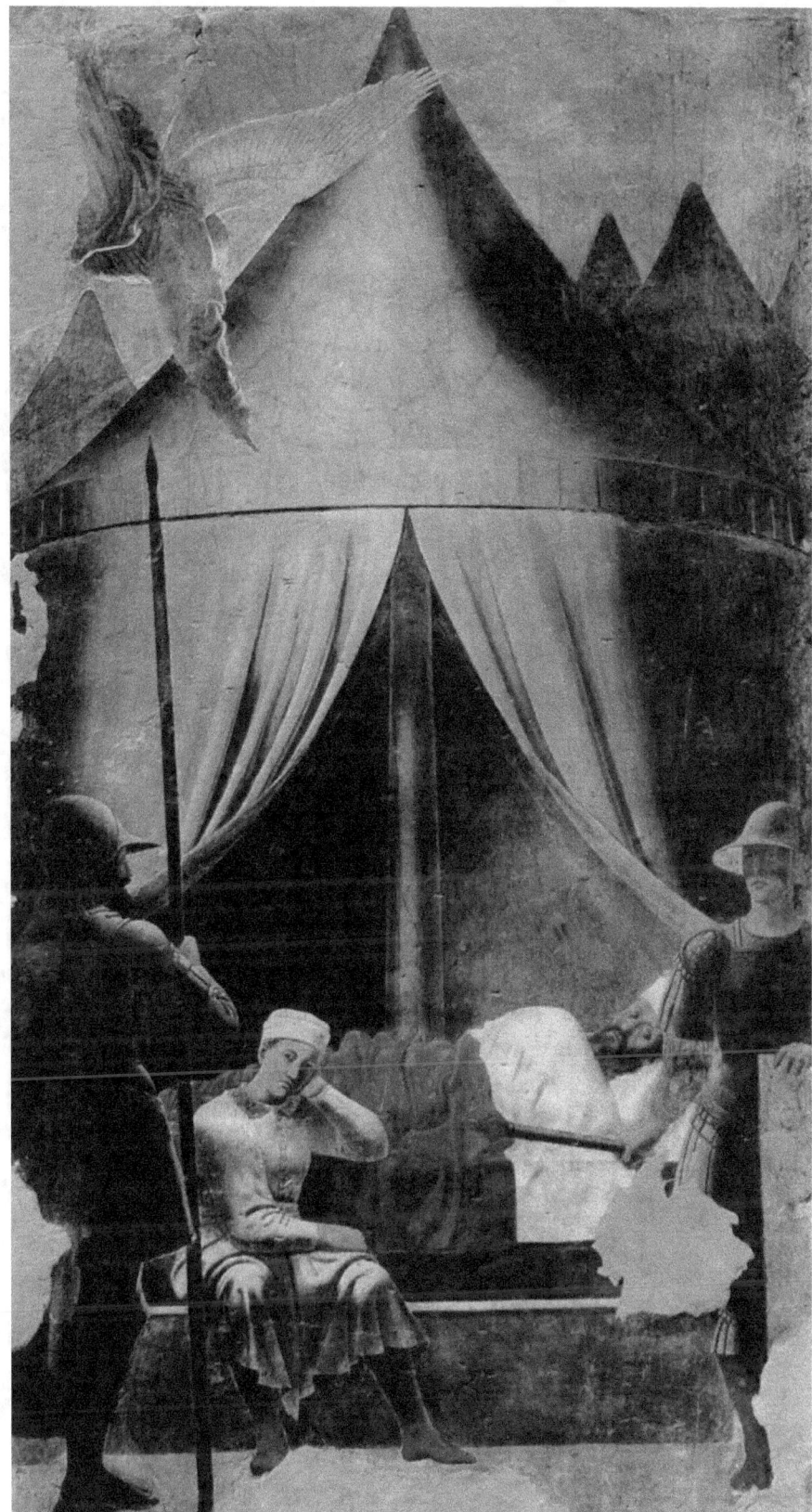

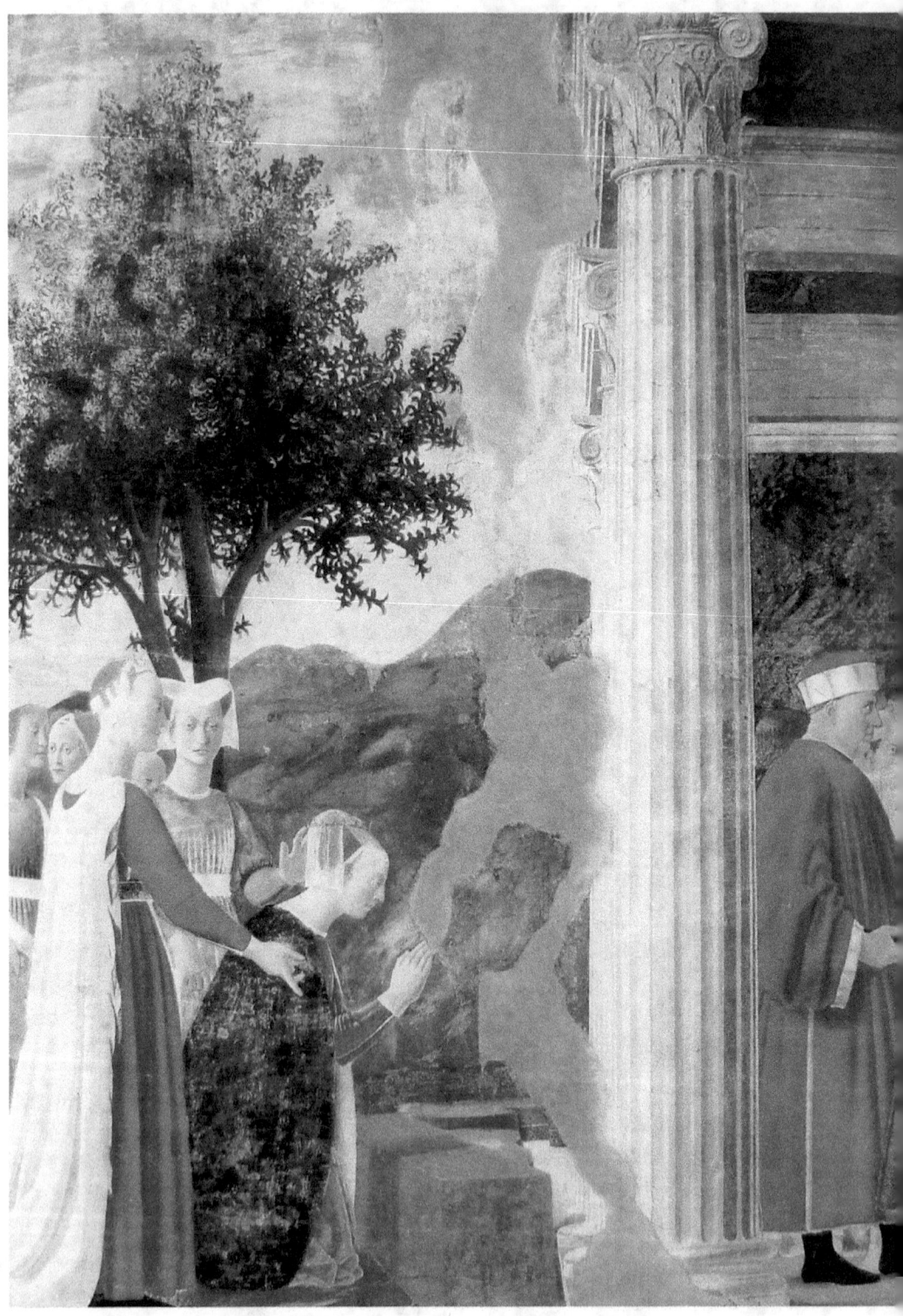

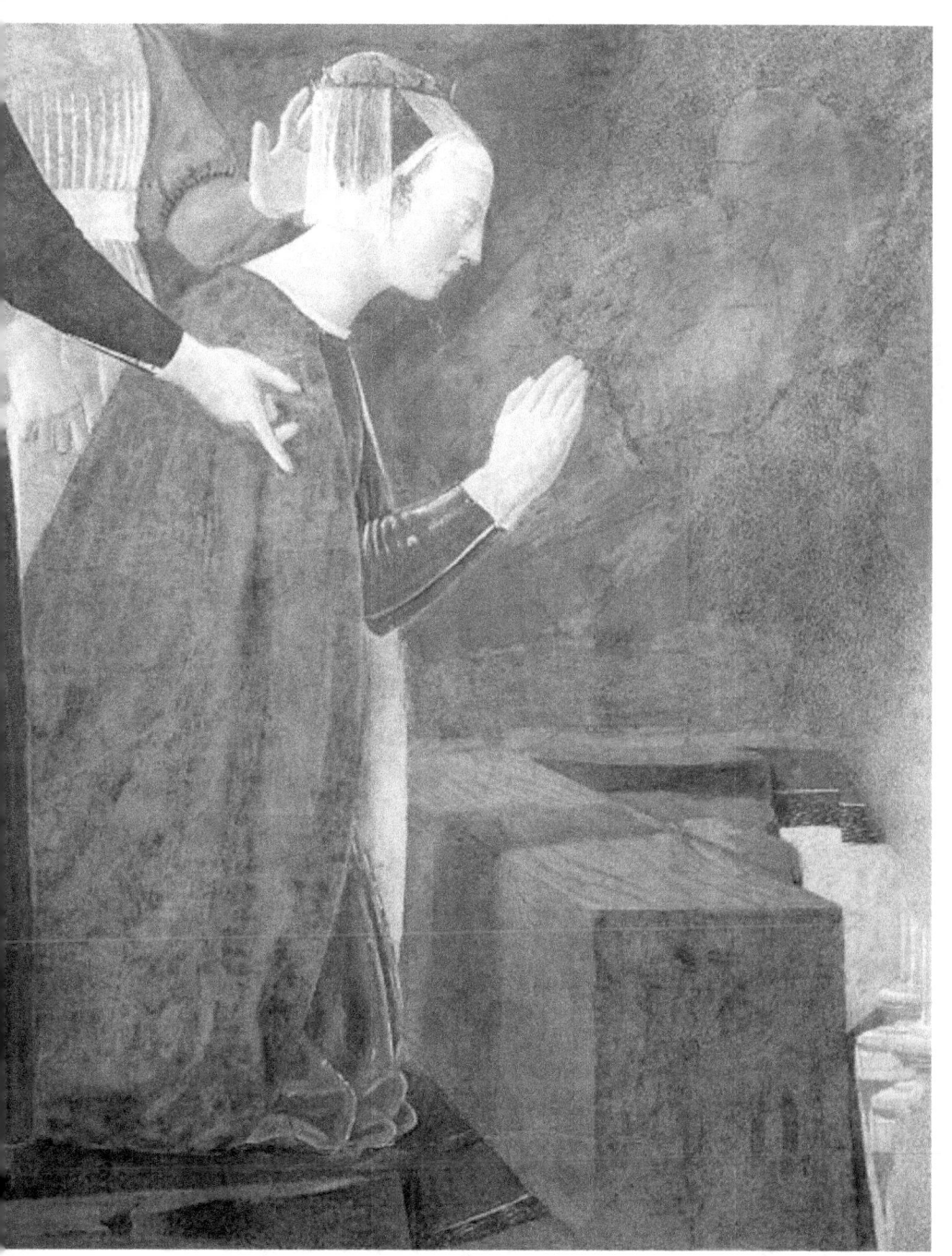

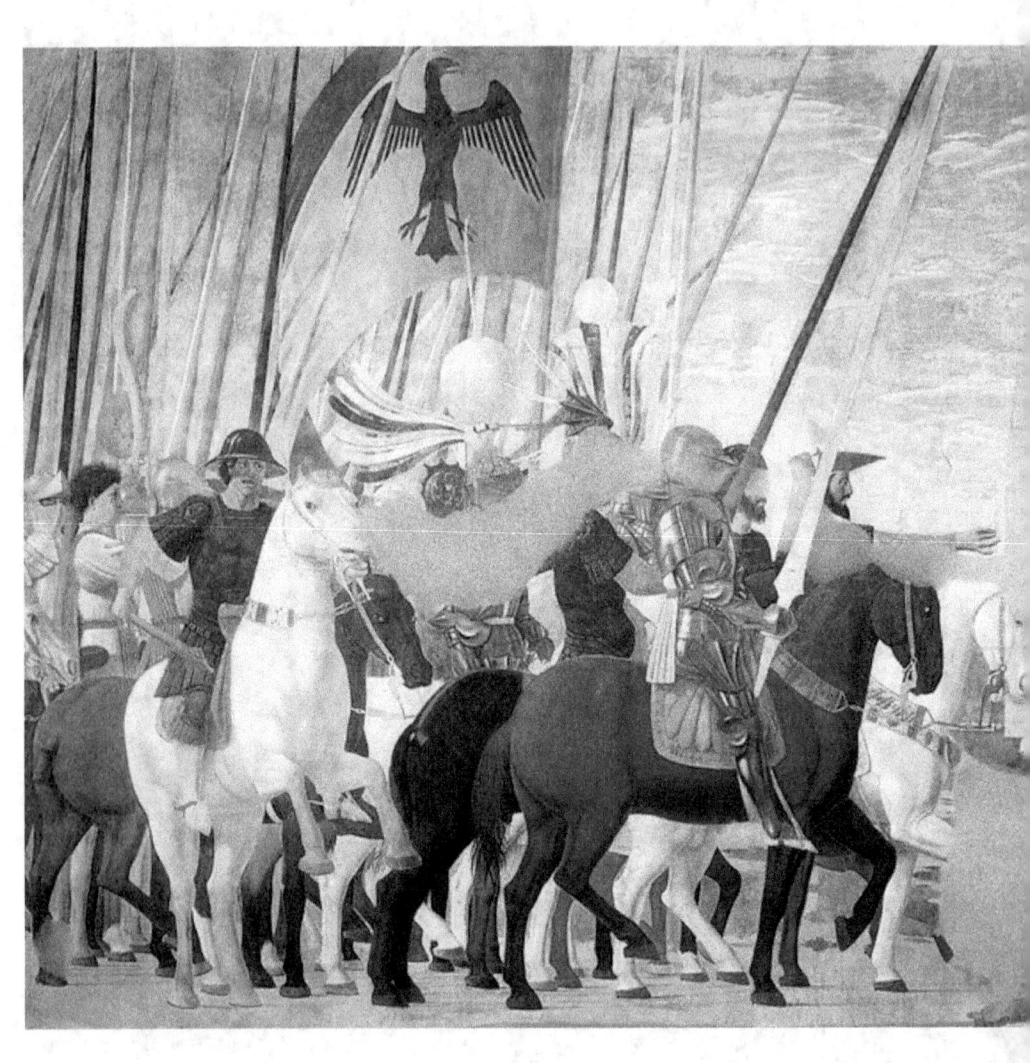

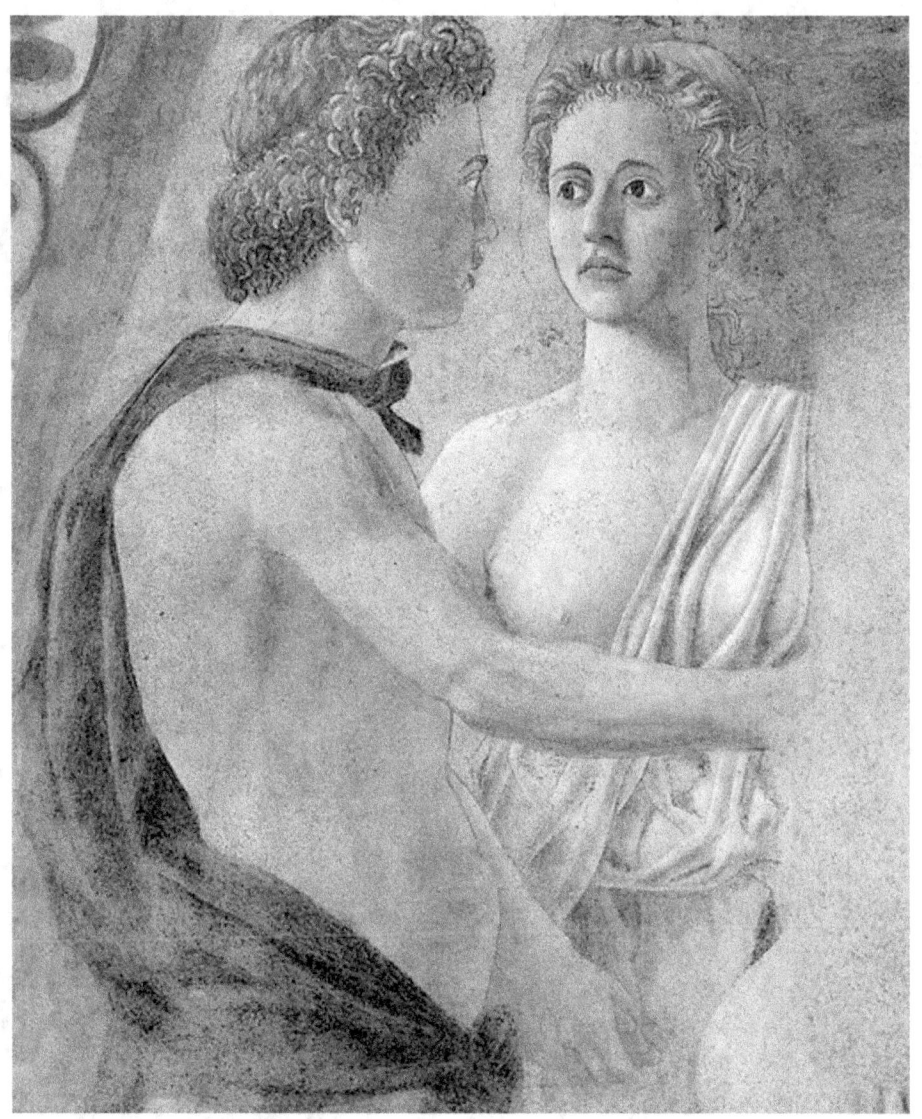

Piero della Francesca, The Death of Adam, detail

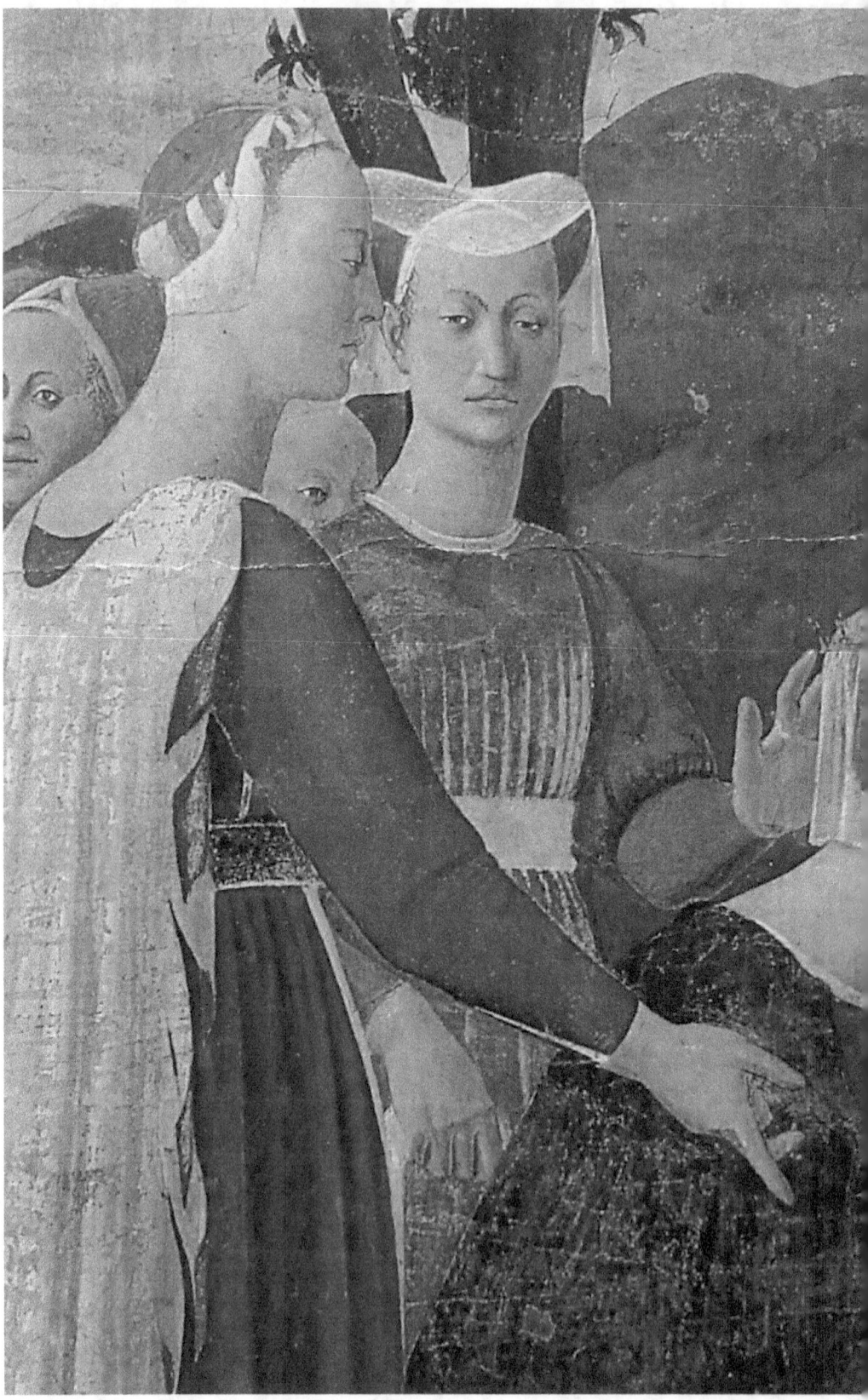

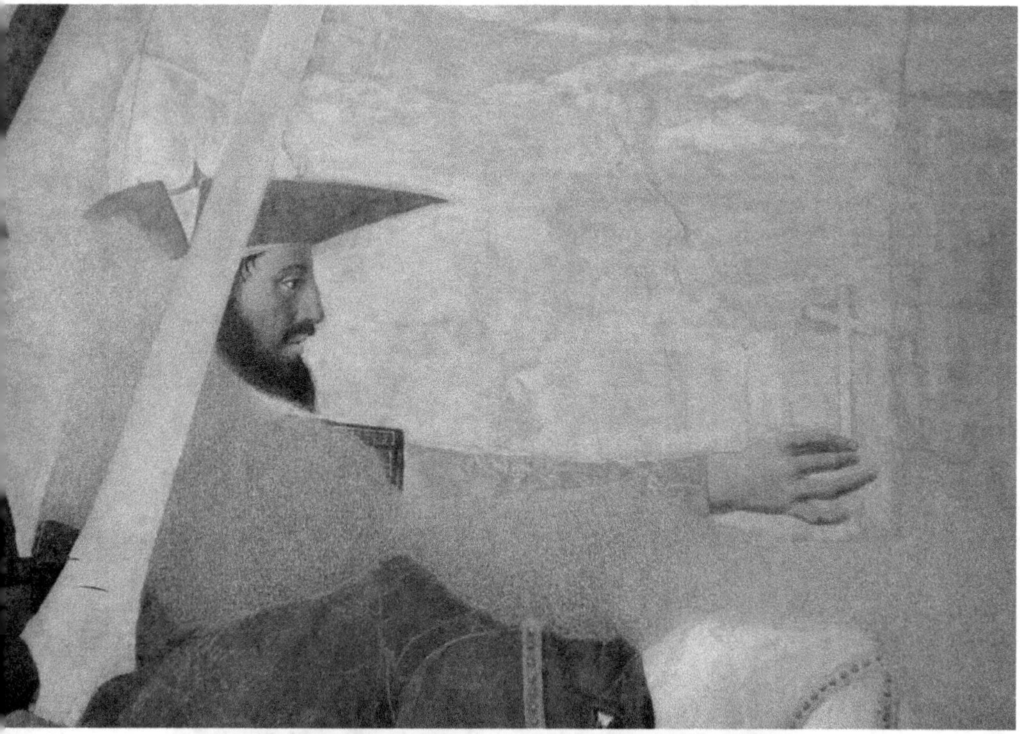

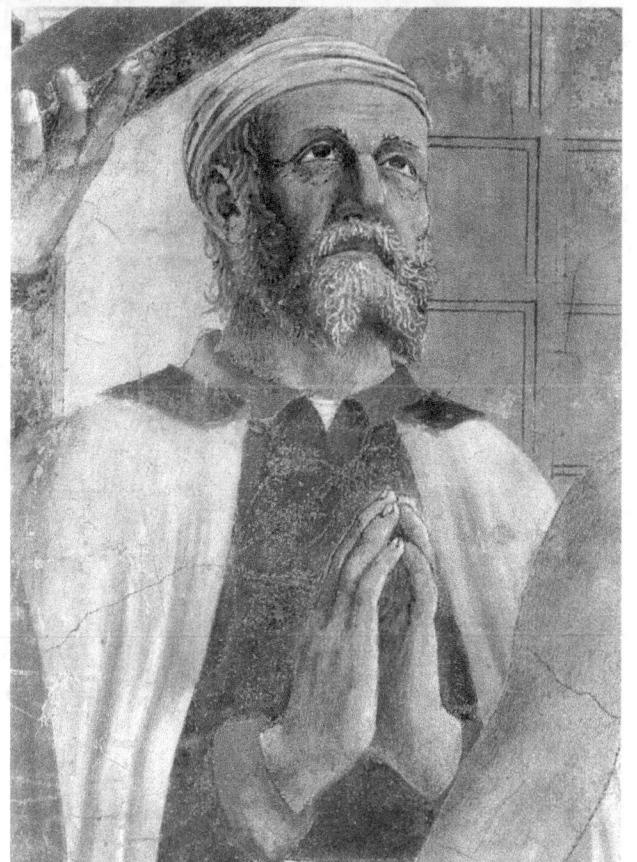

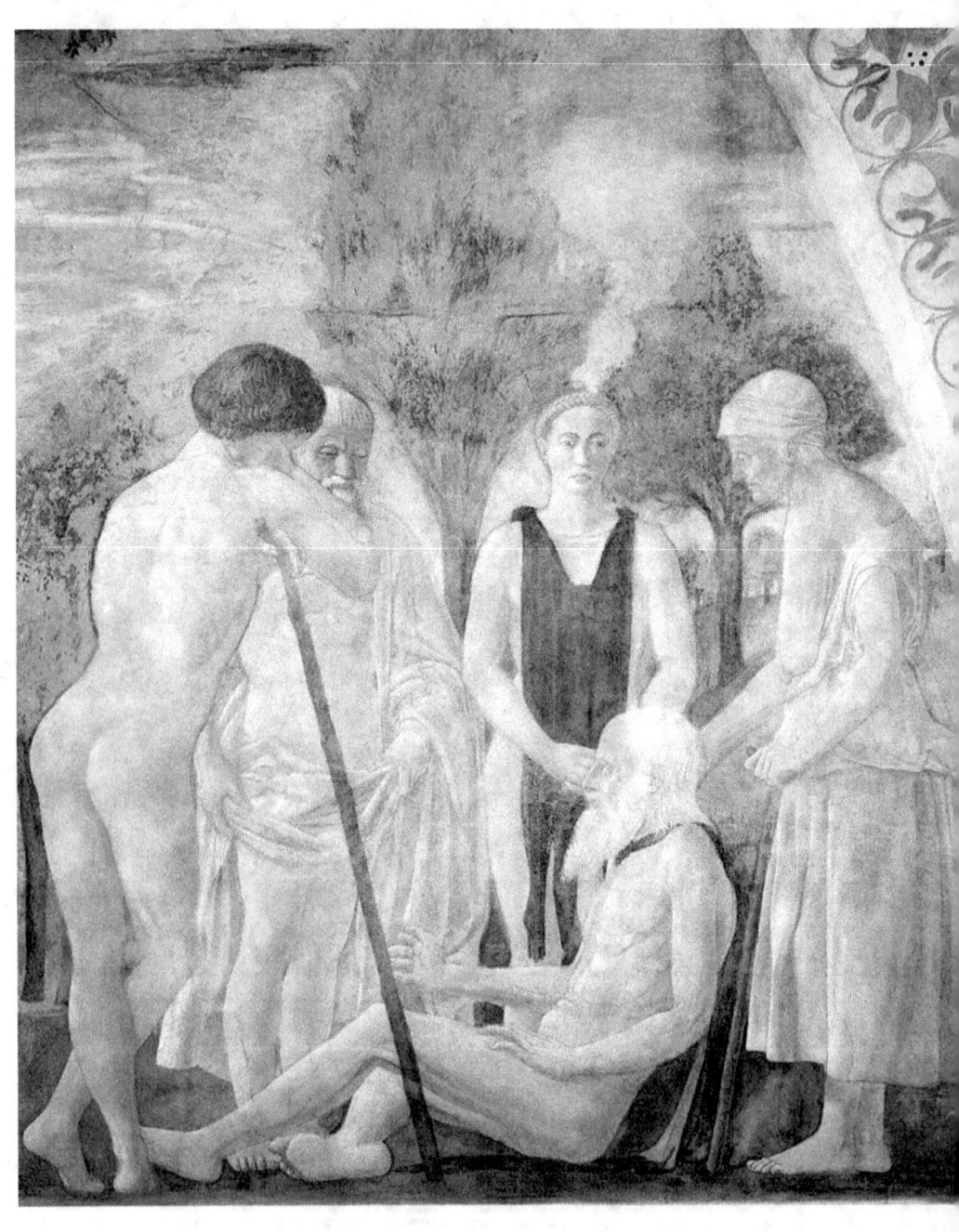

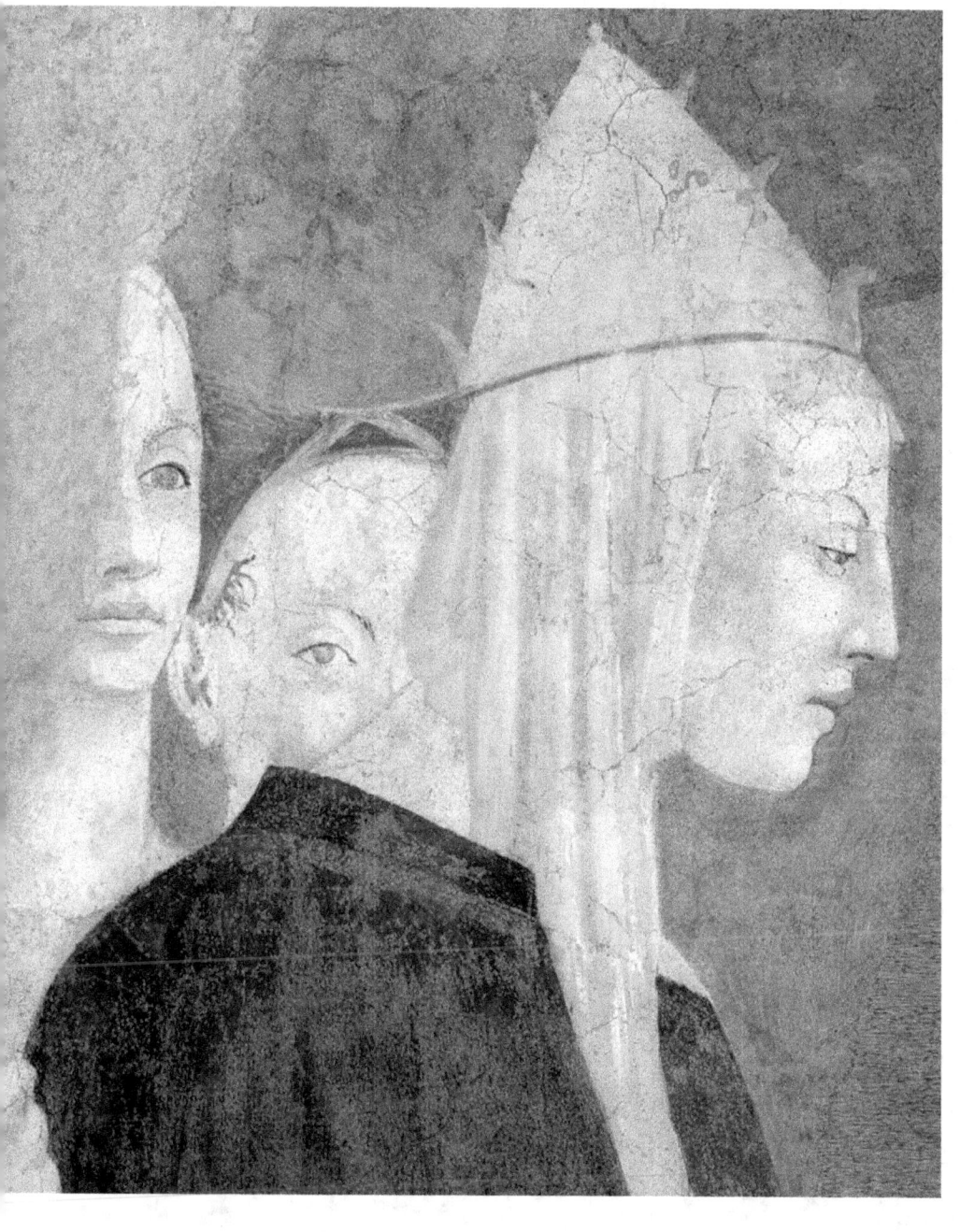

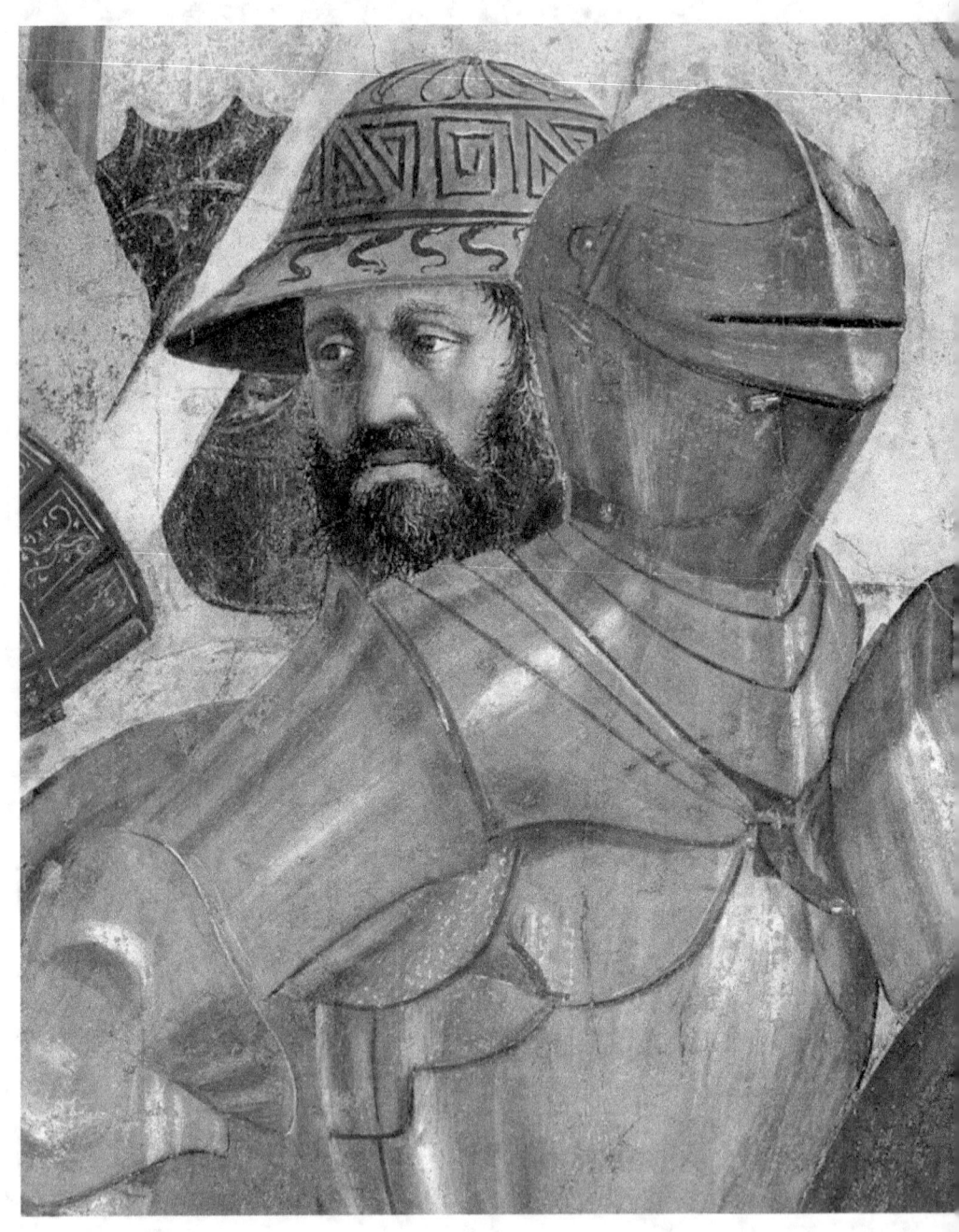

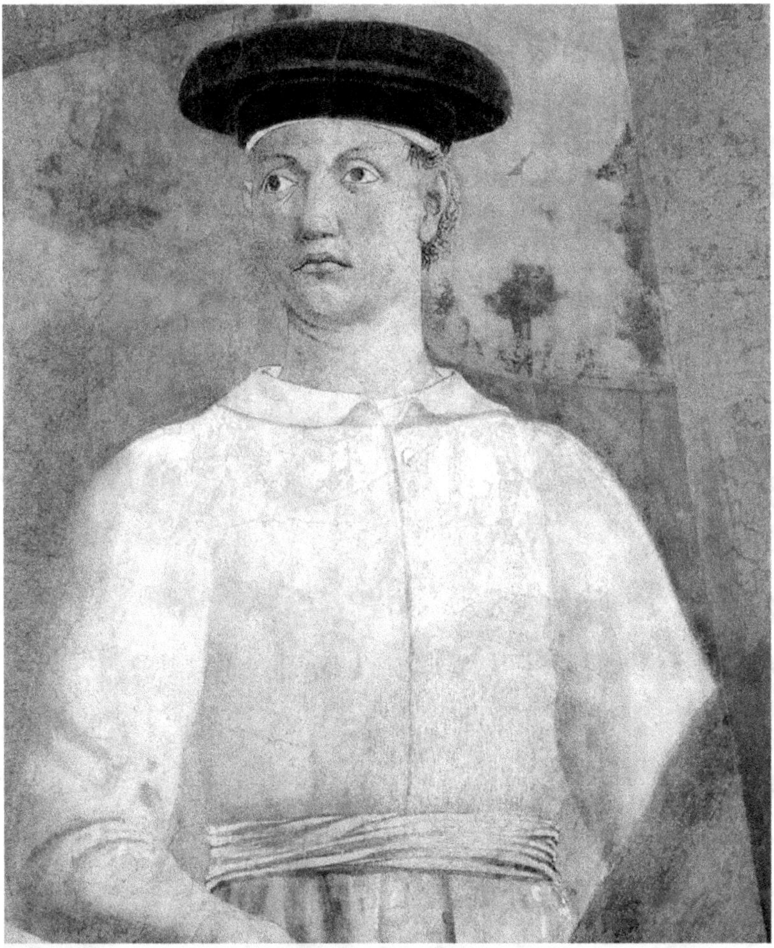

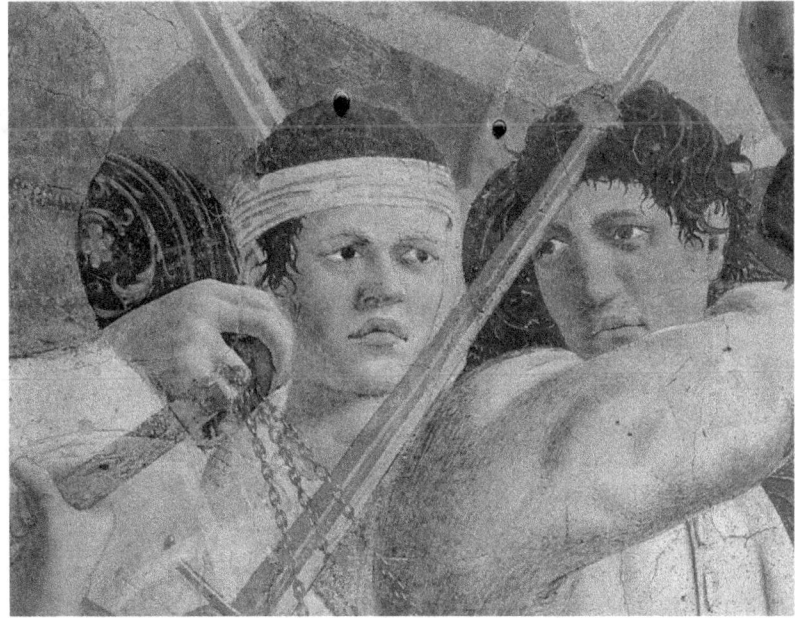

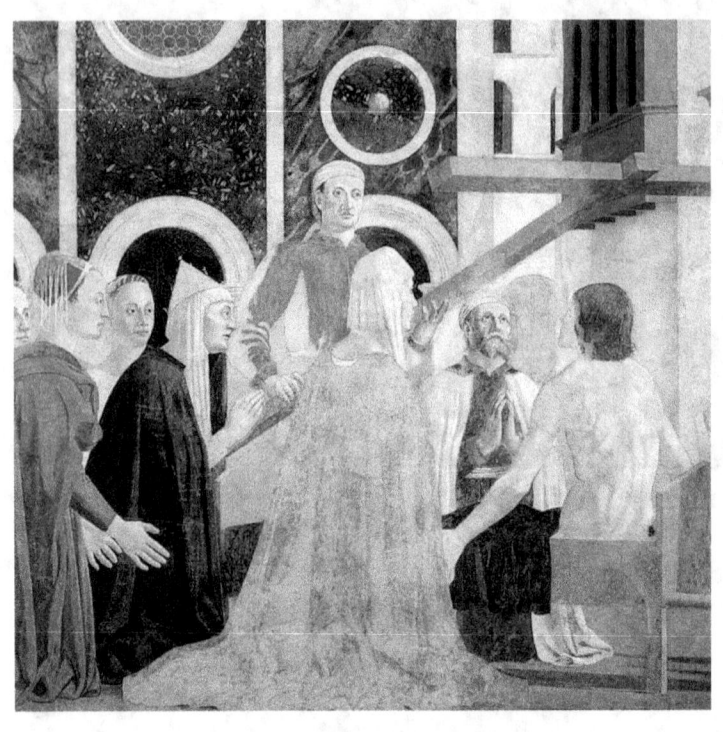

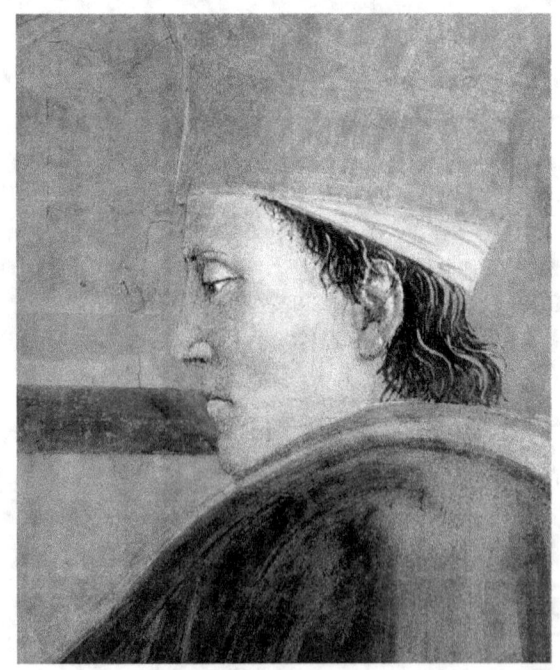

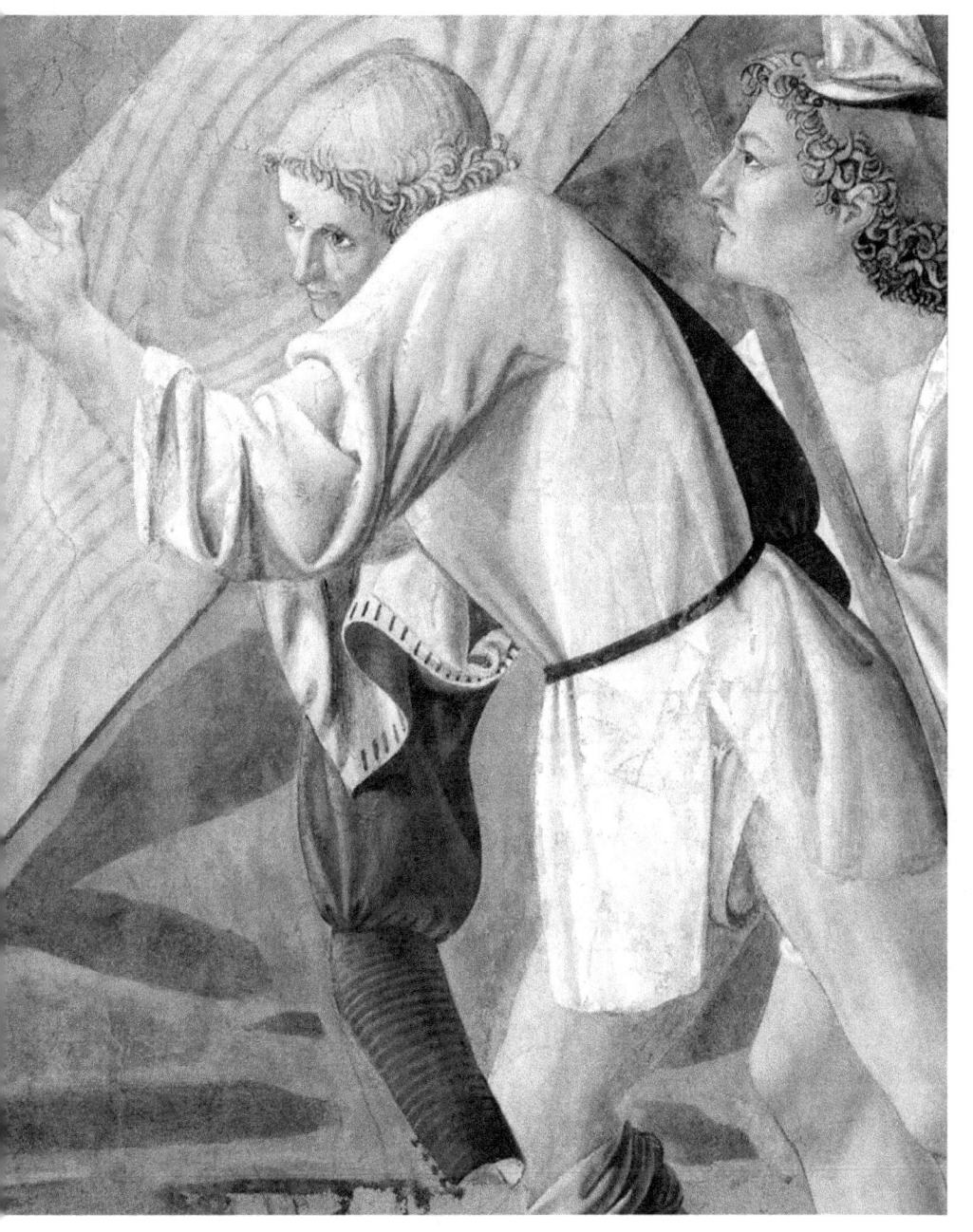

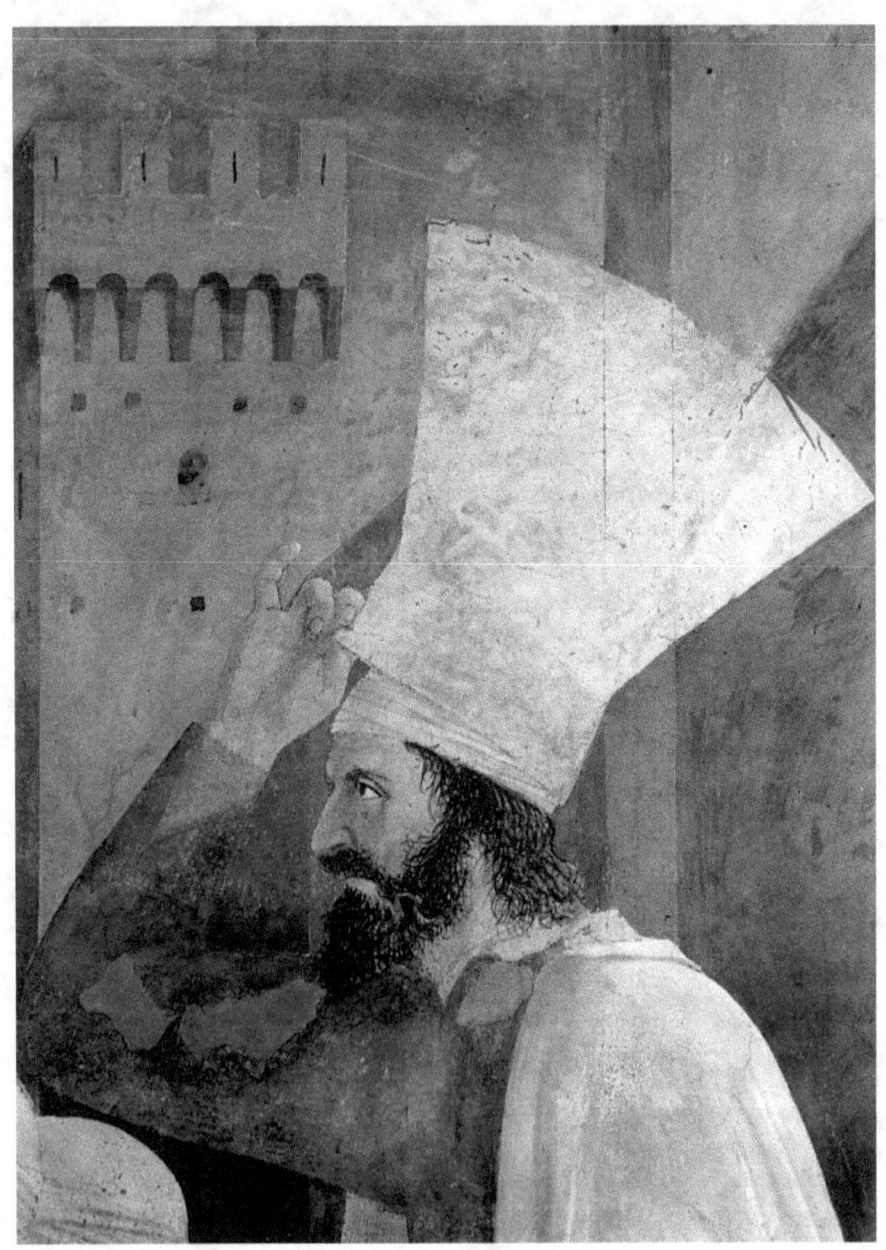

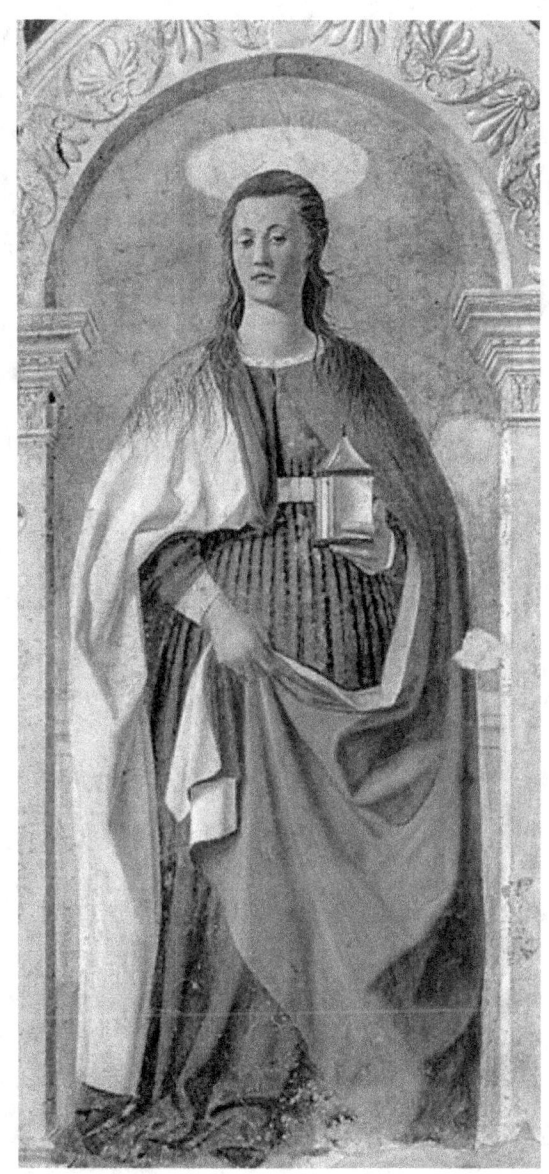

Piero, St Mary Magdalene, Arezzo

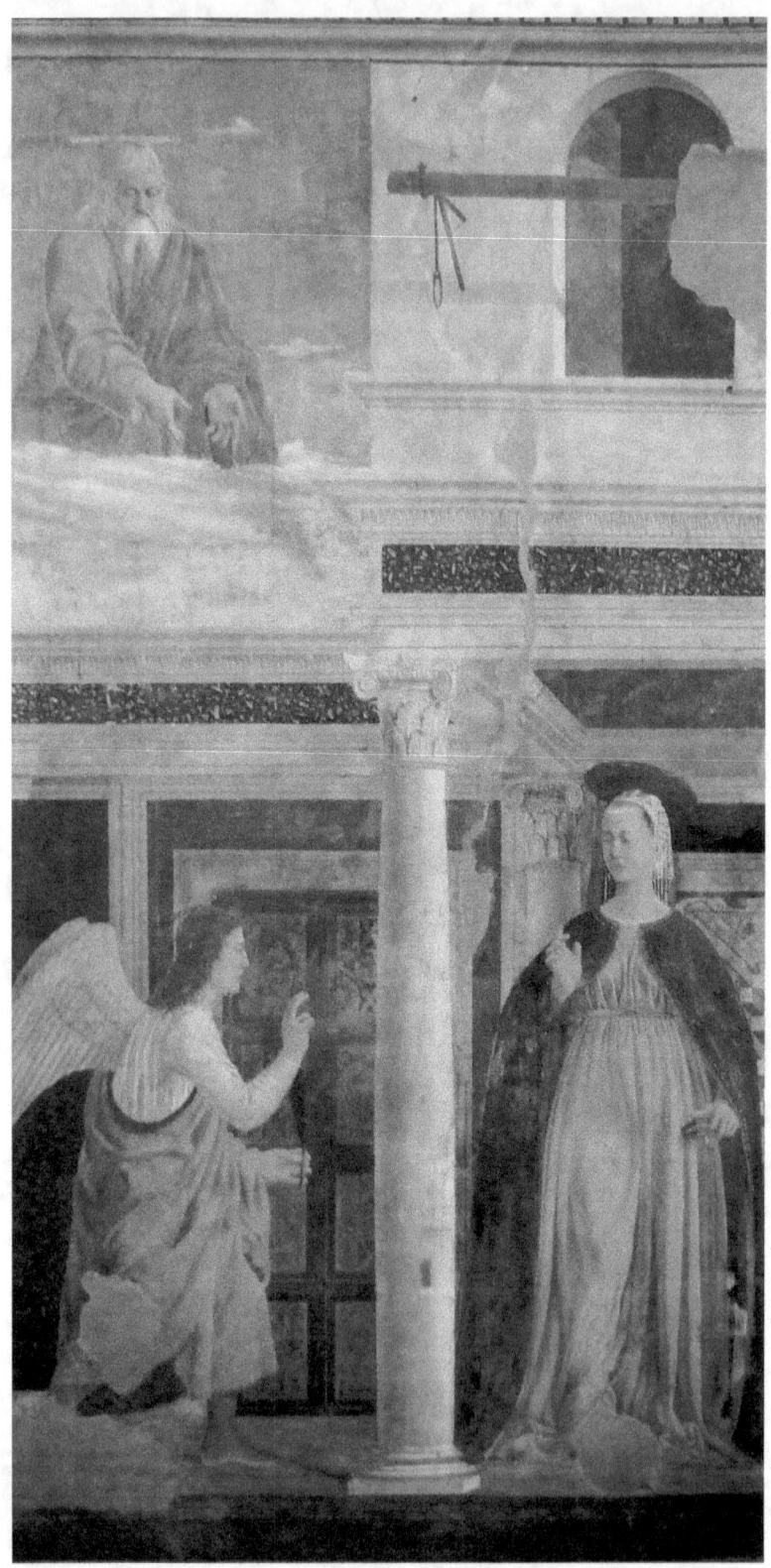

Piero, The Annunciation, Arezzo

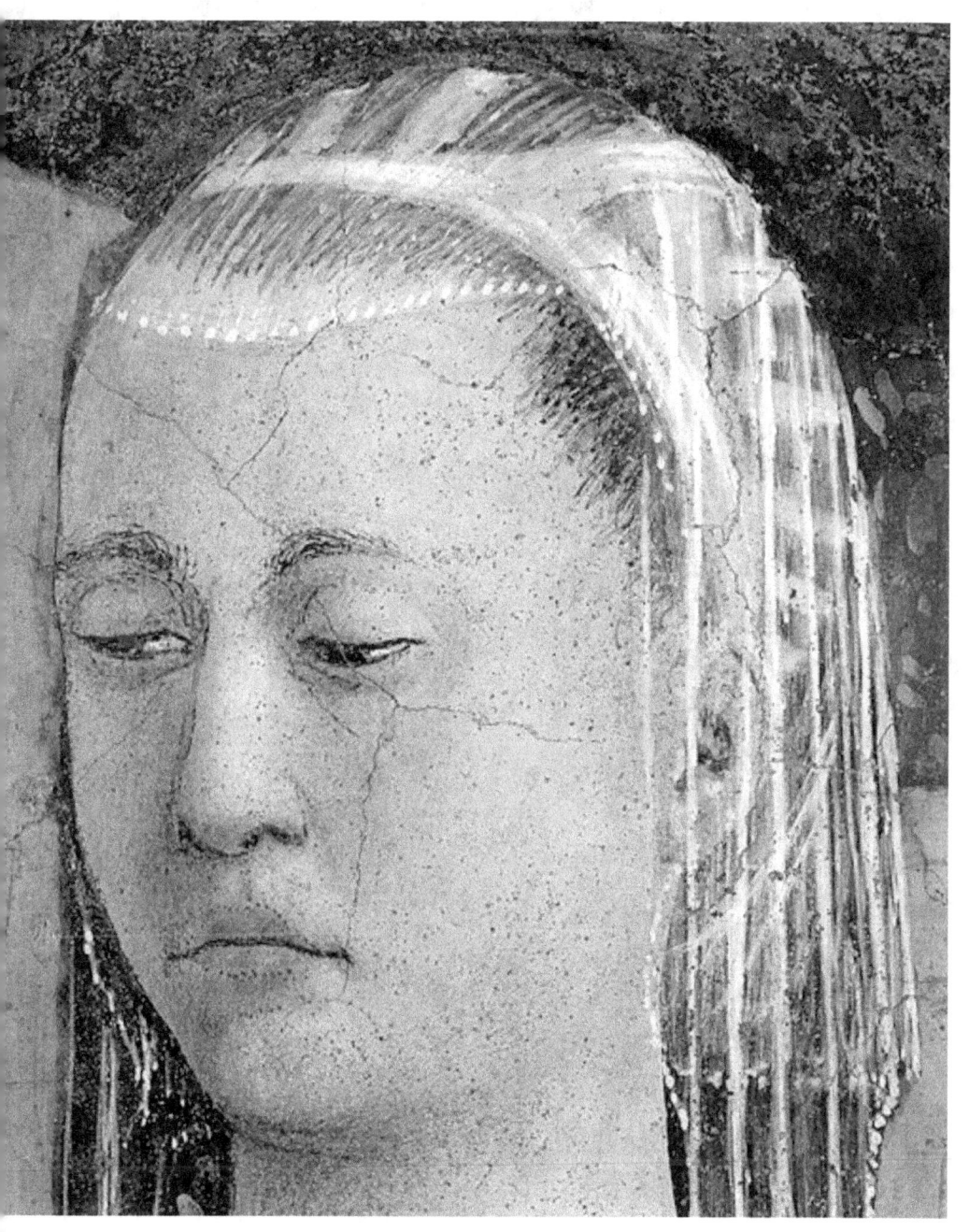

The Annunciate Virgin, detail

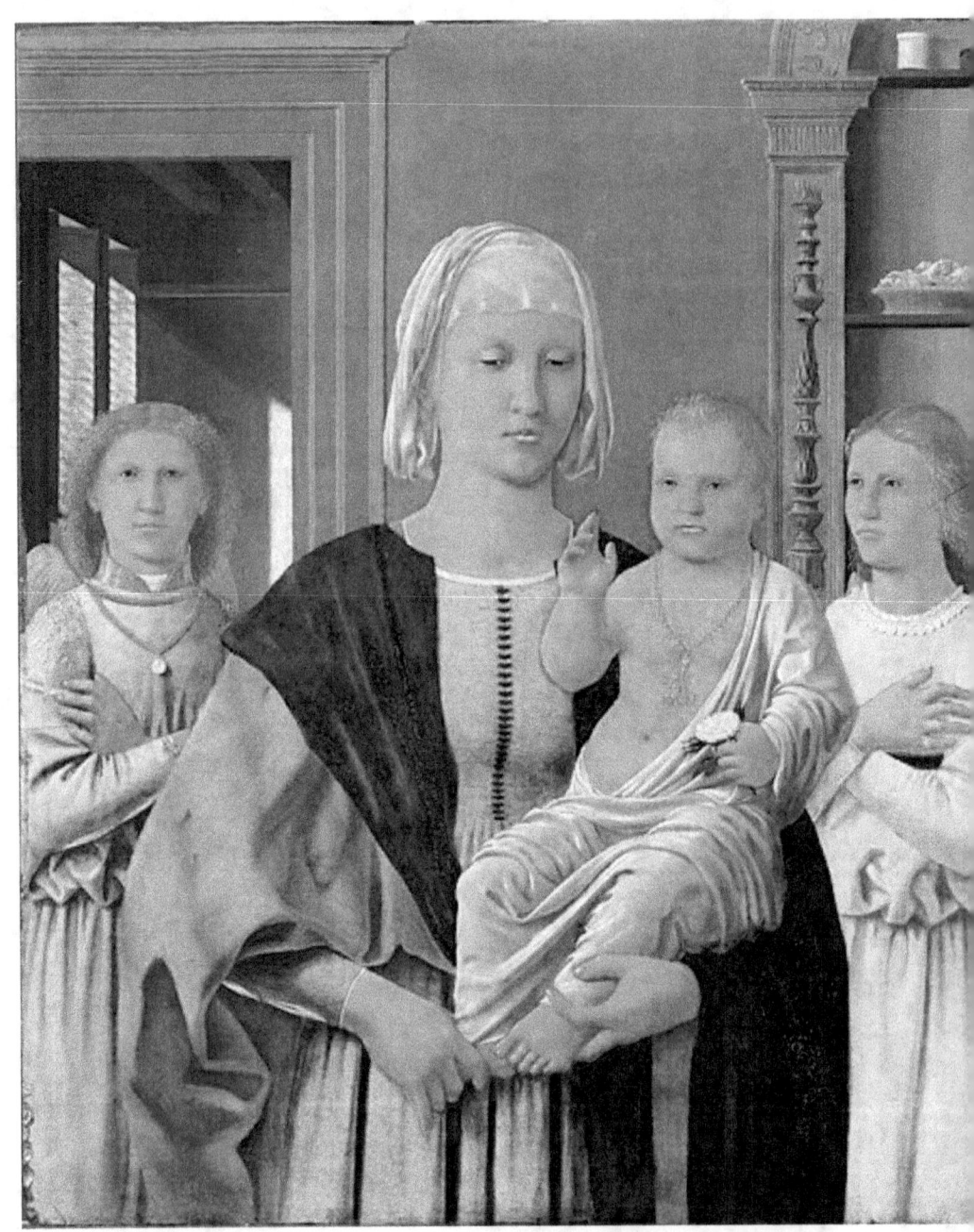

Piero della Francesca, The Brera Madonna

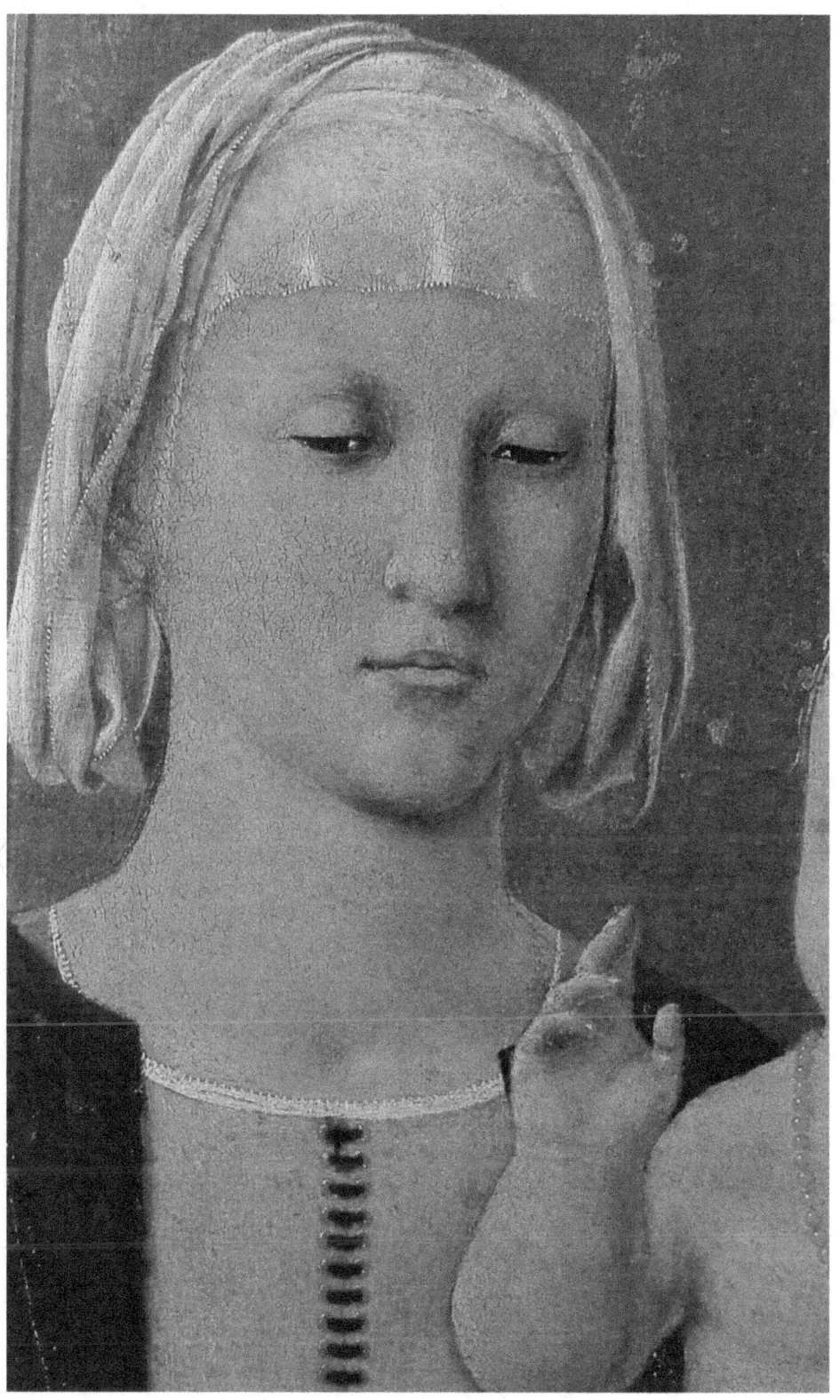

Piero, The Senigallia Madonna, detail

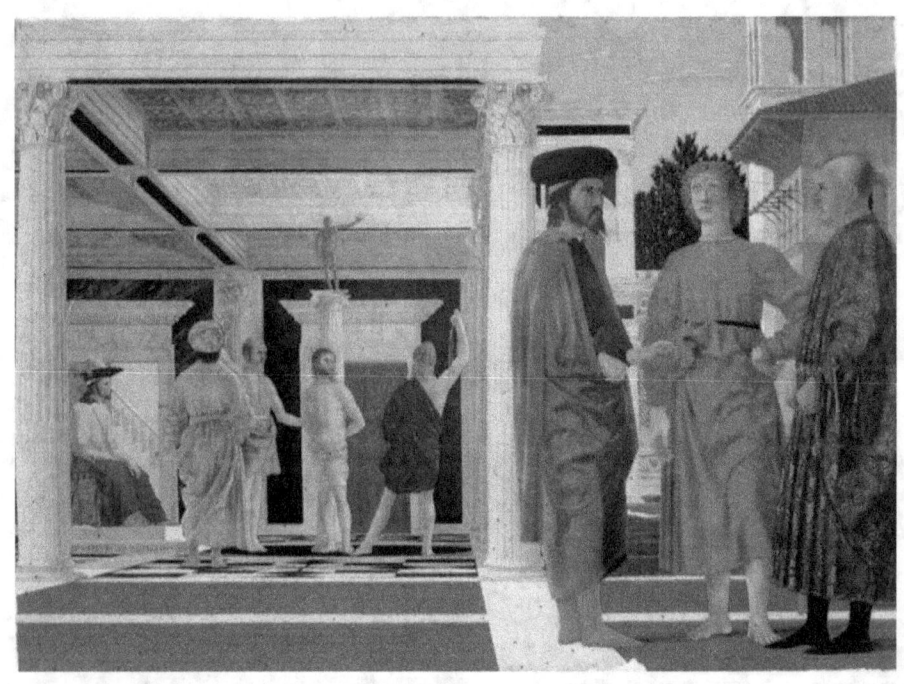

Piero della Francesca, The Flagellation

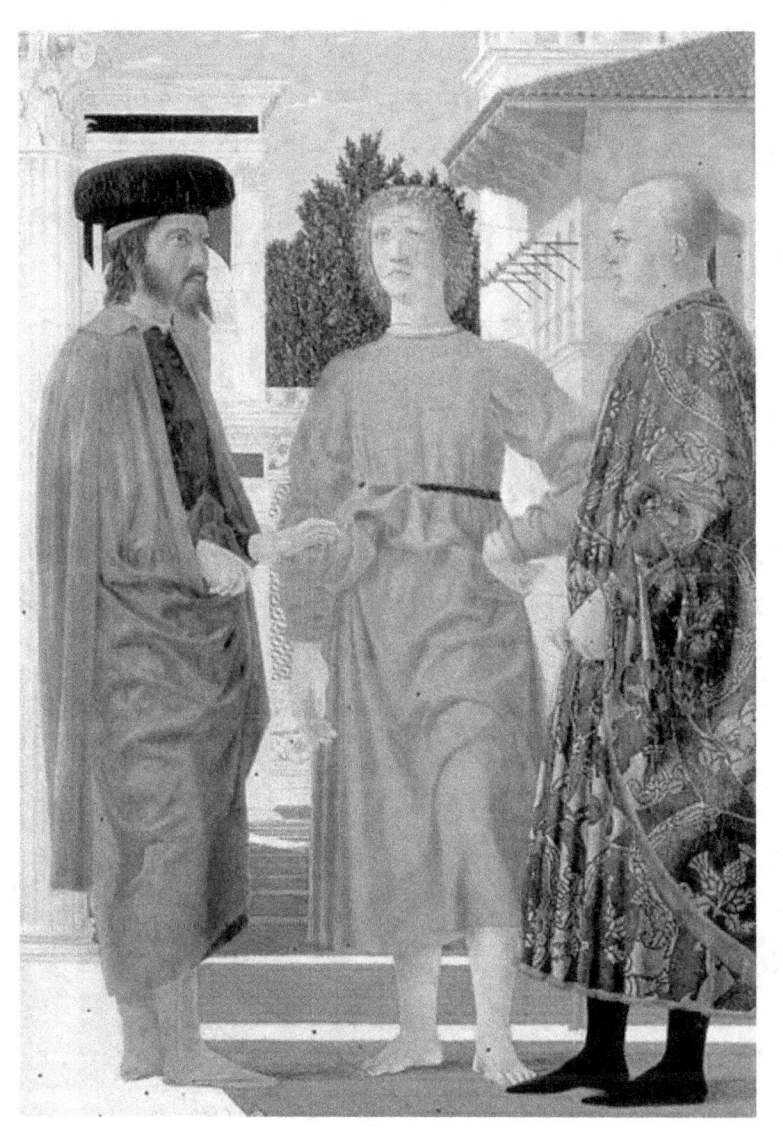

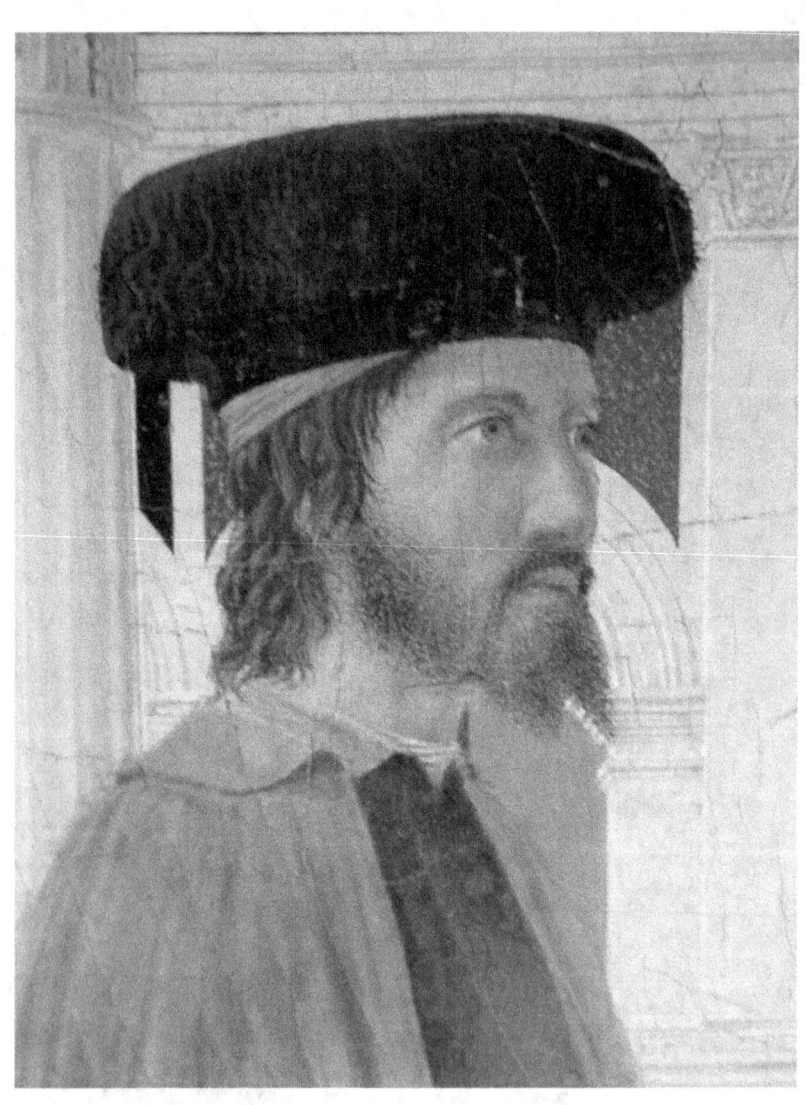

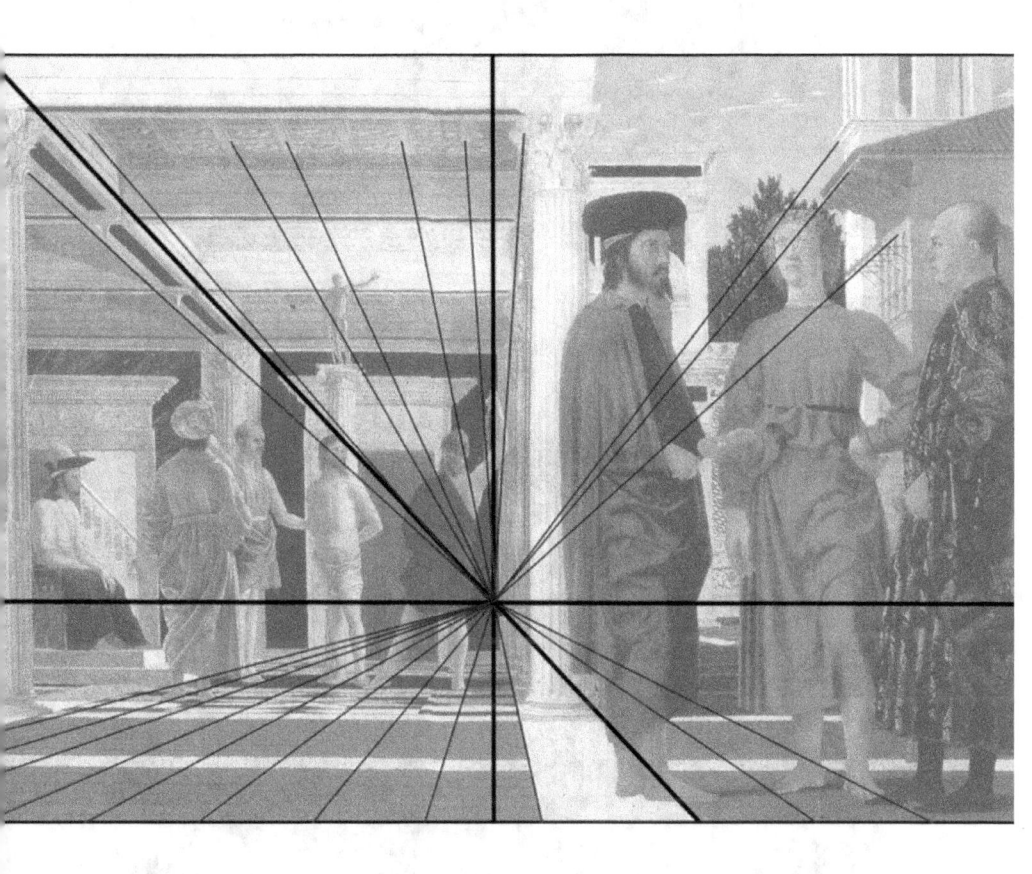

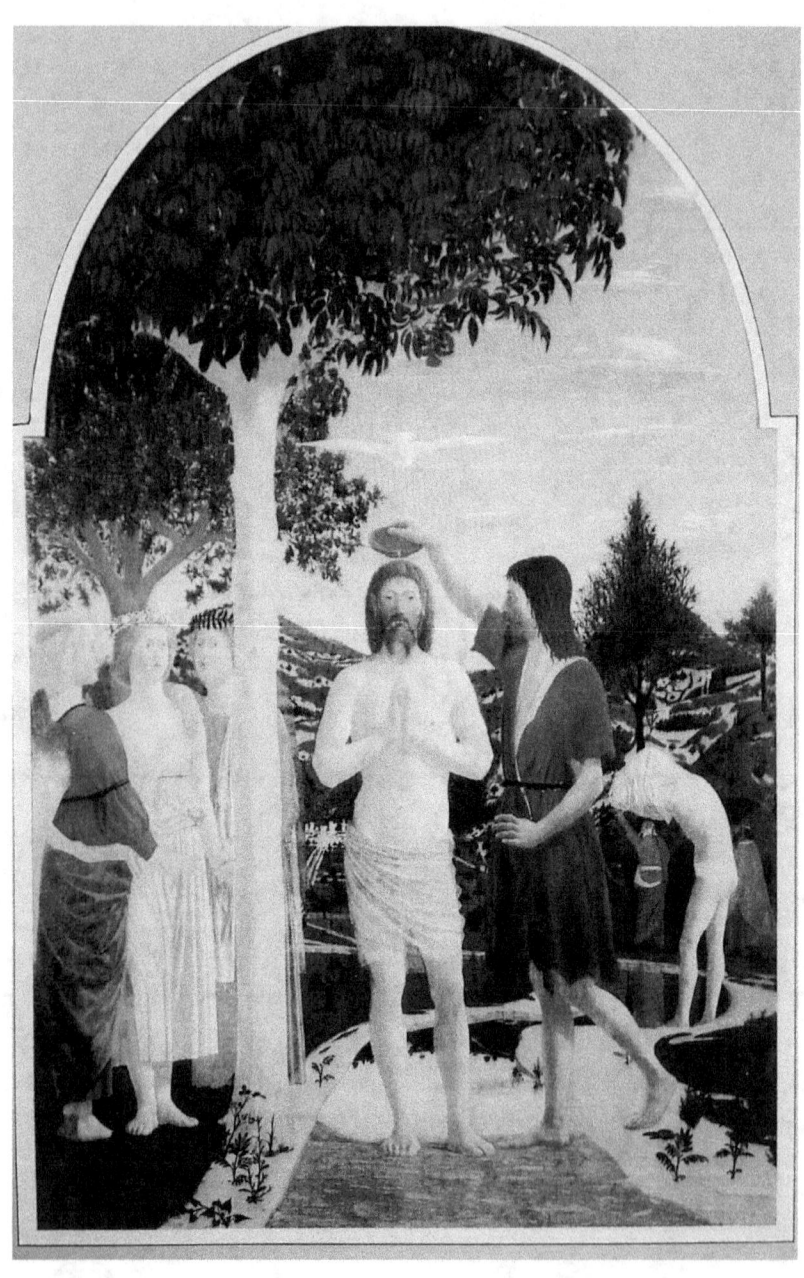

Piero della Francesca, *The Baptism of Christ*, National Gallery, London

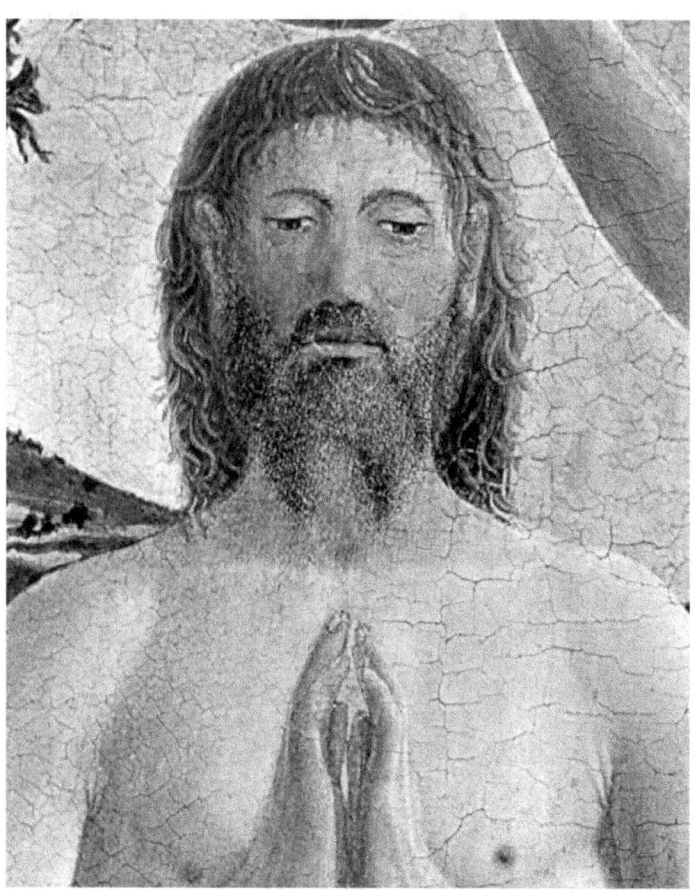

The Baptism, detail

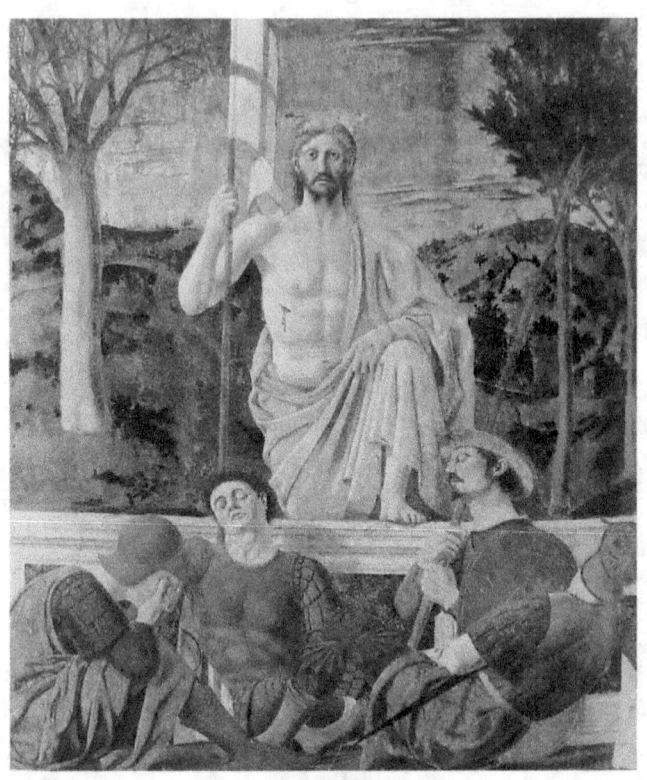

Piero, The Resurrection

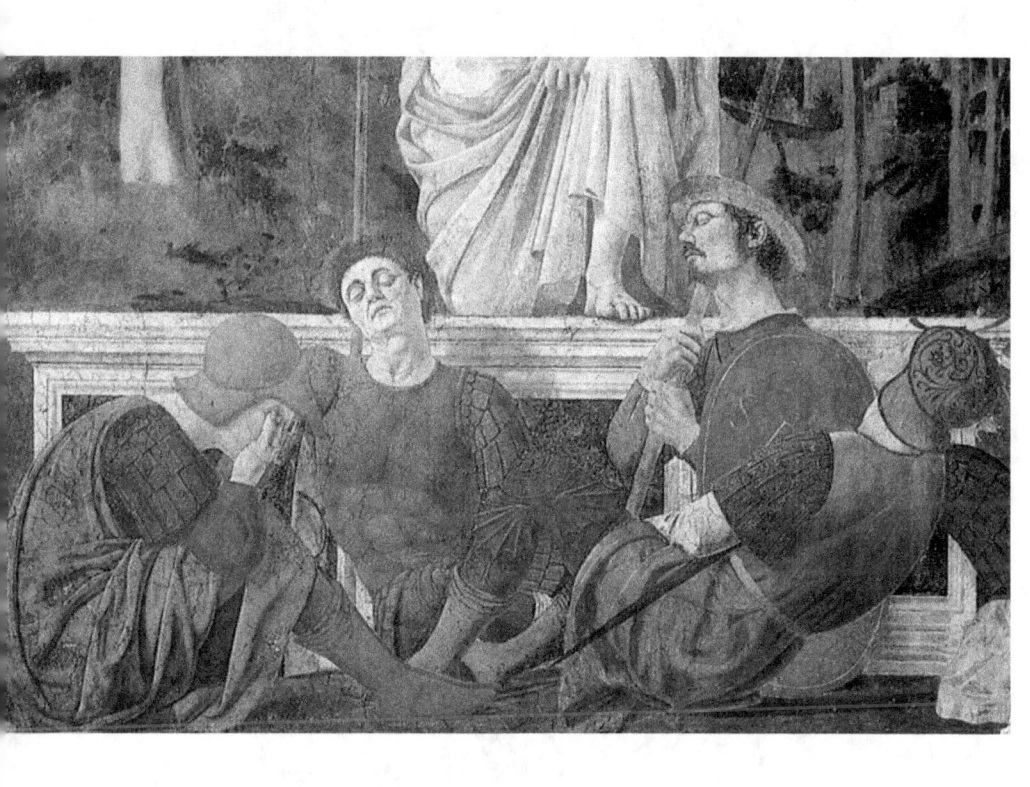

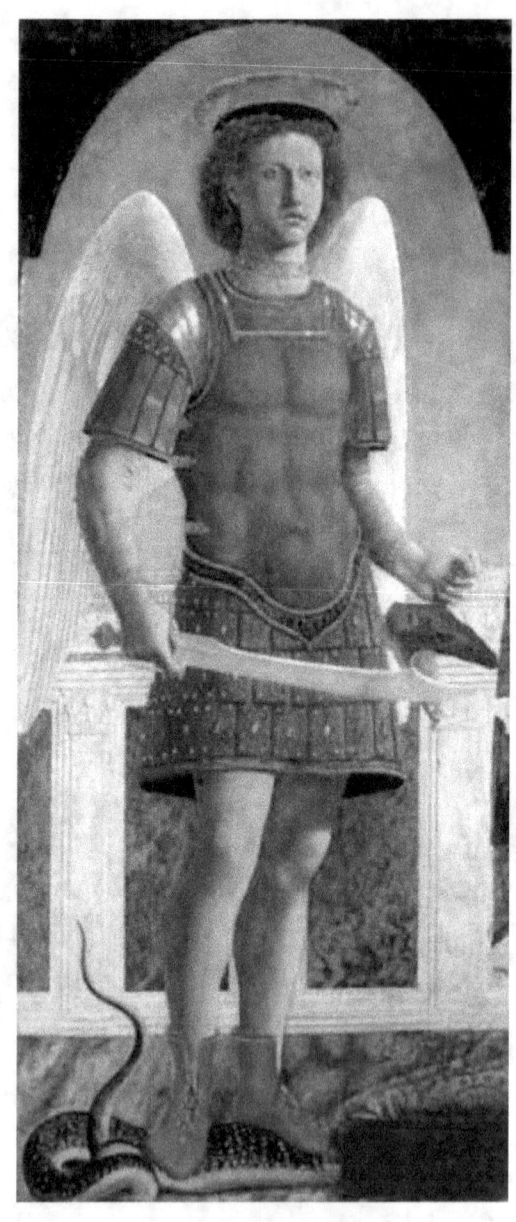

Piero della Francesca, St Michael,
National Gallery, London

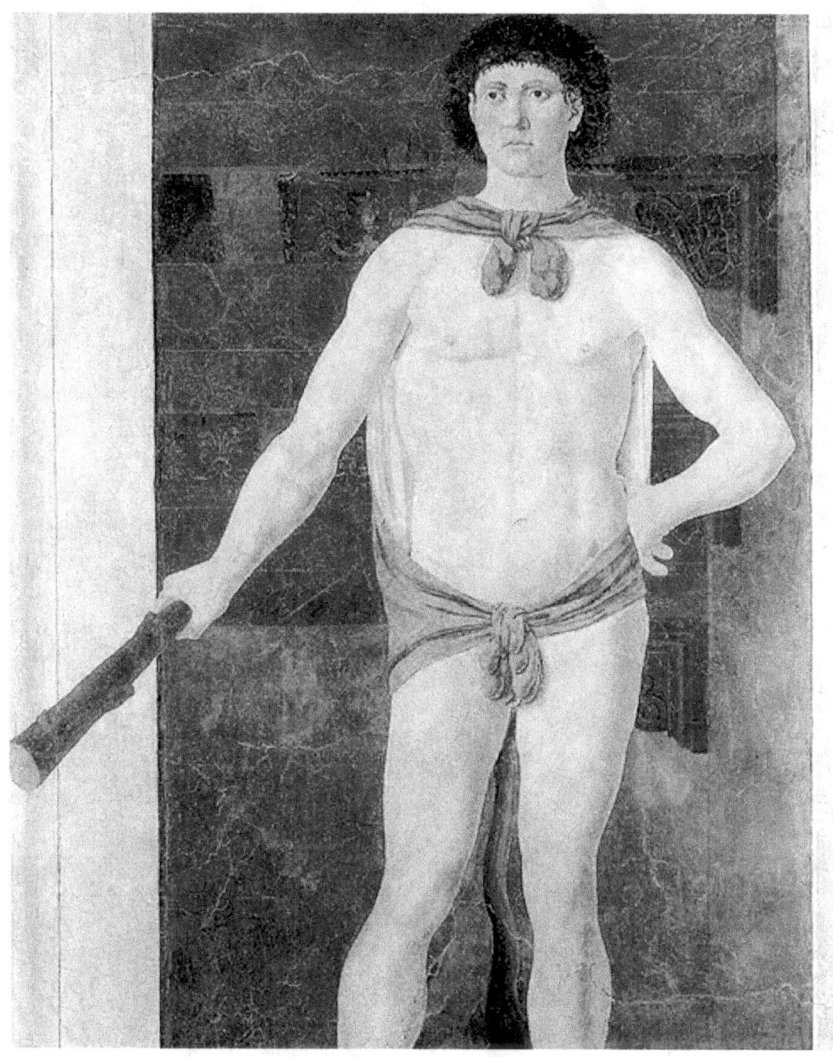

Piero della Francesca, Hercules, after 1465,
Isabella Stewart Gardner Museum

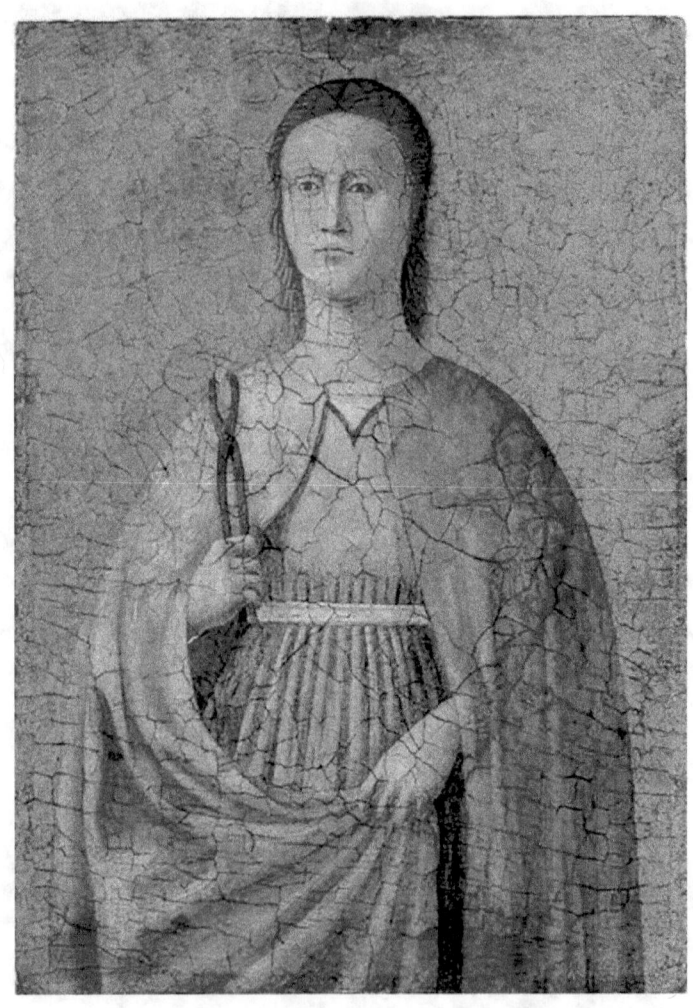

Piero, Sant'Apollonia, c. 1460, National Gallery of Art,
Washington, DC

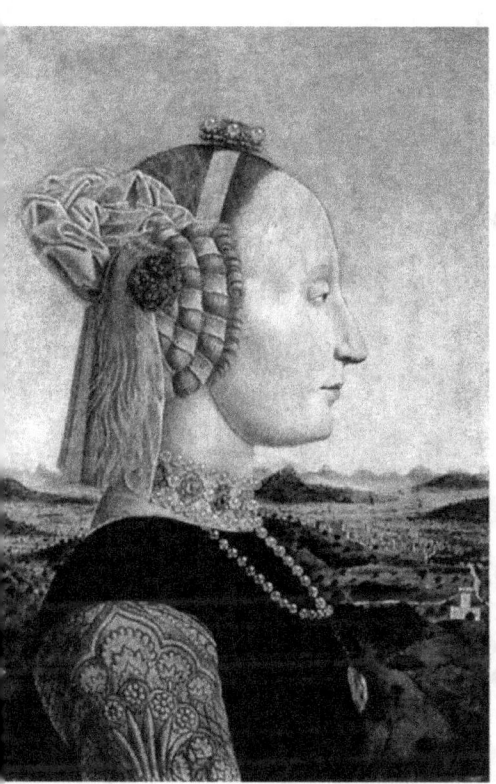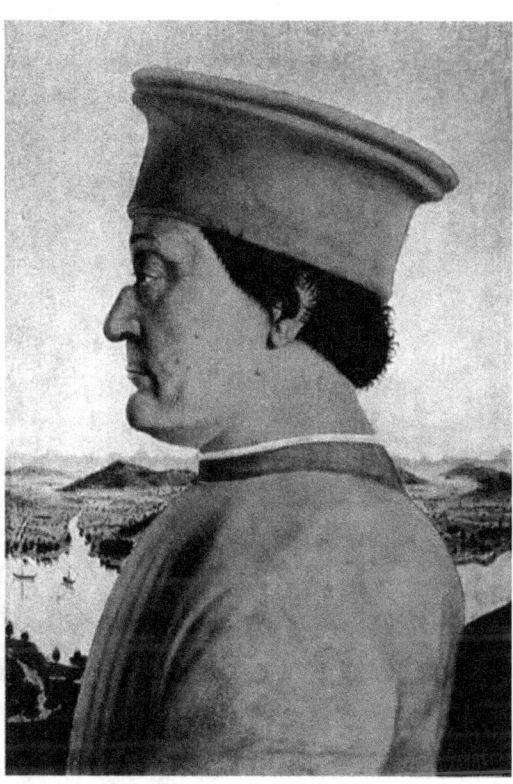

Piero della Francesca, Ritratto di Battista Sforza
and Federico da Montefeltro, 1472, Uffizi Gallery, Florence

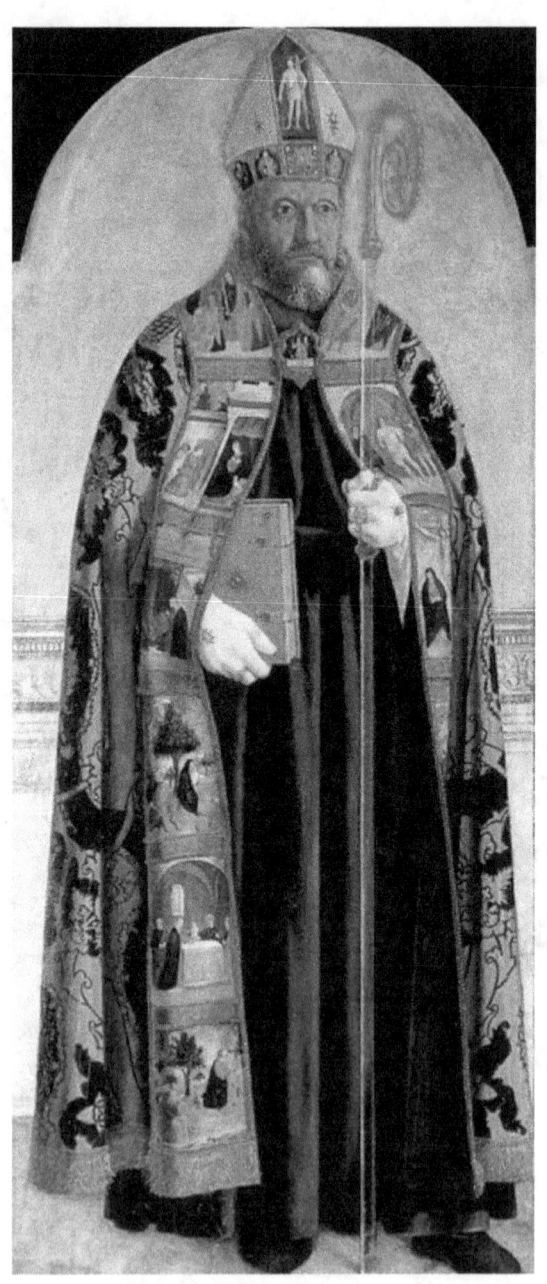

Piero, Polyptych of St Augustine

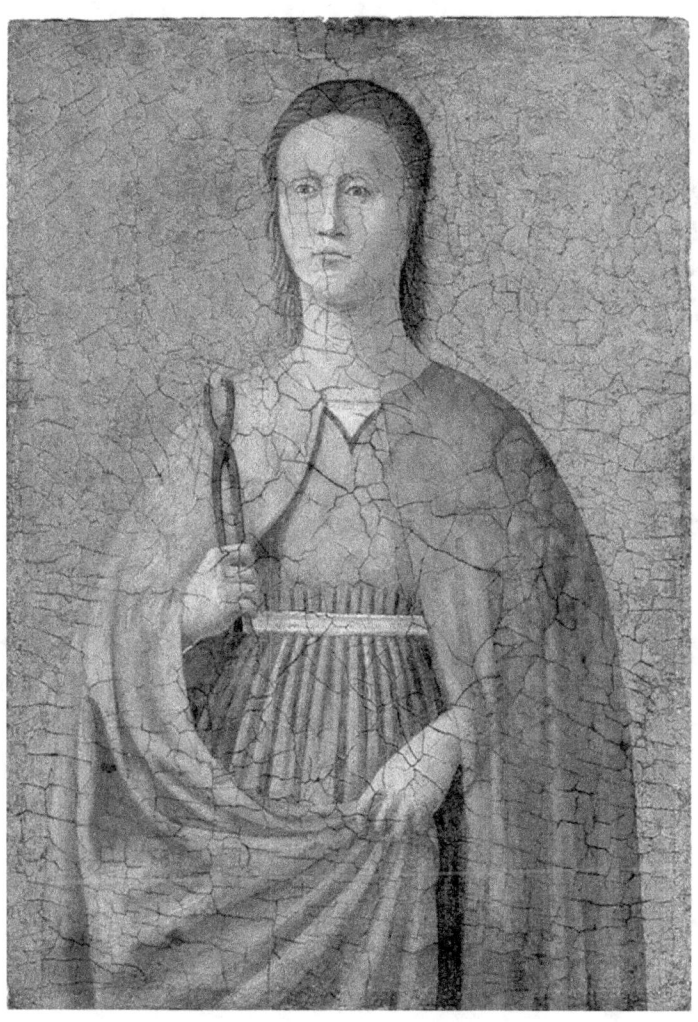

Piero, Sant'Apollonia, 1455-60, Washington

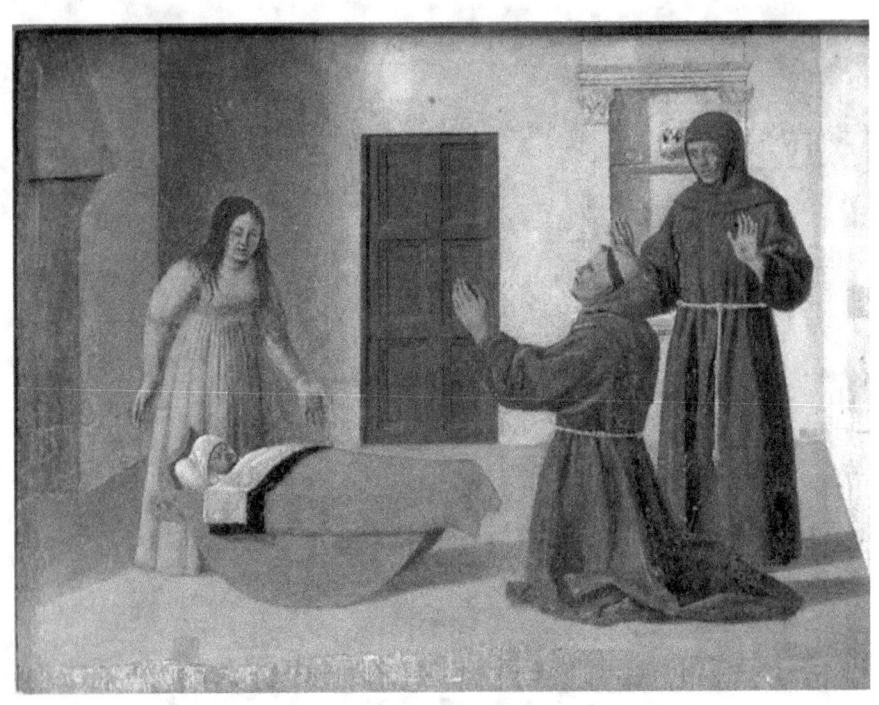

Piero, Polyptych of St Anthony

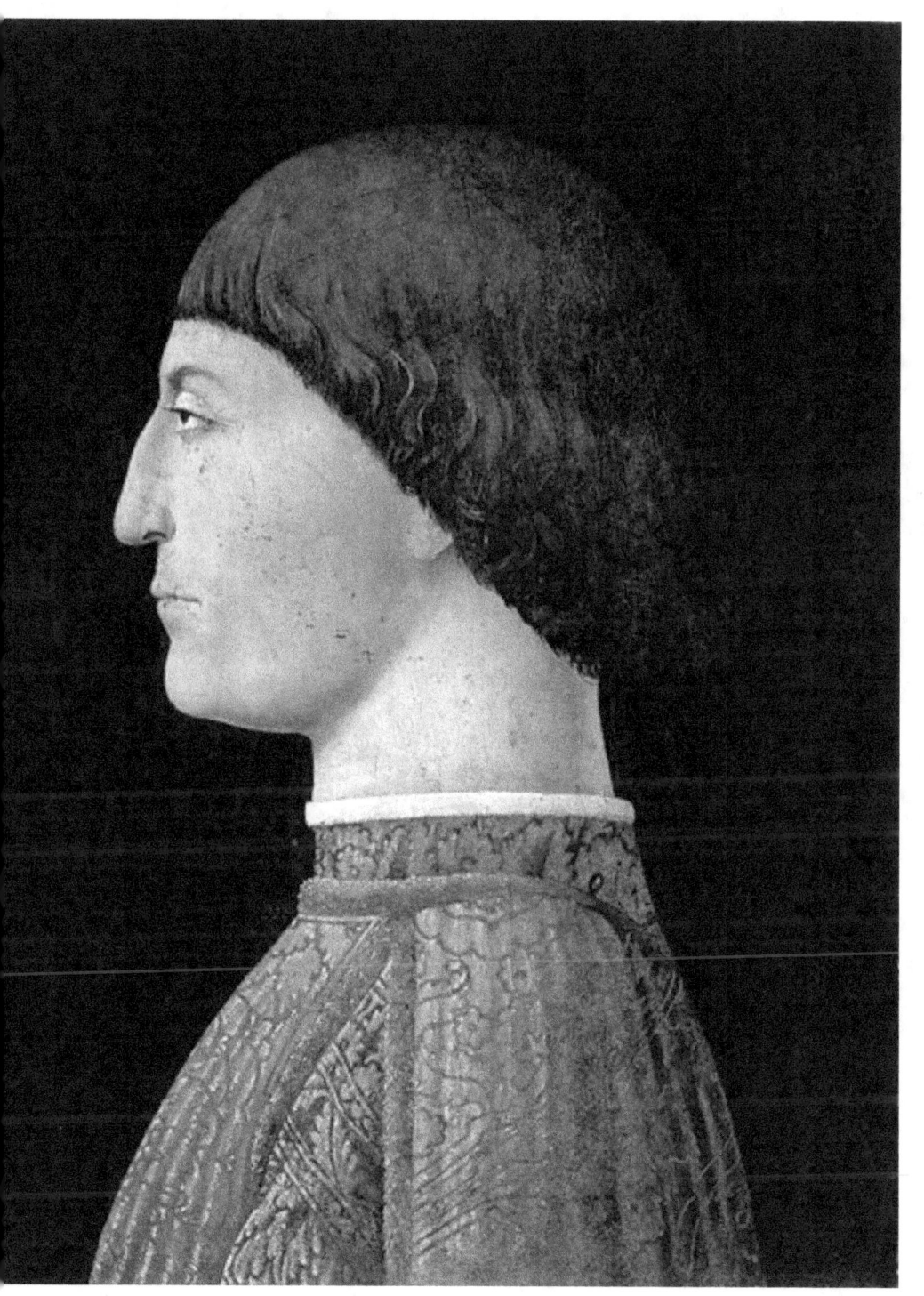

Piero della Francesca, Portrait of Sigismondo Pandolfo Malatesta,
1451, Louvre, Paris

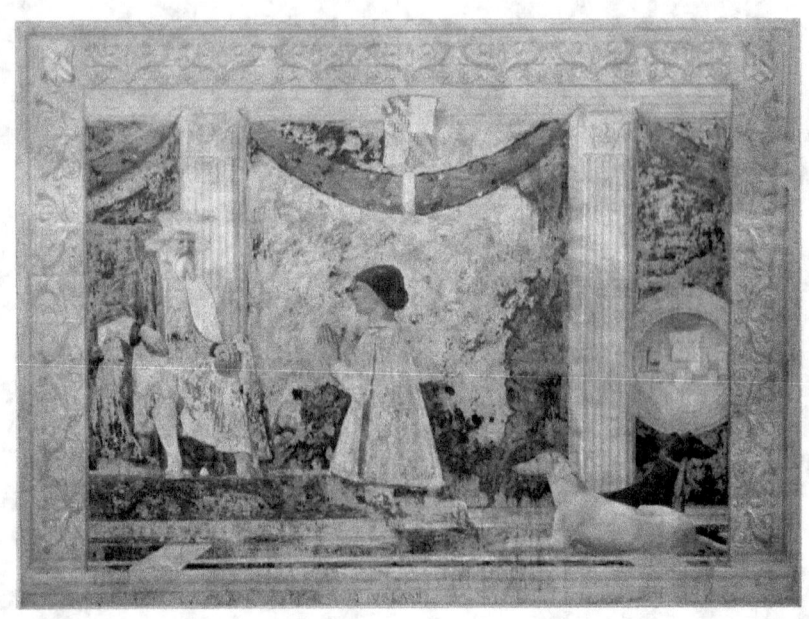

Piero, Malatesta, 1451

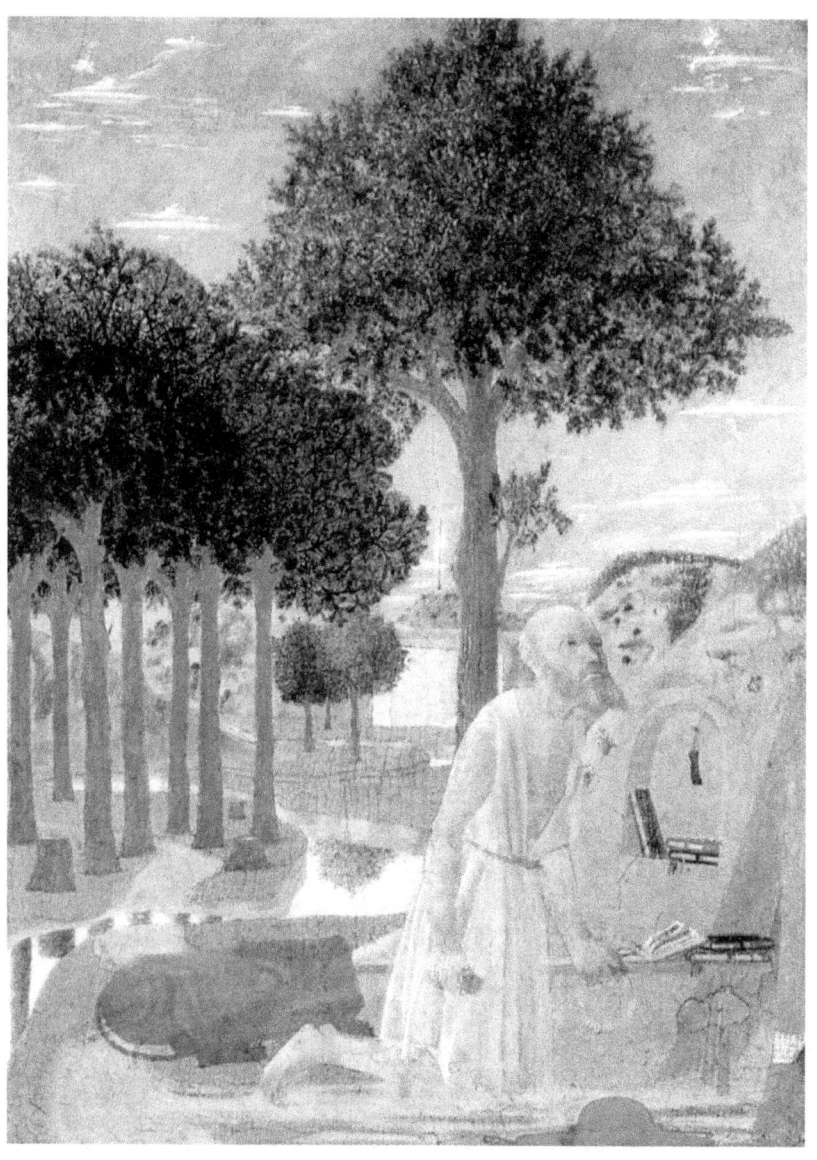

Piero, St Jerome, 1451

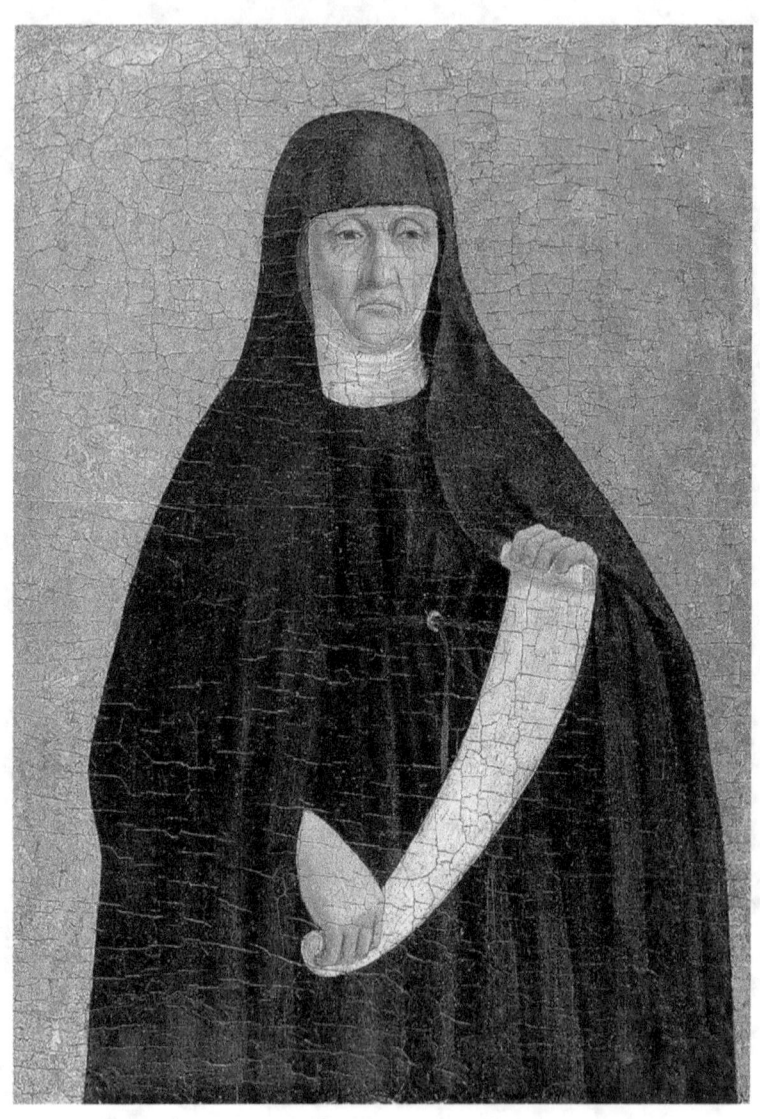

Piero, Santa Monaca, 1455-60, Washington

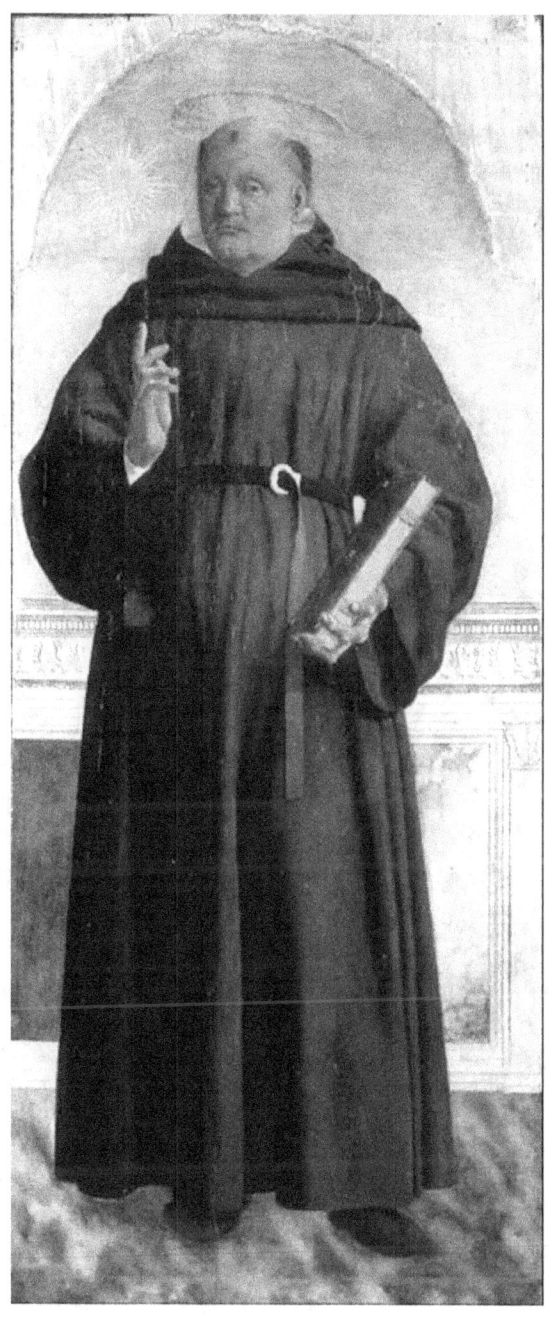

Piero, St Nicholas of Tolentino, 1454-59

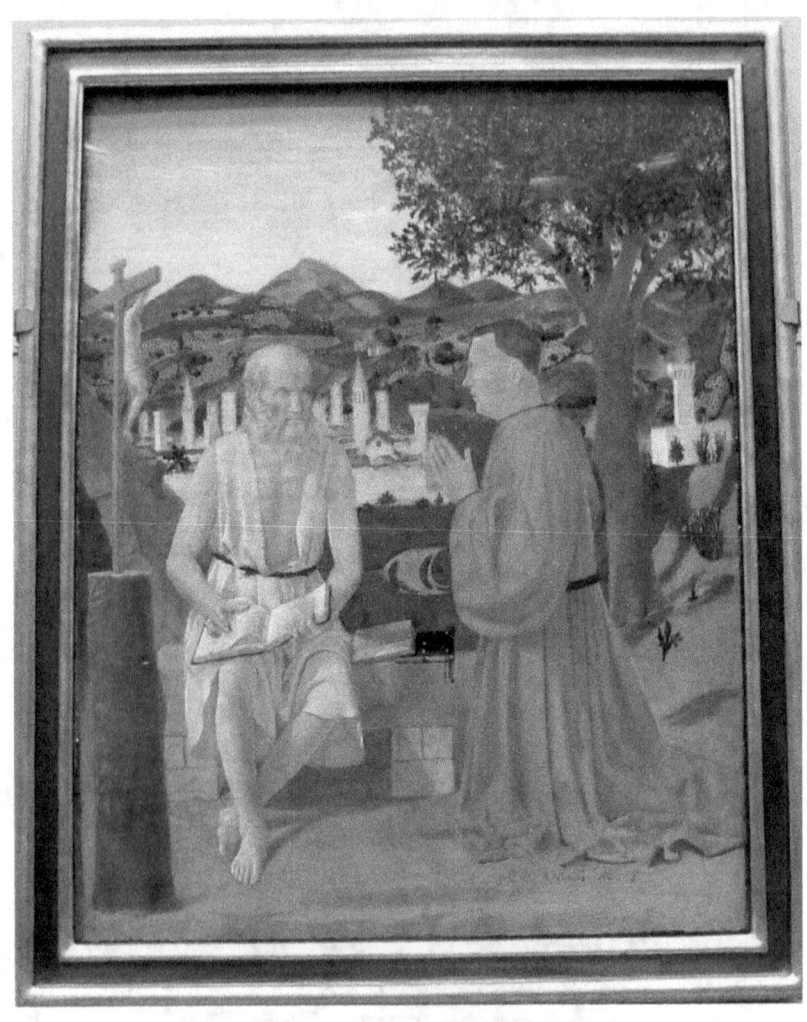

Piero, San Girolamo, 1440-50, Venice

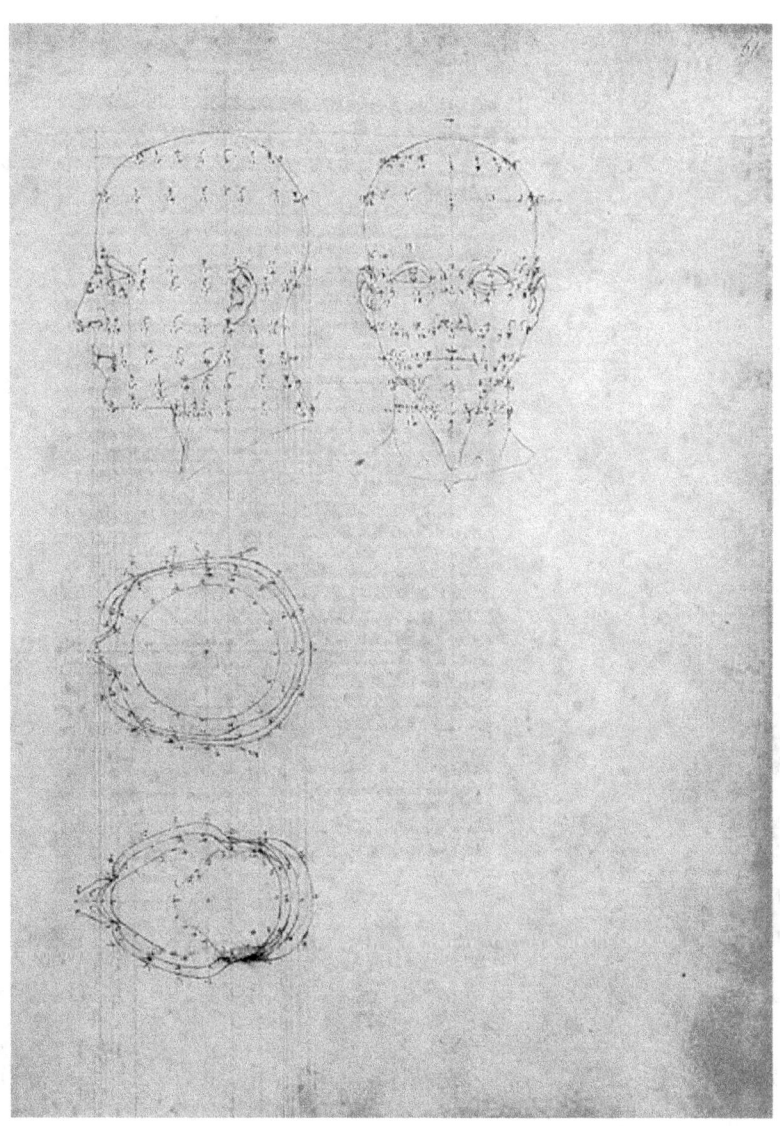

Piero della Francesca, Proiezioni di una testa scorciata dal de prospectiva pingendi, before1482, Biblioteca Ambrosiana, Milan

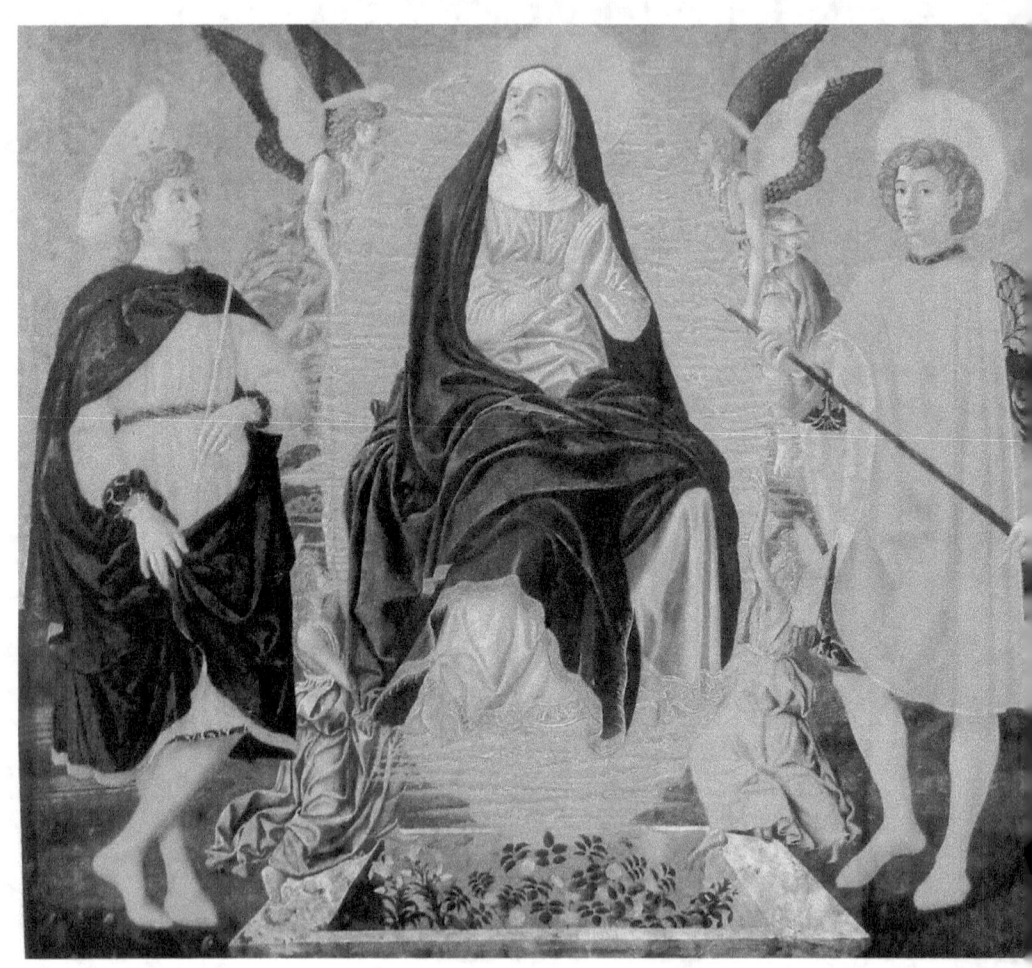

Andrea del Castagno, Assumption, Berlin

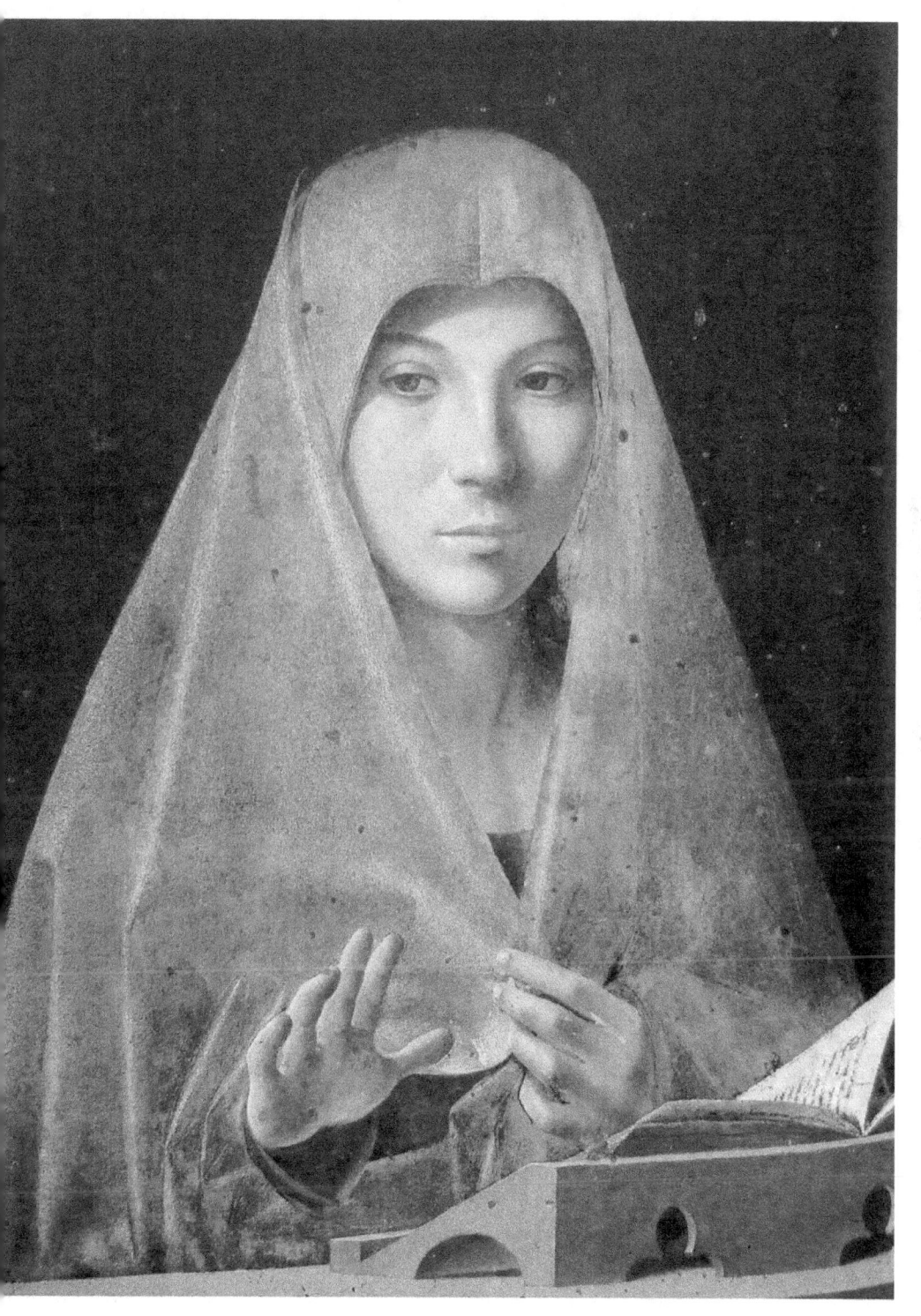

Antonello da Messina, The Virgin of the Annunciation, 1475, Palermo

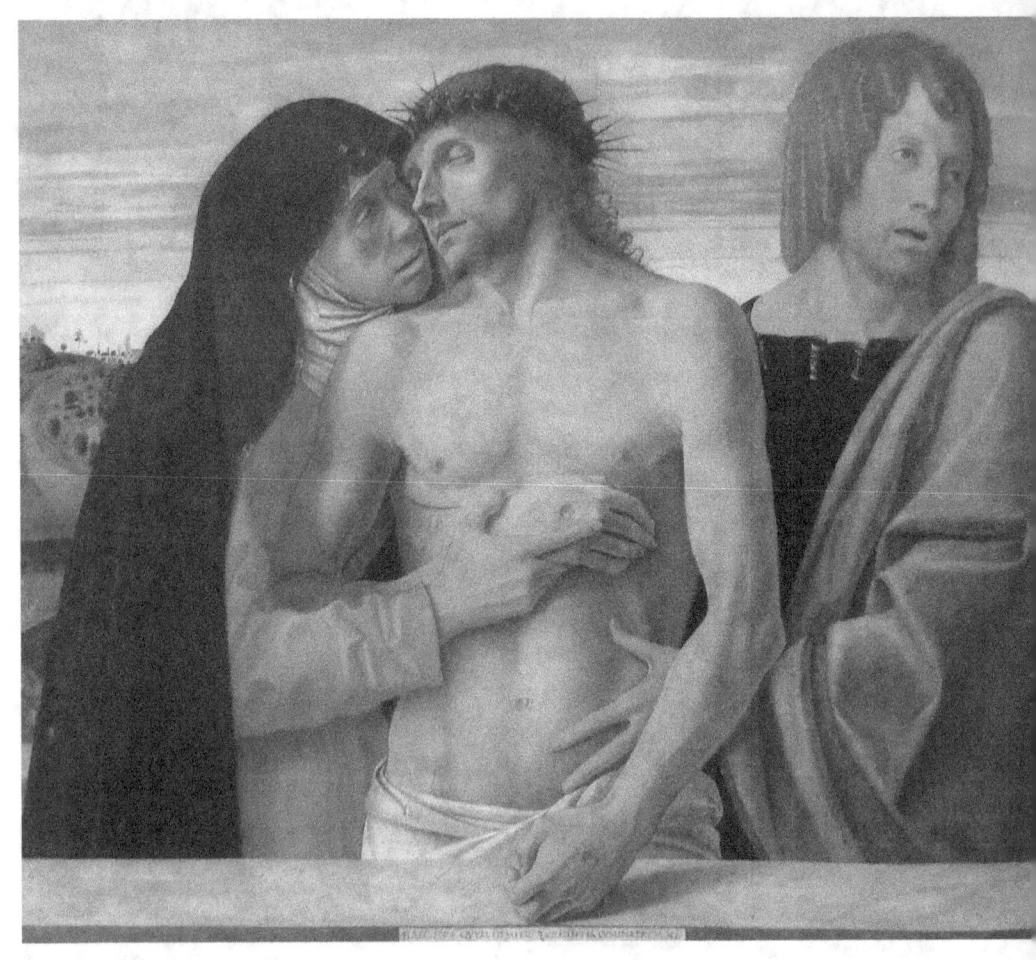

Giovanni Bellini, Pietà, Milan

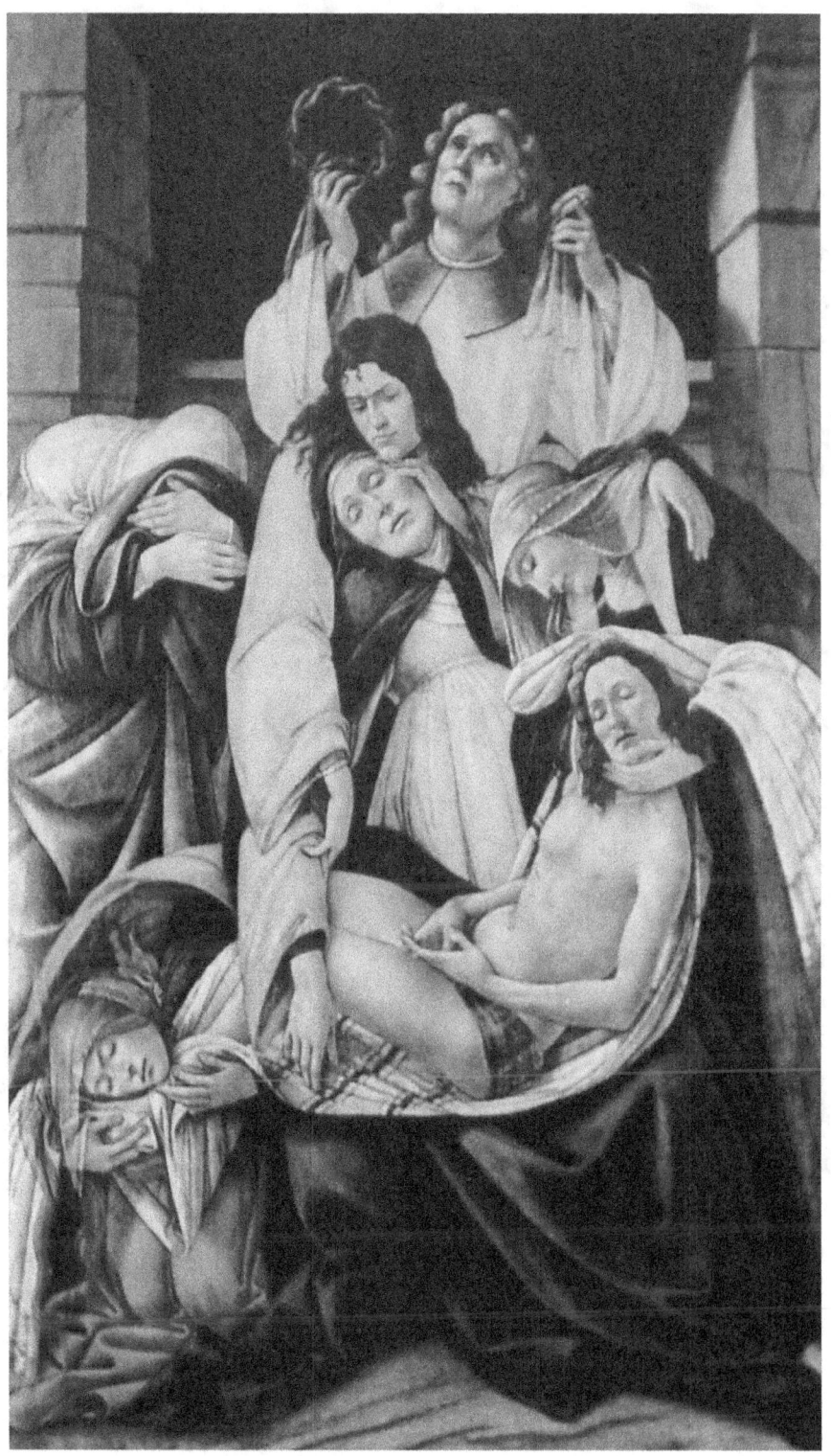

Sandro Botticelli, *Pietà*, Museo Poldi Pezzoli, Milan

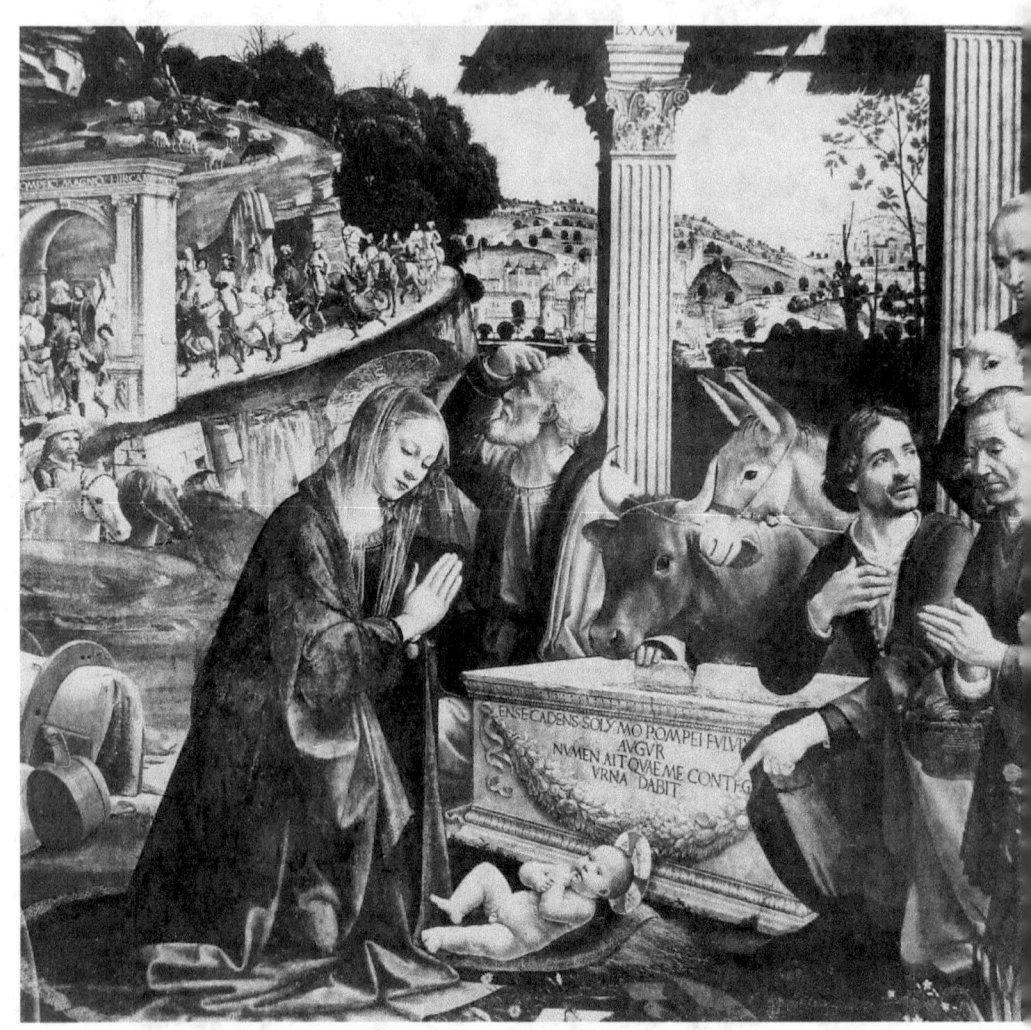

Domenico Ghirlandaio, Adoration of the Shepherds, 1485

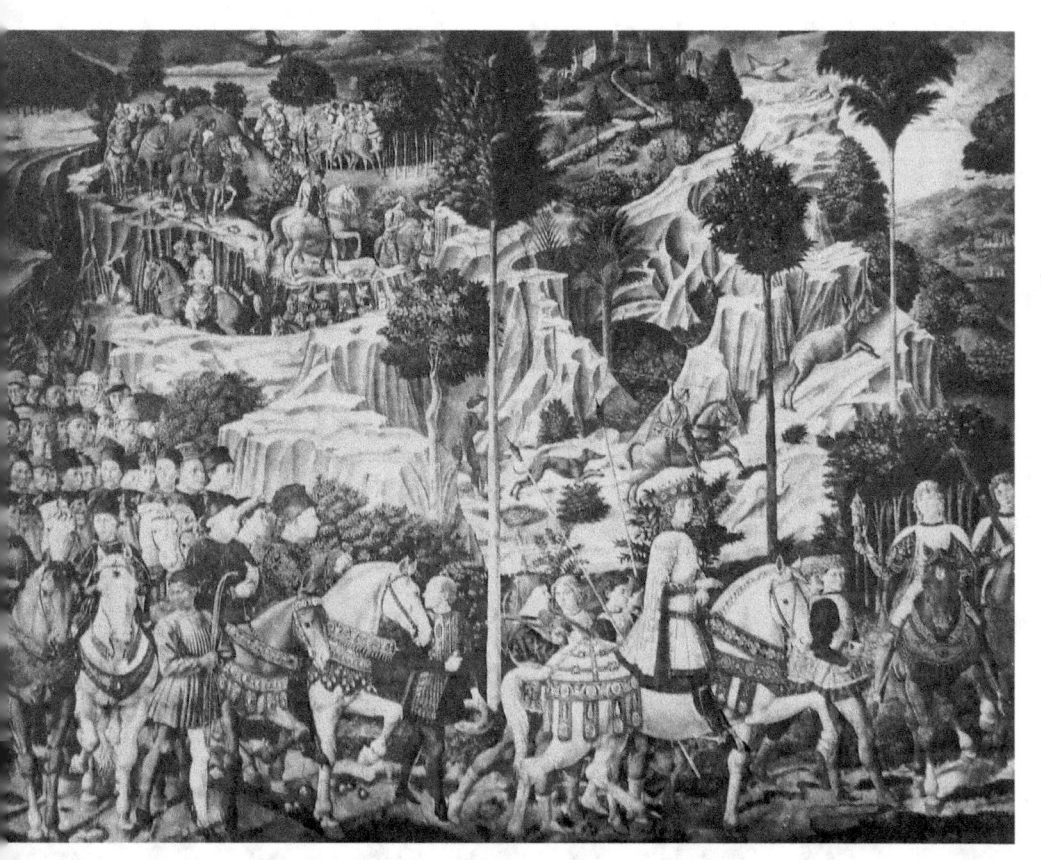

Benozzo Gozzoli, Journey of the Magi

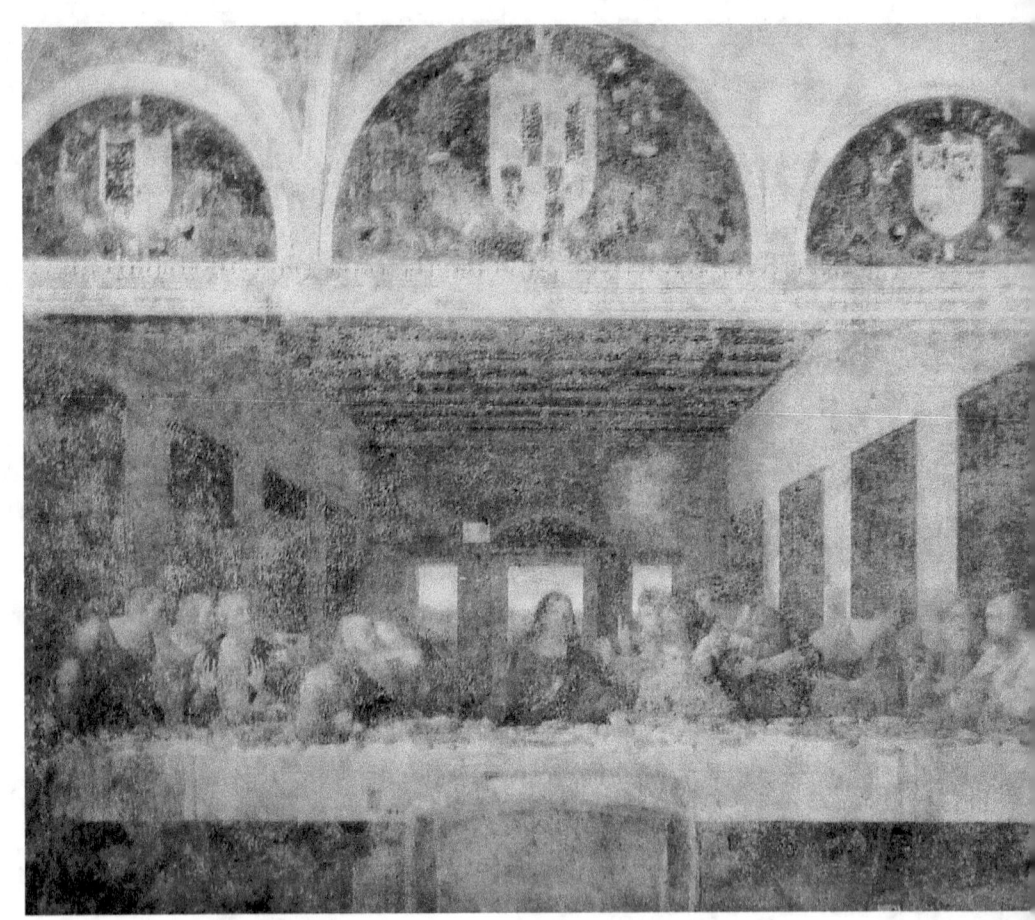

Leonardo da Vinci, The Last Supper, Milan

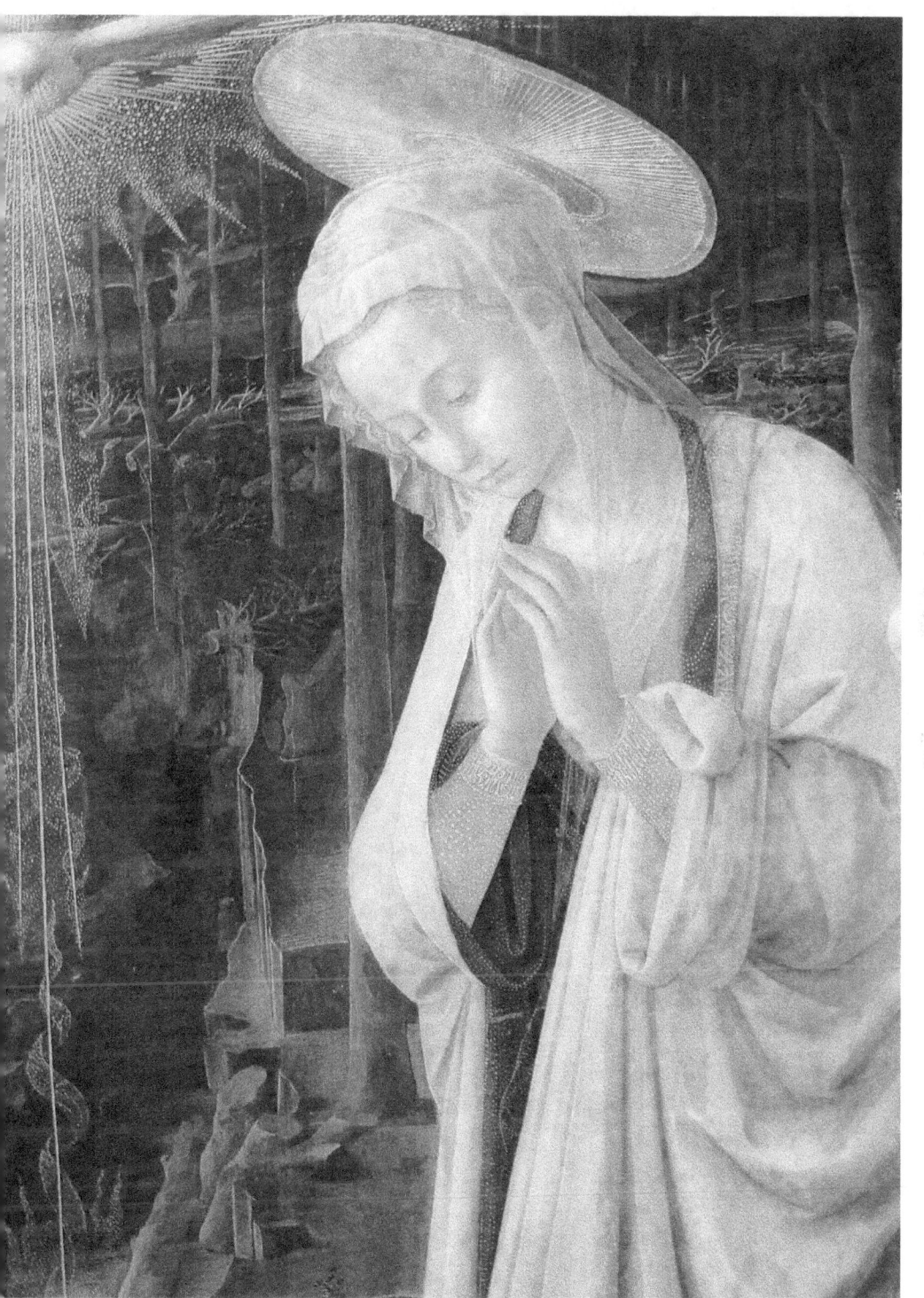

Fra Filippo Lippi, The Adoration of the Virgin, Berlin, detail

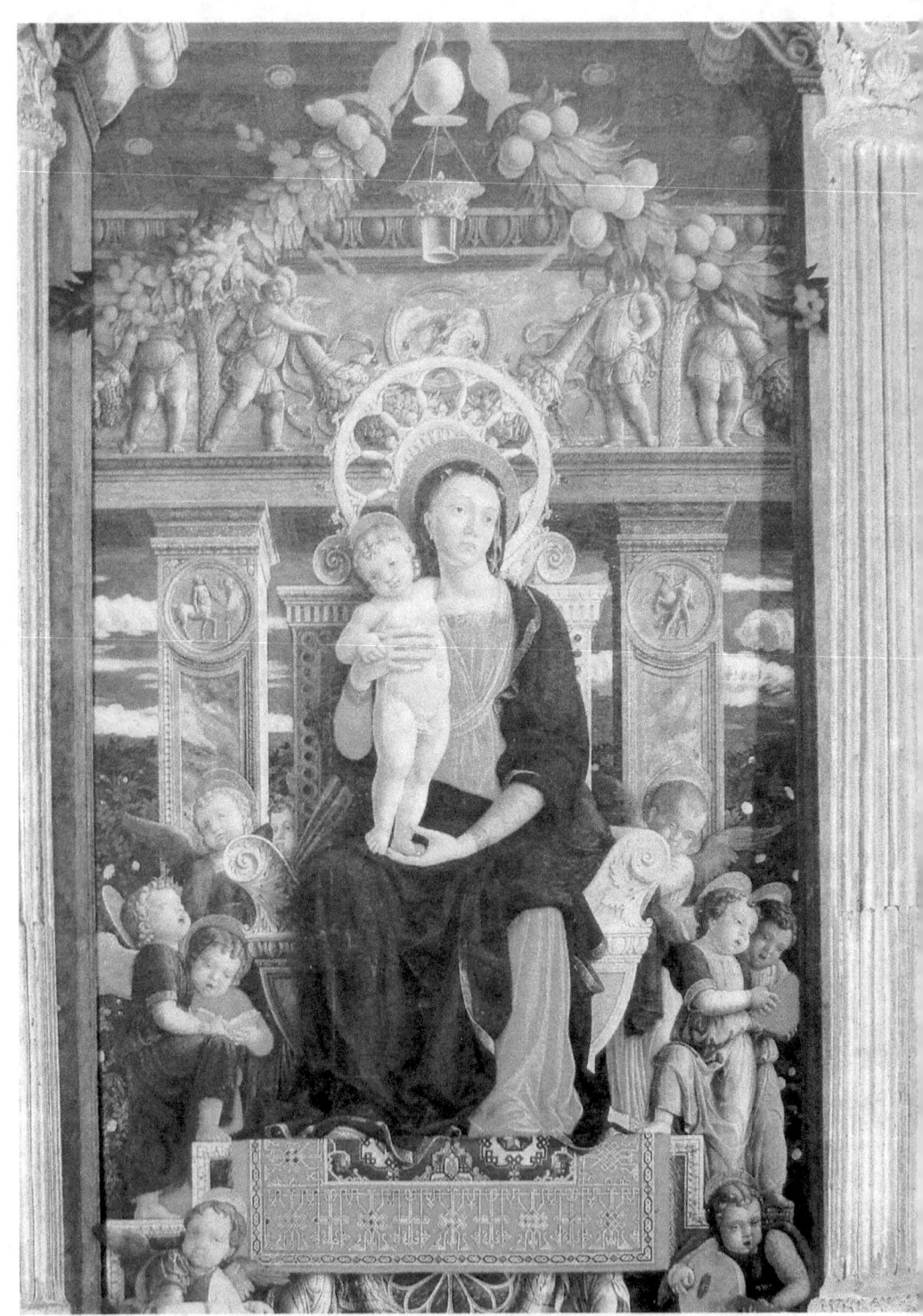

Andreas Mantegna, Madonna and Child Enthroned, 1457-60, Verona

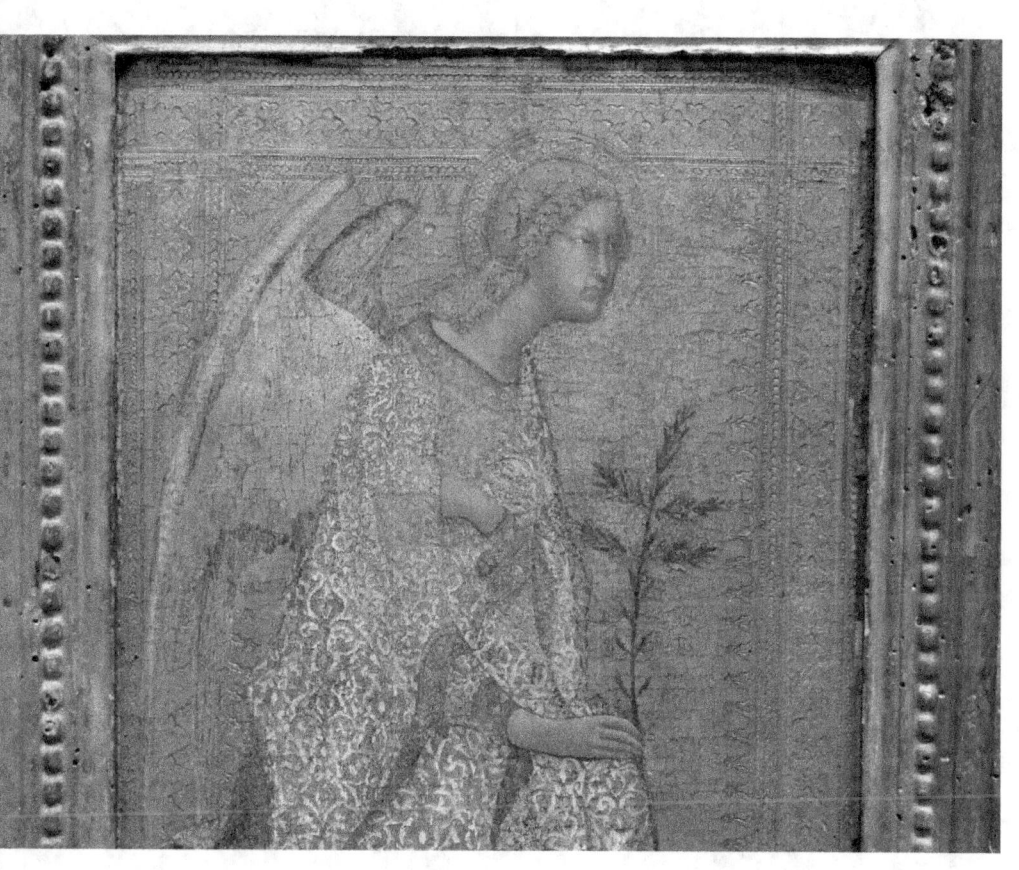

Simone Martini, Annunciation, Metropolitan Museum of Art, New York

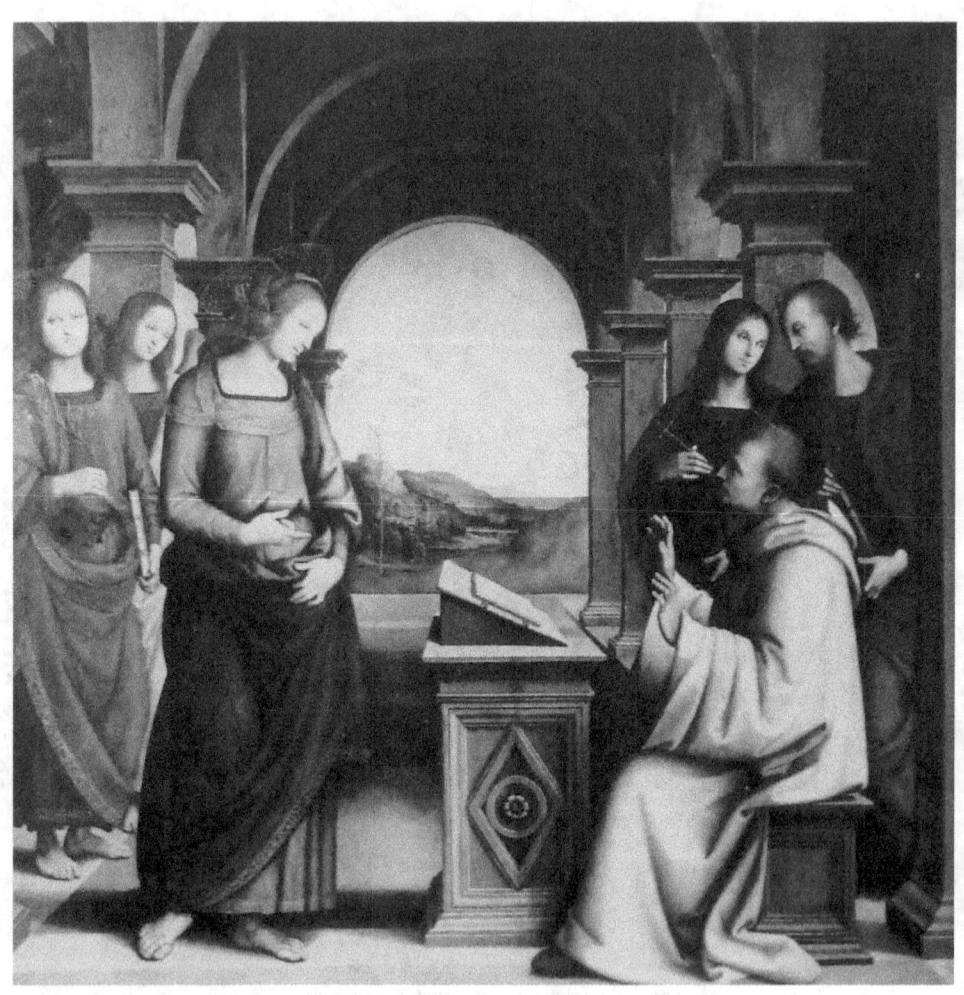

Perugino, Vision of St Bernard, 1488

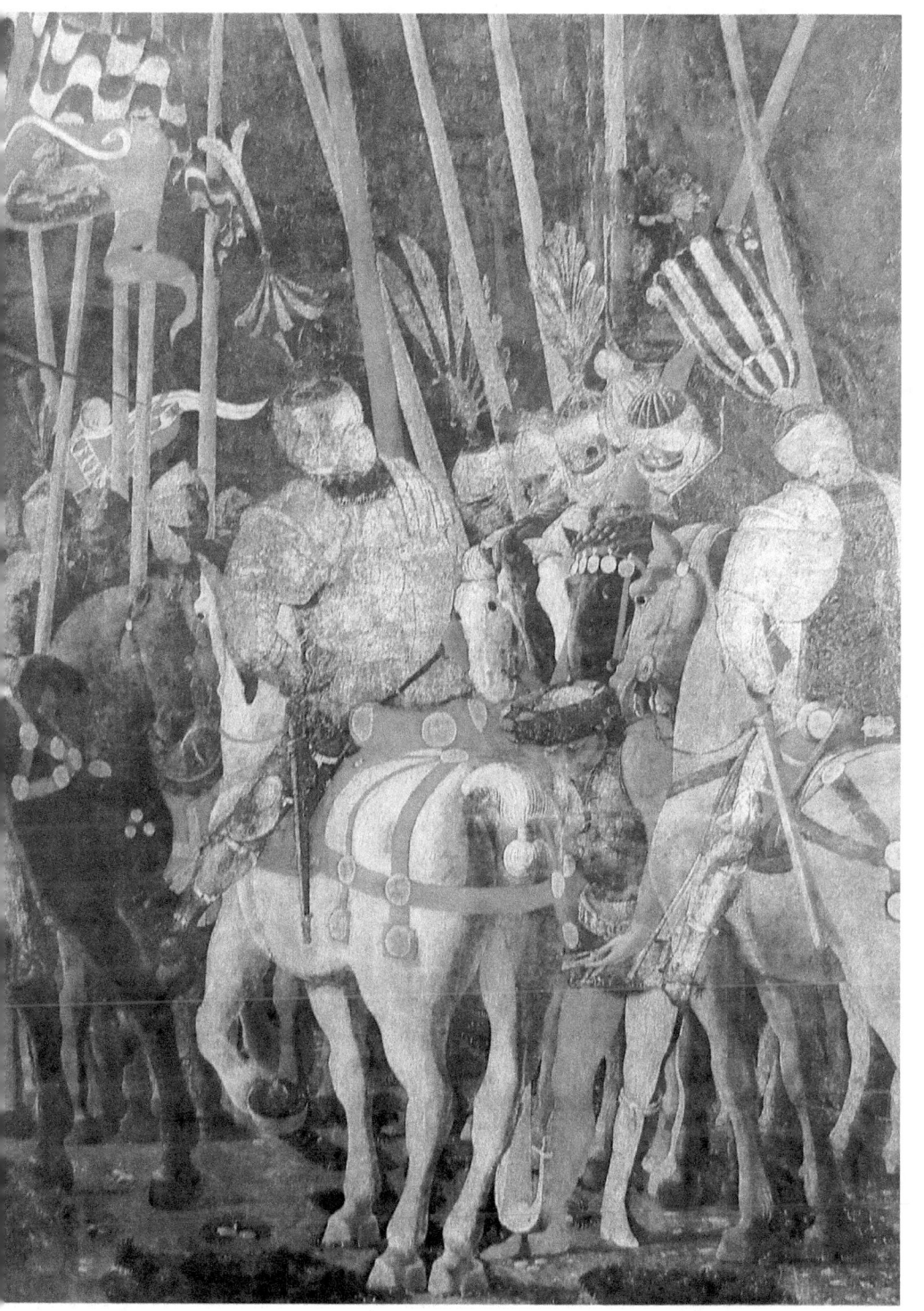

Paolo Uccello, Battle of San Romano, 1456-60, Loure, Paris

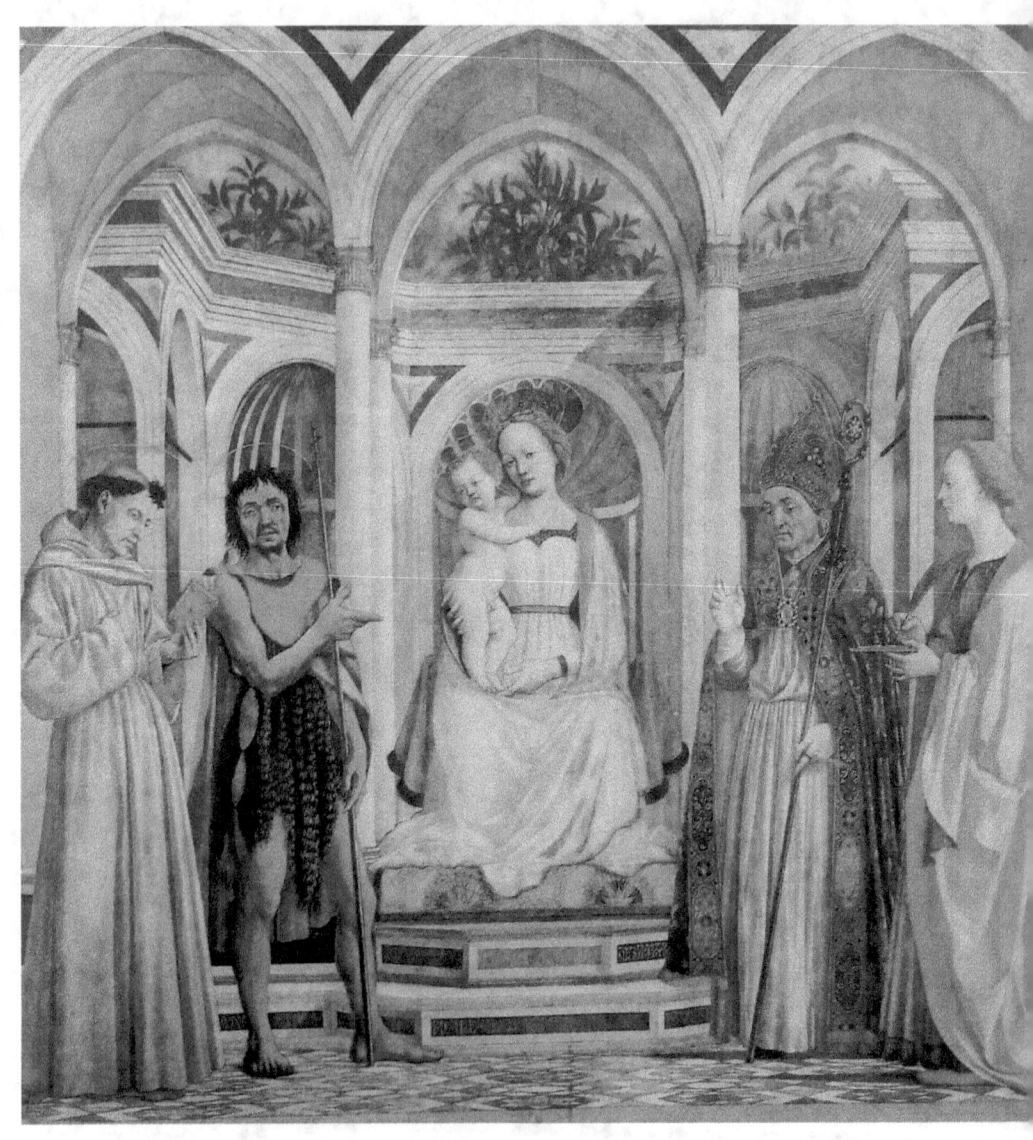

Domenico Veneziano, Madonna and Child With Saints, 1445, Uffizi Gallery

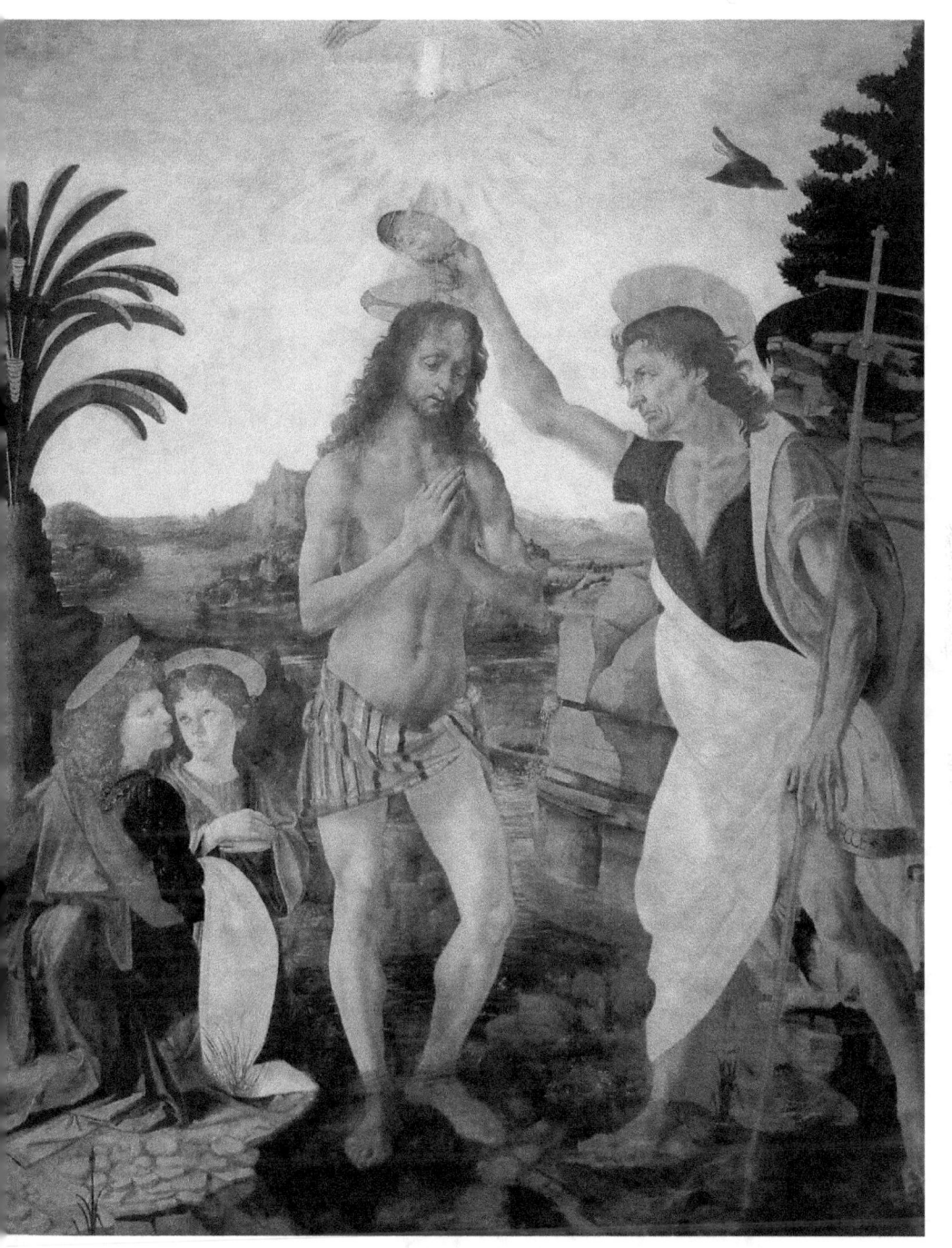

Andrea del Verrocchio, The Baptism of Christ

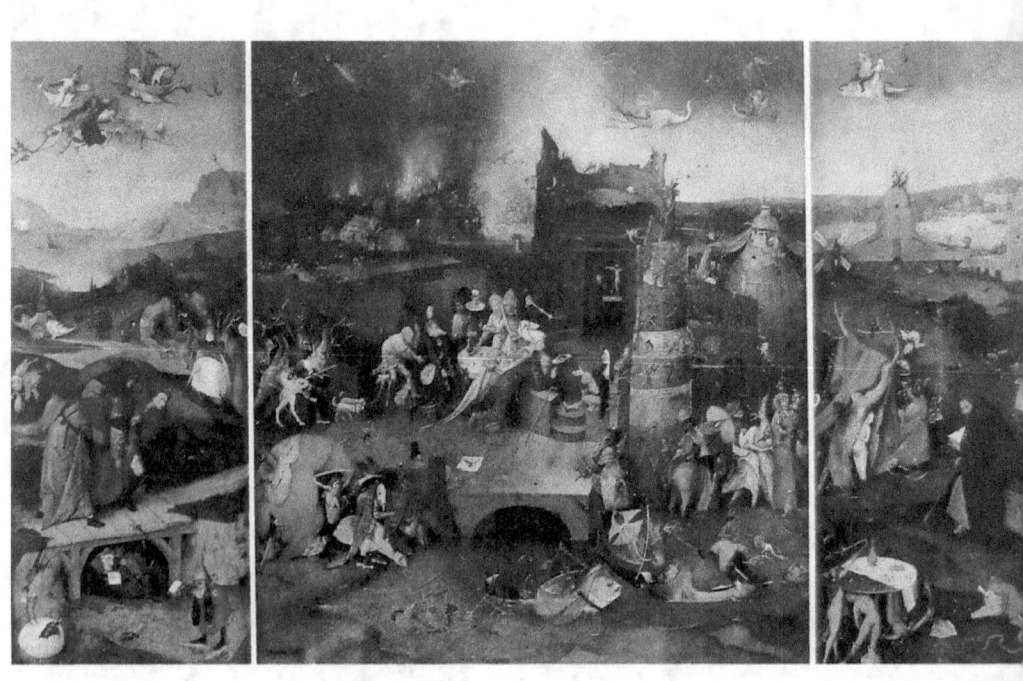

Hieronymous Bosch, The Temptations of St Anthony

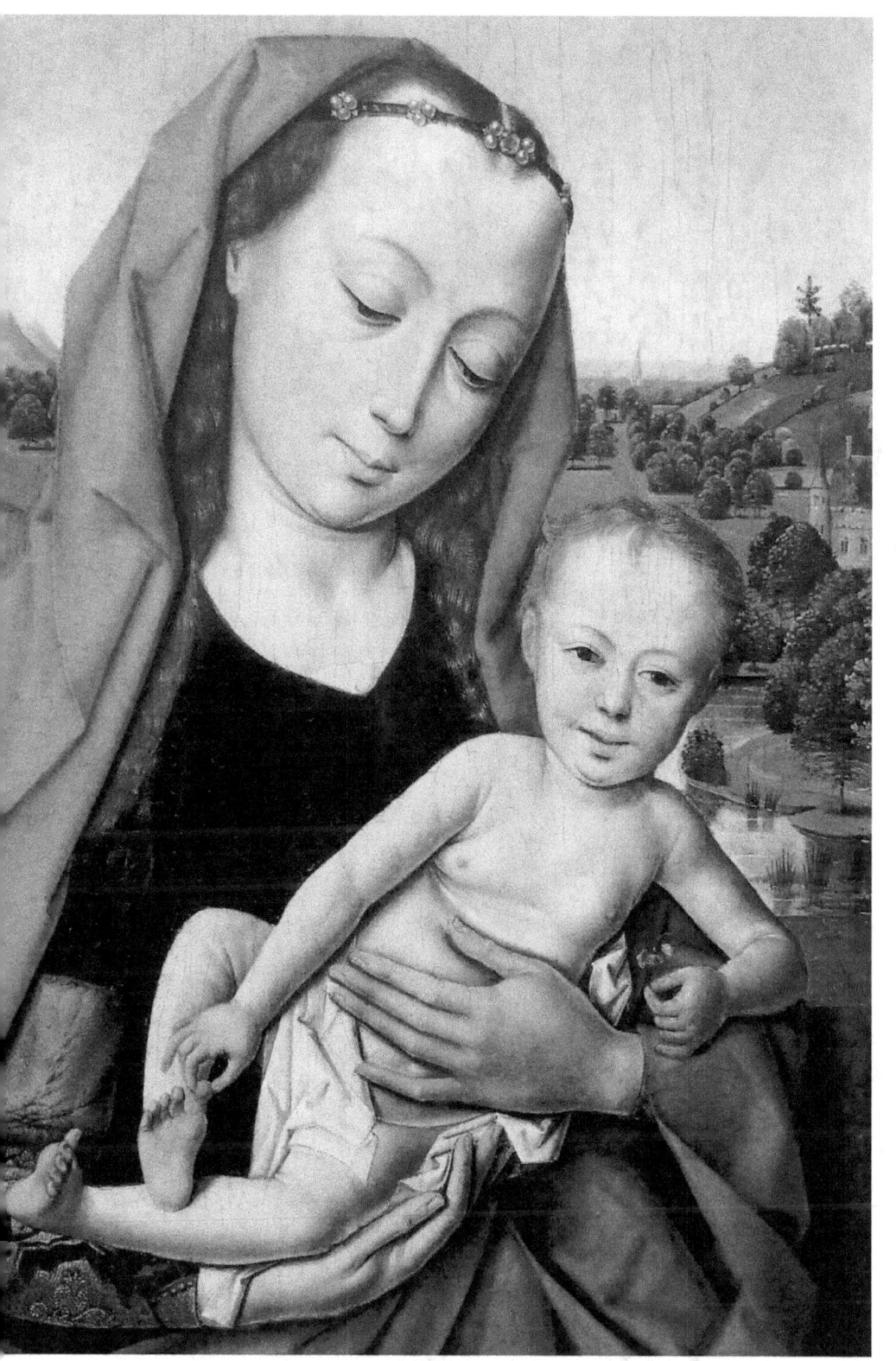

Dieric Bouts (workshop), Virgin and Child, Metropolitan Museum, New York City

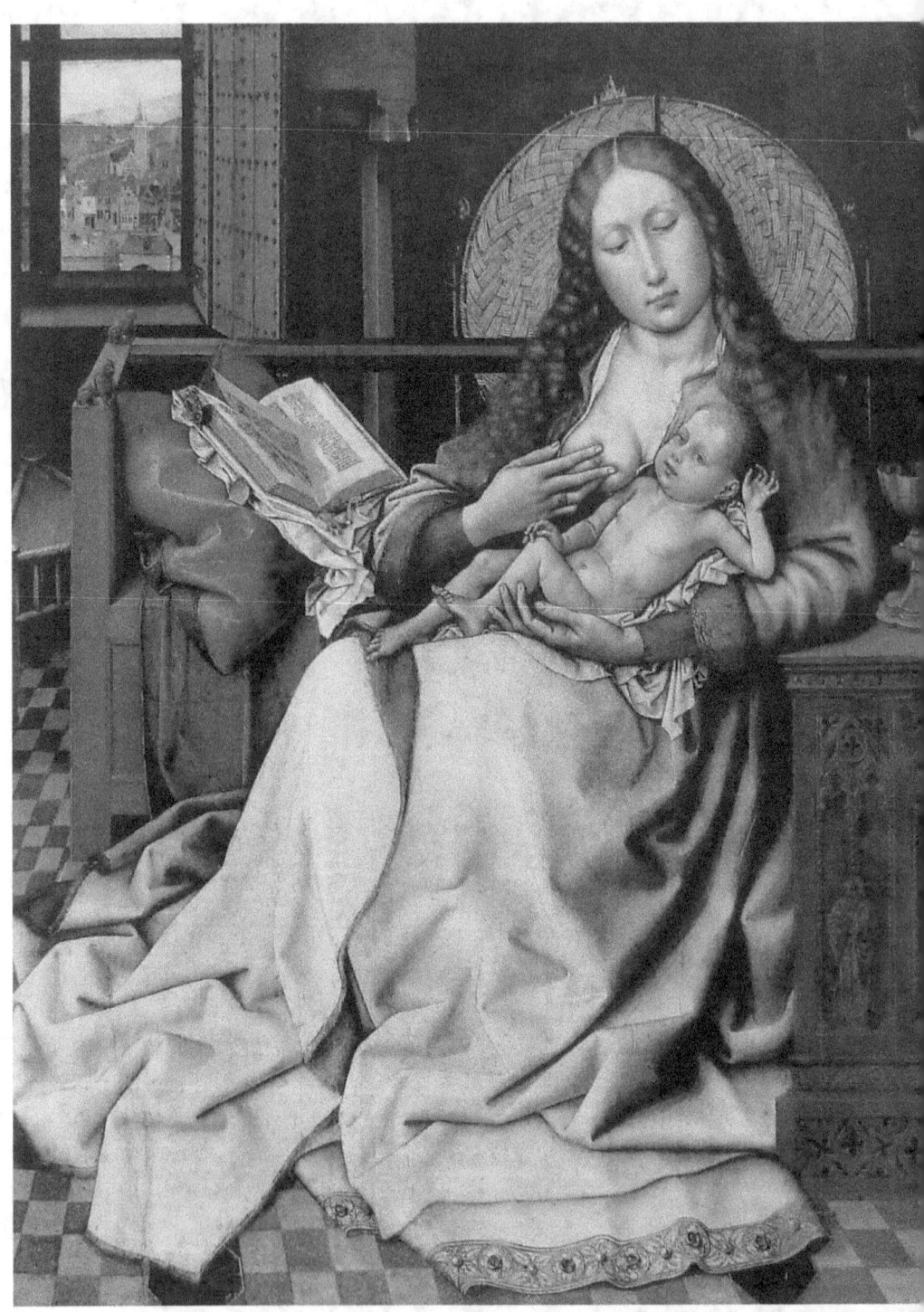

Robert Campin, Madonna With the Firescreen, National Gallery, London

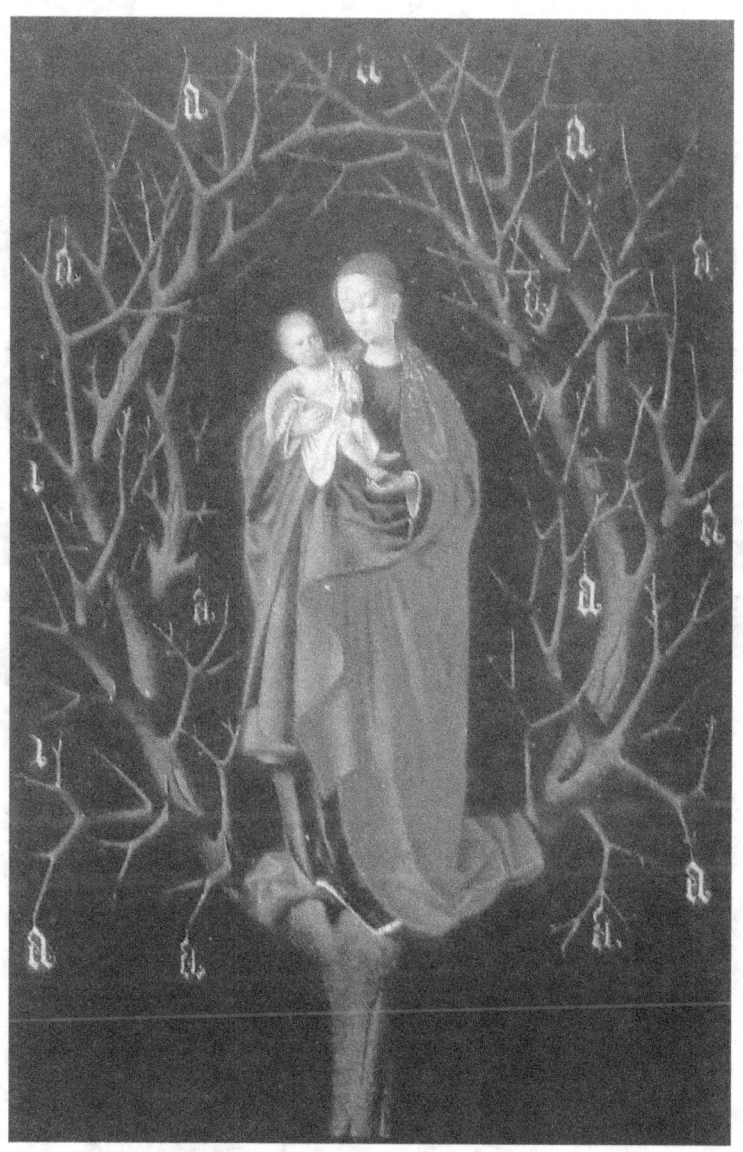

Petrus Christus, Madonna In a Barren Tree, 1450,
Prado, Madrid

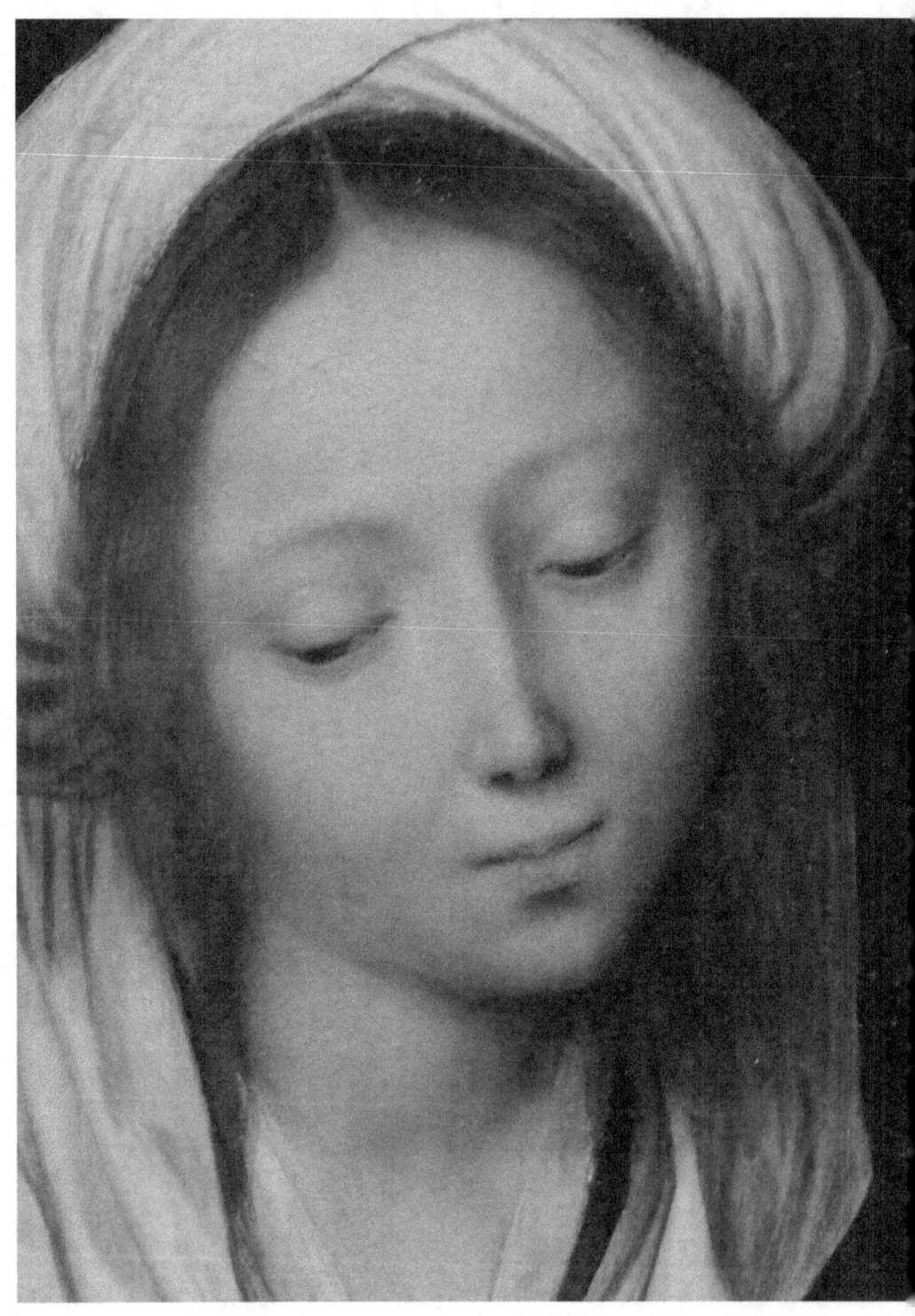

Gerard David, detail of the Adoration, Metropolitan Museum of Art

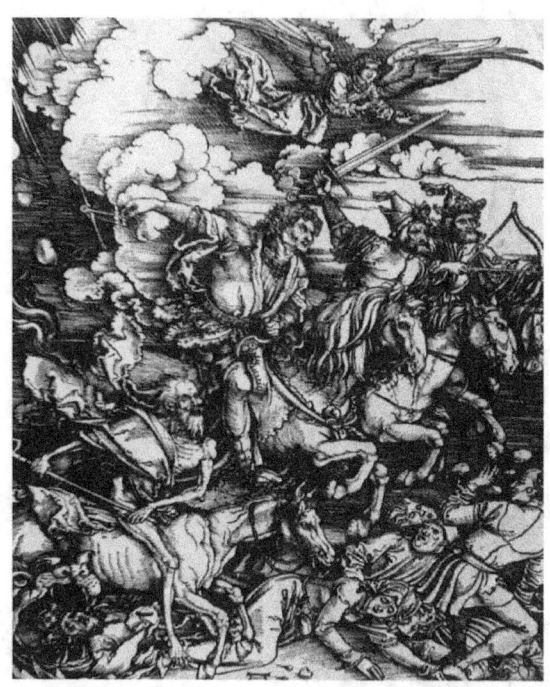

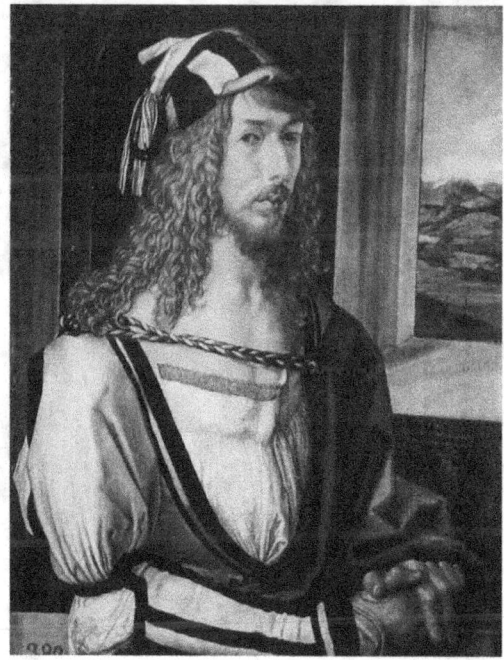

Albrecht Dürer

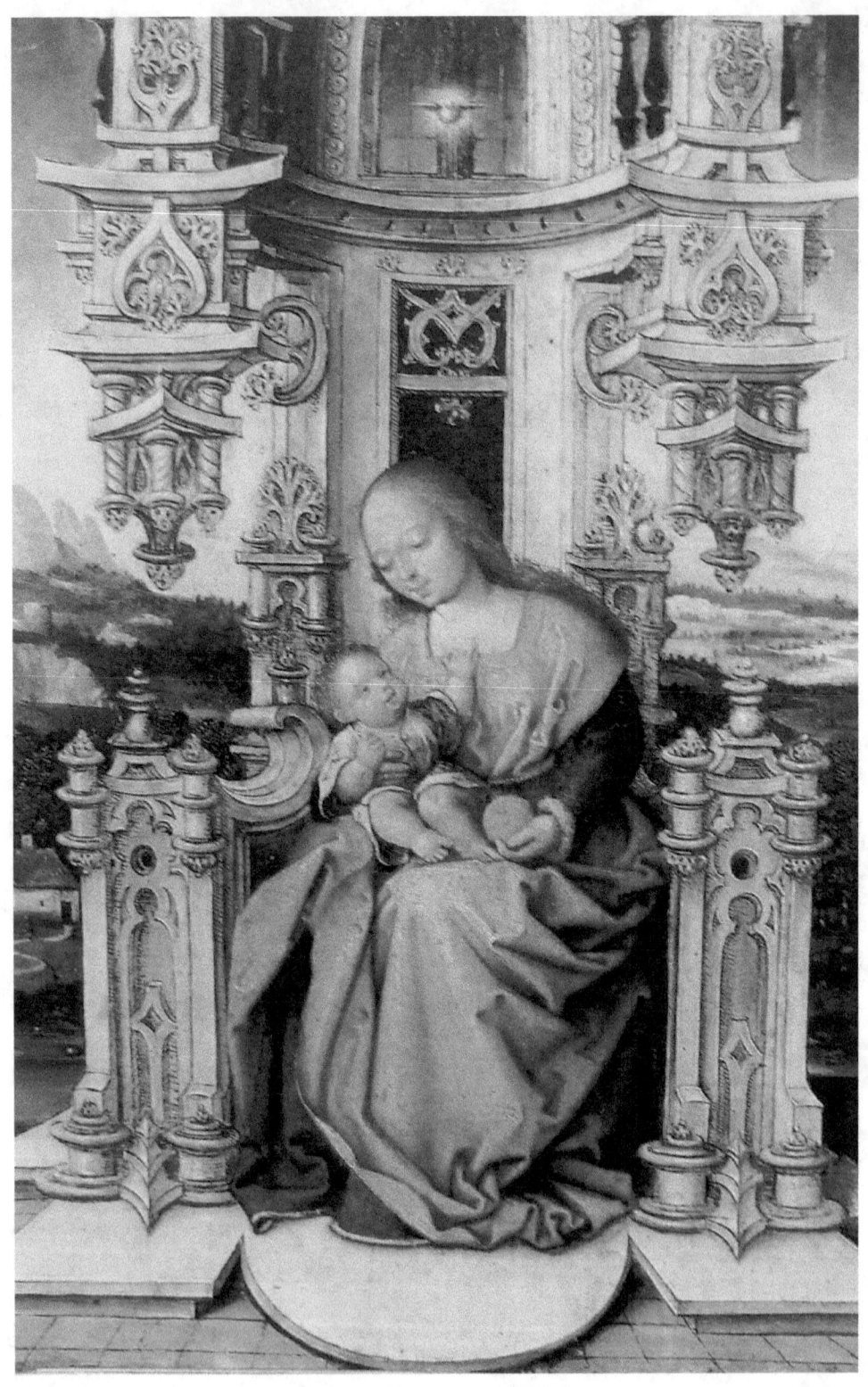

Jan Gossaert, Madonna and Child, Antwerp

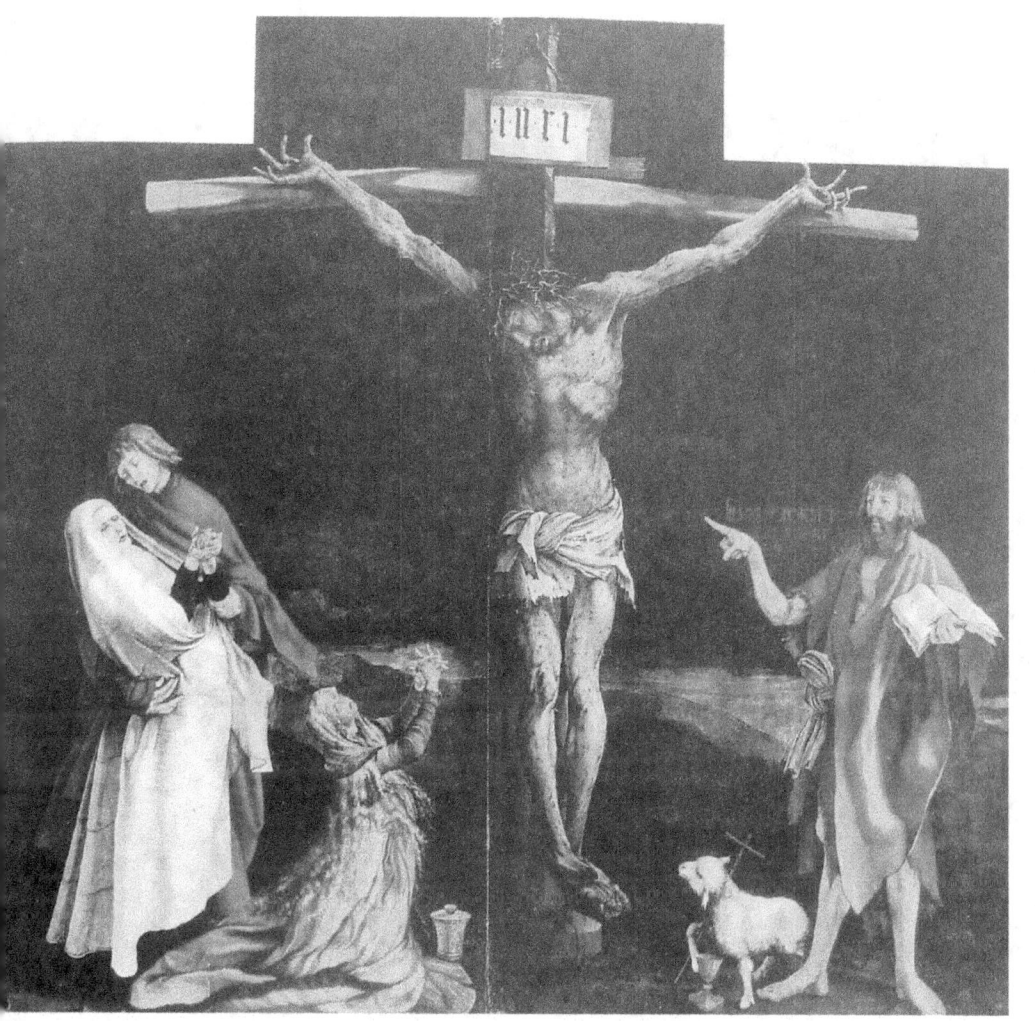

Matthias Grünewald, Crucifixion, Isenheim Altarpiece

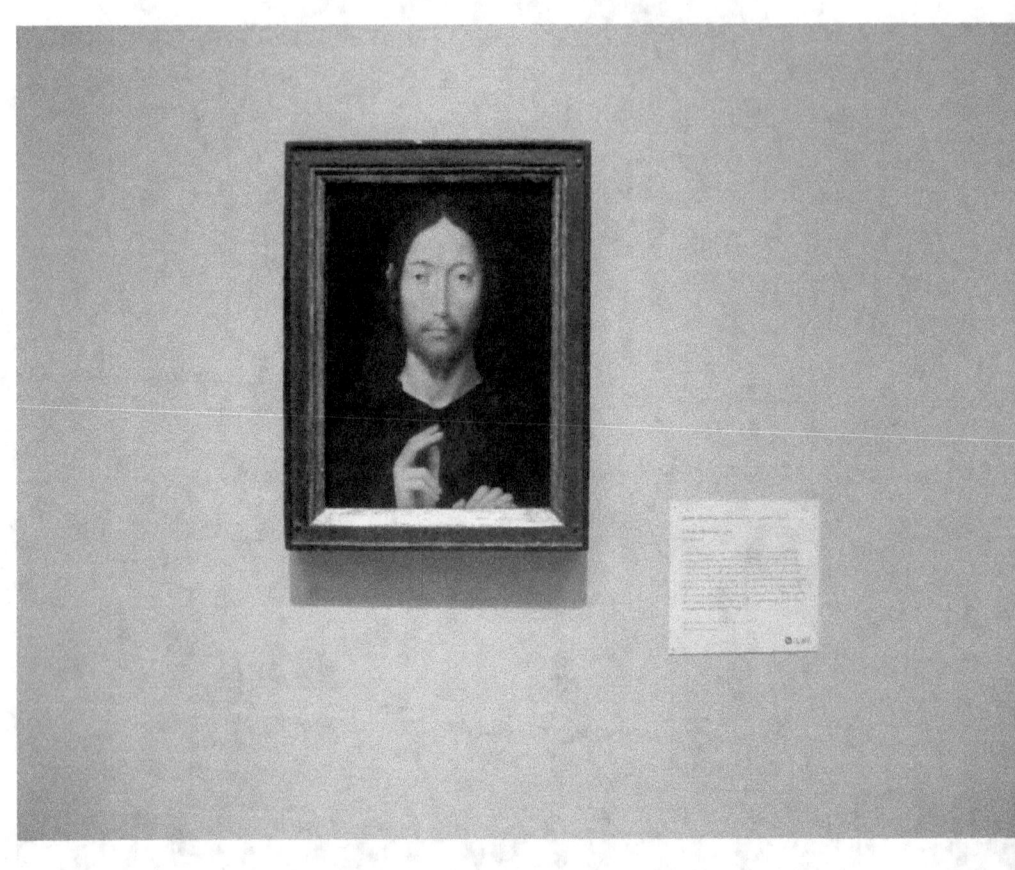

Hans Memling, Christ Blessing, Metropolitan Museum of Art

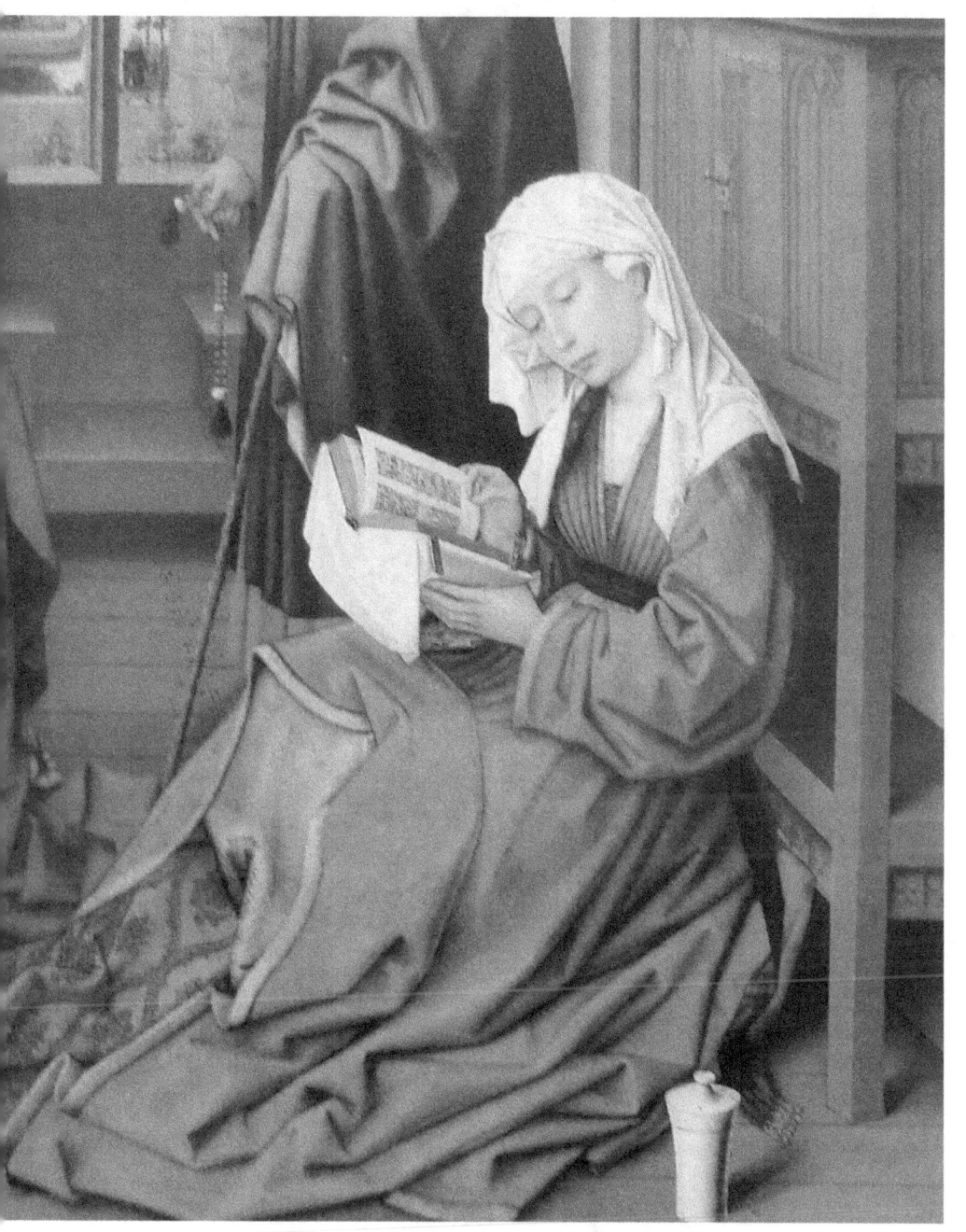

Rogier van der Weyden, Mary Magdalene Reading, detail, National Gallery, London

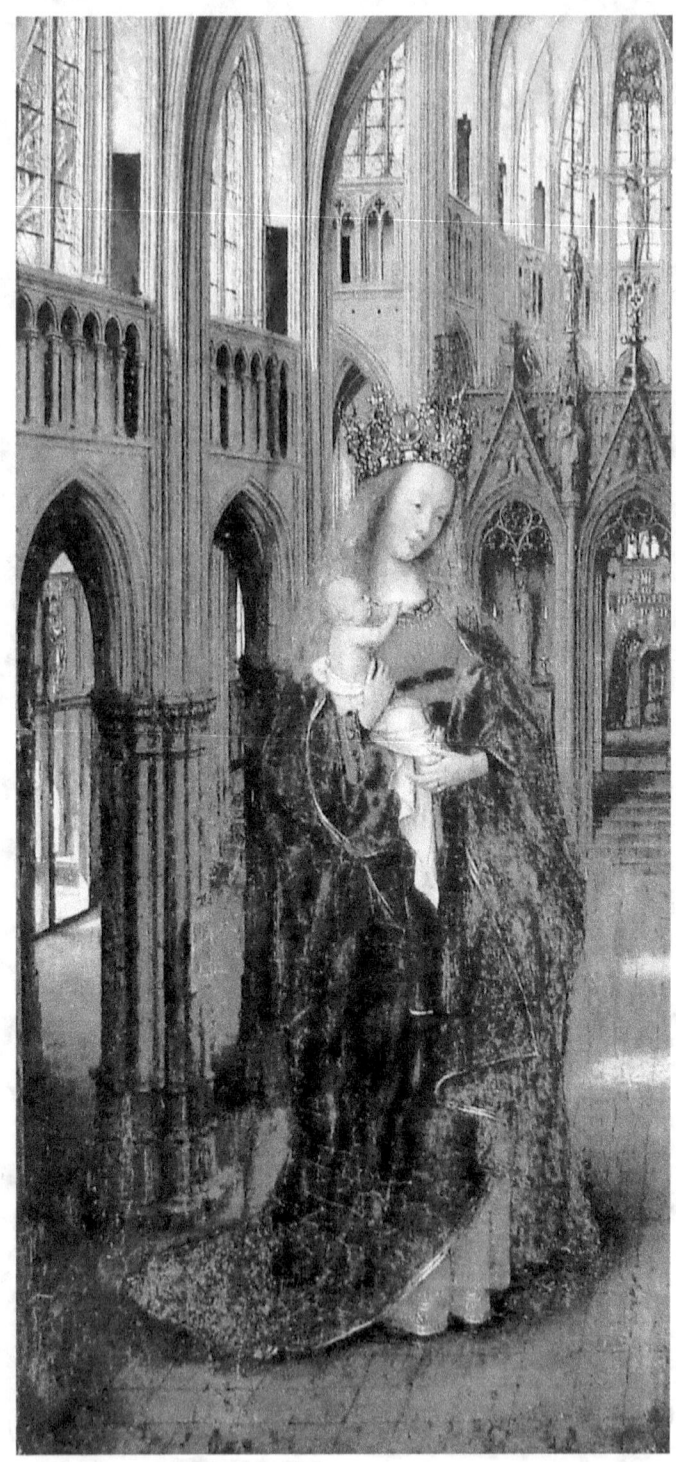

Jan van Eyck, Madonna In a Church, Berlin

# Notes

I : Introduction: Piero della Francesca and Arezzo

1. Dore Ashton: *About Rothko*, Oxford University Press, New York 1983

2. See, for instance C. Gilbert: "Piero della Francesca's 'Flagellation': The Figures in the Foreground", *The Art Bulletin*, LIII, 1971; E.H. Gombrich: "The Repentance of Judas in Piero della Francesca's 'Flagellation of Christ'", *Journal of the Warburg and Courtauld Institutes*, XXI, 1959, 105-7; M. Aronberg Lavin: "Piero della Francesca's 'Flagellation': the Triumph of Christian Glory", *Art Bulletin*, L, 1986, 321-42; R. Wittkower & B.A.R. Carter: "The Perspective of Piero della Francesca's 'Flagellation'", *Journal of the Warburg and Courtauld Institutes*, 16, 1953, 292-302; L. Borgo: "New Questions for Piero's Flagellation", *Burlington Magazine*, CXXI, Sept 1979, 546-53; A. Turchini: "Un'ipotesi sulla Flagellazione di Piero della Francesca", *Quaderni medievali*, XIV, 1982; G. Marchini: "Osservazioni sulla Flagellazione di Piero della Francesca", *Federico di Monfeltro*, Rome 1986, 243-6; J. Hofmann: "Piero della Francesca's *Flagellation:* A Reading from Jewish History", *Zeitschrift für Kunstgeschichte*, XLIV, 1981, 340-357; T. Zanobini Leoni: "La Flagellazione di Cristo di Piero della Francesca", *Sound Sonda*, 3/4, 1978; Bacci, 1979; T. Gouma Peterson: "Piero della Francesca's *Flagellation*: an Historical Interpretation", *Storia dell'Arte*, XXVIII, 1976, 217-233; C. Gilbert: "Piero della Francesca's *Flagellation*", *Art Bulletin*, LIII, March 1971, 41-51

3. Pierluigi de Vecchi, in P, 98

II : Space

1. F. Stella: *Working Space*, 40

2. M. Baxandall, 1985, 107

3. Piero Della Francesca, *De Prospectiva Pingendi*, in Goldwater, 143-4

4. R. Vischer: *Luca Signorelli and the Italian Renaissance*, 1879, in Piero, 10

5. A. Stokes: *The Stones of Rimini*, 1929, in Piero, 11; Clark, 1969, in ib., 12

6. Alberti: *Tratto della Nabilta della Pittura*, 1585, in P, 10

7. Lawrence Wright: *Perspective in Perspective*, Routledge 1983, 75

8. Roberto Longhi, introduction, *Piero della Franscesca*, Batsford 1949, 10. Clark suggests that Piero pinted large areas of colour interspersed with tiny details because he was short-sighted. Piero's sight deteriorated so that a young boy (Marco di Longaro) supposedly led Piero about when he was an old man.

9. F.M. Cornford: *Plato's Cosmology*, Harcourt, Brace, New York 1937

10. Michel Foucault suggests that

the real scandal of Galileo's work lay not so much in his discovery, or rediscovery, that the earth revolved around the sun, but in his constitution of an infinite, and infinitely open space.

(M. Foucault: "Of Other Spaces", *Diacritics*, vol. 16, no. 1)

11. Victor Burgin writes:

The effect of monocular perspective, however, is to maintain the idea that this space does nevertheless have a centre—the observer. By degrees the sovereign gaze is transferred from God to man. With the 'emplacement' of the medieval world now dissolved, this ocular subject of perspective, and of mercantile capitalism, is free to pursue its entrepreneurial ambitions wherever trade winds blow.

("Geometry and Abjection", in Fletcher, 1990, 106)

12. Victor Burgin, op. cit., 107

13. See R. Lawlor, C. Bouleau, *et al.*

14. Frank Stella writes:

We are so conditioned by the window of perspective that we stand motionless in front of it, waiting for painting to organize itself according to our acquired habits...Today, although we claim to be free of the bounds of perspective, we hold slavishly to a notion of a box view of a whole... to put it another way, the flatness of abstraction today, its sense of surface... is simply the forwardmost plane, the windowed picture plane of the fifteenth century perspectival box. (*Working Space*, 51)

III : Mother of God

1. Julia Kristeva: "Motherhood According to Bellini", *Peinture*, December 1975, no 10-11, and in *Desire in Language*, 1982, 243. Page numbers refer to this edition. Also: Julia Kristeva: *Revolution in Poetic Language*, in Kristeva, 1986, 101

2. Andrea Dworkin writes:

this premise about a biologically based morality is used, the woman-superior model of antifeminism is operating to keep women down, not up, in the crude world of actual human interchange. To stay worshipped, the woman must stay a symbol and she must stay good. She cannot become merely a human in the muck of life, morally flawed and morally struggling, committing acts that have complex, difficult, unpredictable consequences. She must not walk the same streets men do or do the same things or have the same responsibilities. Precisely because she is good, she is unfit to do the same things, unfit to make the same decisions, unfit to resolve the same dilemmas, unfit to undertake the same responsibilities, unfit to exercise the same rights. Her nature is different—this time better but still absolutely different—and therefore her role must be different. The worshipping attitude, the spiritual elevation of women that men invoke whenever they suggest that women are finer than they, proposes that women are what men can never be: chaste, good. In fact men are what women can never be: real moral agents, the bearers of real moral authority and responsibility. Women are not kept from this moral agency by biology, but by a male social system that puts women above or below simple human choice in morally demanding situations. The spiritual superiority of women in this model of ludicrous homage isolates women from the human acts that create meaning, the human choices that create both ethics and history. It separates women out from the chaos and triumph of human responsibility by giving women a two-dimensional morality, a stagnant morality, one in which what is right and good is predetermined, sex-determined, biologically determined.

(*Right-Wing Women: The Politics of Domesticated Females*, Women's Press 1983, 205-6)

3. J. Kristeva, 1982, 243

4. Julia Kristeva writes:

The face of his Madonnas are turned away, intent on something else that draws their gaze to the side, up, above, or nowhere in particular, but never centres it in the baby. (1991, 247)

5. J. Kristeva writes:

The language of art, too, follows (but differently and more closely) the other aspect of maternal jouissance, the sublimation taking place at the very moment of primal repression within the mother's body, arising perhaps unwittingly out of her marginal position. At the intersection of sign and rhythm, of representation and light, of the symbolic and the semiotic, the artist speaks from a place where she is not, where she knows not. (ib, 242)

6. J. Kristeva, *Desire in Language,* 246

IV : The Monumental Madonna

1. 'To be gilded with fine gold and coloured with fine colours, especially with ultramarine blue', quoted in M. Baxandall, 20. Latin text from *Nuovi documenti per la storia dell'arte toscana*, G. Milanesi, Rome 1893, 91

2. J. Kristeva: "Stabat Mater", in 1986, 170

V : The Exaltation of Pregnancy

1. The pomegranate is linked, symbolically, with Classical myths of resurrection and fucundity, such as that of Demeter/ Prosperine and the rebirth of the Nature in Spring. In Christianity, the pomegranate is a symbol of the Resurrection. Sometimes, in *Madonna and Child* paintings, the Christ child is seen holding a pomegranate.

2. See Benjamin Walker: *Gnosticism: Its History and Influence,*

Aquarian Press 1983

VII : The Triumph of Architecture

1. R. Lawlor, 96f; C. Bouleau, 95f. C.L. Ragghoanti has extended the architecture in the *Brera Altarpiece* beyond the frame, to reconstruct how it may have looked before it was possibly cut down (P, 106f). Carlo Bertelli writes of the painting as it might have been:

Before Berruguete repainted the Madonna's headdress, adding a brazenly natural milk-white, the star jewel on the forehead of the Madonna, like those on the heads of the archangels, must have grouped these five figures together, compared to all the others. Five daisies of pearls, rubies, sapphires, and emeralds glittered in sunlight at the centre of the painting and established a contrast with the opaque surface of the egg and the gold chain from which it hangs. The contrast in luminosity and texture between the Madonna's forehead and the egg should have instantly established the depth of scale between the two. (Bertelli, 138)

2. Alessandro Angelini writes of the *Brera Altarpiece* thus:

In this painting...the artist's mastery of proportions is remarkable; it is almost symbolized by the large ostrich egg hanging from the shell in the apse. The shape of this symbolic element is echoed by the near perfect oval of the Madonna's head, placed in the absolute centre of the composition. Piero's extraordinary invention of an architectural apse echoed below by another apse, consisting in the figures of the saints gathered around the Madonna, was taken up time and time again by artists working at the end of the 15th century and at the beginning of the 16th... (Angelini, 70)

3. The addition of the two saints (behind Bernardino and Peter Martyr) spoils the circle of figures and overcrowds the painting.

4. J. Cooper, 60; M. Meiss in F. Hartt, 1987, 281; Peter Fingesten. *The Eclipse of Symbolism*, University Press of California, 1970, 120.

5. Piero is said to have influenced Bellini. They were about the same age, but Bellini lived longer than Piero, into the 2nd decade of the 16th century. Piero's *Brera Altarpiece* may have influenced some of Bellini's later works.

VIII: Virgin and Whore

1. Piero may have known Early Netherlandish art at the court of Federico

da Montefeltro at Urbino, or in Florence.

2. M. Meiss: *The Great Age of Fresco*, Phaidon 1970, 134. Another critic wrote of the *Senigallia Madonna:*

Here however he finds an equilibrium never again achieved between a monumental expression, to which the ancient group of the Virgin and Child certainly belong (a possible Christologic meditation), and the direct dialogue between the work and the spectator, who is provoked to see, in those extremes of night and day...which provide an allusion to an individual destiny. The contrasting primary colours, present in Piero's more youthful work, are here muted to the point of placing a rose-peach colour opposite to an ash-colour at the two extremes of the picture. The Madonna does not wear jewels, and the lining of her mantle (a solution Piero has always loved) creates a grey zone in an important area. The lips of all the figures are a surprising bold cyclamen-rose colour against the pallid ochre of the face, while on top of the general intonation, blue-grey as in the *pietra serena* of the walls, the sulphureous yellows break out with brilliant novelty. (C. Bertelli, 163)

IX: The Life of Christ

1. Mircea Eliade: "Divinities: Art and the Divine", *Encyclopedia of World Art*, McGraw-Hill, New York 1961, vol 4, 382

2. Mircea Eliade: "Divinities: Art and the Divine", op.cit, 387

3. From the *Oxyrhynchus Sayings of Jesus*, in Happold, 195. Also the pagan deities of the Etruscans and Romans, former inhabitants of Piero's homeland.

4. *Corpus Hermeticum*, in Ferguson, 1976, 76

5. J. Risset, in Serge Gavronsky, ed: *Toward a New Poetics: Contemporary Writing in France*, University California Press, Berkeley 1994, 144

6. C. Bertelli writes:

The gesture of the man with the raised arm marks the moment of the apparition, as Christ's halo is formed before our eyes, as if it were from strands of gold united at the moment in which the water falls from the bowl...We are witnessing the creation of things. (C. Bertelli, 58)

7. C. Bertelli writes:

Piero's Jesus concentrates completely on himself and on his mission; his body is outlined beneath the transparent loincloth that girds him, as a small mound of waves surrounding Christ's body would have done in ancient representations. As with the forehead in the Rimini *St Sigismund*, here the arm traces a lunette on his torso, underling the angle formed by the wrist and the hand under the breastbone. This sacred body, given solidity by the shadow, is fundamentally untouchable. An inviolable area is cut between the arm and the foot of the Baptist, and the entre figure of Jesus. John's taut left hand, outstretched in suspended action, which does not pass over this border, further emphasizes this separation. (C. Bertelli, 54)

8. C. Ginzburg, 1985, 19f; C. de Tolnay: "Conceptions religieuse dans la peinture de Piero della Francesca", *Arte antica e moderna*, VI, 1963; M. Tanner: "Concodria in Piero della Francesca's *Baptism of Christ*", *Art Quarterly*, XXXV, 1972, 1-20; Battisti, I, 117; J. Gill: *The Council of Florence*, Cambridge 1959

9. The 'Three Baptisms' are by water, blood (*Baptismus sanguinis*) and spirit (*Baptismus flaminis*). See M. Baxandall, 1985, 123; S. Antonio: *Summa Theologica*, XIV. xiii, xiv. ii. 1

10. 'Piero's light is pure and unwavering, an ethereal manifestation of divinity on earth'. (B. Cole, 1991, 51)

11. Michael Levey writes of *The Flagellation* in a more controlled manner than some critics, but the enthusiasm is still there: 'Piero's sophisticated science and deliberate emotional control result in a painting of Christ's Passion as effective as any more disturbed, more realistically presented scene. It invests with dignity even the moment of being tortured' (Levey, 1967, 130).

12. 'The picture seems to retain its locked-up secret, even while appearing at first glance to be all openness and lucidity.' Michael Levey, 1967, 129

13. M. Lavin, 1981; A. Martone in O. Calabrese, 1984; C. Bertelli, 122; Carter, 1953

14. See Bruce Cole: *Agnolo Gaddi*, Oxford 1977; M. Boskovits: "In margine alla bottega di Agnolo Gaddi", *Paragone*, 355, 1979, 54-62; De Tolnay, 222-6; Gilbert, 77f

15. Piero was among the first painters to use cartoons so extensively. Bruce Cole reckons that Piero would not have been able to complete the

complex interweaving of figures and drapery without using cartoons. (1991, 96)

# Bibliography

On Piero della Franscesca

J. Alazard: *Piero della Francesca*, Paris 1948

F. Ames-Lewis: "Fra Filippo Lippi and Flanders", *Zeitschrift für Kunstgeschichte*, XLII, 1979, 255-273

A. Angelini: *Piero della Francesca*, Scala, Florence 1985

M. Bacci: *Piero della Francesca. La Pittura*, Florence 1979

E. Bairati: *Piero della Francesca*, Milan 1991

E. Battisti: *Piero della Francesca*, Milan 1971

Carlo Bertelli: *Piero della Francesca*, Yale University Press, New Haven 1992

Anthony Bertram: *Piero della Francesca*, Studio Publications 1949

Piero Bianconi: *Piero della Francesca*, tr Paul Colacicchi, Oldbourne, 1962

R. Black: "The Uses and Abuses of Iconology: Piero della Francesca and Carlo Ginzburg", *The Oxford Art Journal*, IX, 2, 1986, 67-71

O. Calabrese, ed: *Piero teorico dell'arte*, Rome 1984

E. Cassée: "La Madonna del Parto", in *Paragone*, XXIX, 1978, 94-97

Kenneth Clark: *Piero della Francesca*, Phaidon 1969

C.H. Clough: "Piero della Francesca: Some Problems of His Art and Chronology", *Apollo*, XCI, April 1970, 278-289

Bruce Cole: *Piero della Francesca: Tradition and Innovation in Renaissance Art*, Harper Collins, New York 1991

R.M. Cooke: "Piero della Francesca and the Development of Italian Landscape Painting", in *The Burlington Magazine*, CXXII, September 1980, 627-31

V. Dini & L. Sonni: *La Madonna del Parto: Imaginario e realtà nella cultura agropastorale*, Rome 1985

C. Feudle: "The Iconography of the *Madonna del Parto*", *Marsyas*, VII, 1954, 8-24

C. Gilbert: *Change in Piero della Francesca*, New York 1968

Carlo Ginzburg: *The Enigma of Piero: Piero della Francesca, The Baptism, The Arezzo Cycle, The Flagellation*, Verso 1985

# Piero della Francesca

B. Giorni, ed: "La Madonna del Parto di Piero della Francesca e la chiesa di Santa Maria a Nomentana", in *Monterchi e la sua storia*, Città di Castello 1972

—*La Madonna del Parto di Pietro della Francesca*, Sansepolcro 1977

C. Goldner: "Notes on the iconography of Piero della Francesca's *Annunciation* in Arezzo", in *The Art Bulletin*, LVI, Sept 1974, 343-3

J. & M. Guillaud: *Piero della Francesca, Poet of Form. The Frescoes of San Francesco in Arezzo*, New York 1988

P. Hendy: *Piero della Francesca and the Early Renaissance*, London 1968

Marilyn Aronberg Lavin: *Piero della Francecsa's Baptism of Christ*, Yale University Press 1981

—*Piero della Francesca: The Flagellation*, Penguin 1972

—*Piero della Francesca, The Flagellation,* New Haven 1981

—"The Altar of Corpus Domini in Urbino: Paolo Uccello, Joos van Ghent, Piero della Francesca", *Art Bulletin*, 49, 1967, 1-24

—"Piero della Francesca's Montefeltro Altarpiece: A Pledge of Fidelity", *Art Bulletin*, 51, 1969, 367-71

Robert Longhi: *Piero della Francesca,* Milan 1955

D. Mateescu: *Piero della Francesca*, Bucharest 1981

*Convegno internazionale sulla 'Madonna del Parto' di Piero della Francesca*, Monterchi 24 May 1980, Monterchi 1980

A. Paolucci: *Piero della Francesca. Catalogo completo*, Florence 1990

Piero della Francesca: *The Complete Paintings of Piero della Francesca*, intr. Peter Murray, notes by Pierluigi de Vecchi, Penguin, 1985 [abbr. as P]

—*Frescoes,* intr. Robert Longhi, Batsford 1949

—*Piero*, Institutio Italiano d'Arti Grafiche, Bergamo 1956

P. Dal Poggetto: *Piero della Francesca*, Florence 1971

John Pope-Hennessy: "Whose Flagellation?", *Apollo*, Sept 1986, 162-5

G. Renzi: *Piero della Francesca*, Arezzo 1990

D. Schmidt: *Piero della Francesca*, Leipzig 1970

L. Schneider: "The Iconography of Piero della Francesca's Frescoes Illustrating the Legend of the True Cross in the Church of San Francesco in Arezzo", *Art Quarterly*, 32, 1969

John Shearman: "The Logic and Realism of Pierdo della Francesca", in *Festschrift Ulrich Middeldorf*, ed Antje Kosegarten & Pieter Tigler, Berlin 1968, I: 180-6

Lionello Venturi: *Piero della Francesca,* Geneva 1954, Skira, Paris 1959

H. Wohl: "In detail: Piero della Francesca's Resurrection Fresco", *Portfolio*, II, 1981, 38-43

Others

C.G. Argan: *The Renaissance*, Thames & Hudson 1969

Karen Armstrong: *The Gospel According to Woman; Christianity's Creation of the Sex War in the West*, Pan 1987

Karen Arthurs: *A Survey of the Notions Behind, and the Mechanics of, Harmony Within the Composition of Art From Prehistory to the Renaissance*, BA thesis, Newcastle Polytechnic 1984

Geoffrey Ashe: *The Virgin: Mary's Cult and the Re-emergence of the Goddess*, Arkana 1987

—*Discovering the Goddess: A Personal Testimony*, Crescent Moon 1994

Dore Ashton: *American Art Since 1945*, Thomas & Hudson 1982

Michael Baxandall: *Painting and Experience in 15th Century Italy*, Oxford University Press 1988

—*Patterns of Intention: On the Historical Explanation of Pictures*, Yale University Press 1985

James Beck: *Italian Renaissance Painting*, Harper & Row, New York 1981

Ean Begg: *The Cult of the Black Virgin*, Routledge 1985

Bernard Berenson: *The Italian Painters of the Renaissance*, Phaidon 1952/ Fontana 1960

—*Looking at Pictures with Bernard Berenson*, selected by Hann Kiel, Abrahams, New York 1974

Pamela Berger: *The Goddess Obscured*, Robert Hale 1988

Bruce Bernard: *The Queen of Heaven: A Selection of Painting the Virgin from the Twelfth to the Eighteenth Centuries*, Macdonald/ Orbis 1987

—*The Bible and Its Painters*, Orbis 1983

Botticelli: *The Complete Paintings of Botticelli*, Granada 1980

Charles Bouleau: *The Painter's Secret Geometry: A Study of Composition in Art*, tr Jonathan Griffin, Thames & Hudson 1963

Serge Bramly: *Leonardo: The Artist and the Man*, Michael Joseph 1992

Allan Brahama: *Italian Renaissance Painters of the Sixteenth Century*, National Gallery 1985

Robert Briffault: *The Mothers: A Study of the Origins of Sentiments and Institutions*, Allen & Unwin, 3 vols 1927

Helmut Brinker: *Zen in the Art of Painting*, Routledge & Kegan Paul 1987

Stephanie Brown: *Religious Painting*, Phaidon 1979

Jacob Burckhardt: *The Altarpiece in Renaissance Italy*, Phaidon 1988

Titus Burckhardt: *Sacred Art in East and West*, Perennial Book, Middlesex 1967

Ritchie Calder: *Leonardo and The Age of the Eye*, Heinemann 1970

Joseph Campbell: *The Power of Myth*, with Bill Moyers, ed. Betty Sue Flowers, Doubleday, New York 1988

Michael P. Carroll: *The Cult of the Virgin Mary*, Princeton University

Press, New Jersey 1986

Richard Cavendish: *Visions of Heaven and Hell*, Orbis 1977

Andre Chastel: *Art of the Italian Renaissance*, tr Peter & Linda Murray, Alpine Fine Arts Collection 1985

—*The Studios and Styles of the Renaissance, Italy 1460-1500*, tr Griffin, Thames & Hudson 1966

Herschel B. Chipp, ed. *Theories of Modern Art,* University Press of California, Los Angeles 1968

Bruce Cole: *The Renaissance Artist at Work*, John Murray 1983

Pierre Courthion: *Flemish Painting*, Thames & Hudson 1958

Charles D. Cuttler: *Northern Painting From Pucelle to Bruegel*, Holt, Rineheart & Winston, New York 1968

Jean-Luc Daval: *History of Abstract Painting*, Art Data 1989

Martin Davies: *Rogier van der Weyden*, Phaidon 1972

Elisabeth Dhanens: *Hubert and Jan van Eyck*, New York 1980

Lene Dresen-Coenders, ed: *Saints and She-Devils: Images of Women in the 15th and 16th Centuries*, Rubicon Press 1987

Andrea Dworkin: *Intercourse*, Arrow 1988

—*Pornography: Men Possessing Women*, Women's Press 1984

Donald Ehresmann: "Some Observations on the Role of the Liturgy in the Early Winged Altarpiece", *Art Bulletin*, LXIV, 1982

Colin Eisler: *Early Netherlandish Painting: The Thyssen-Bornemisza Collection*, Sotheby's Publications 1989

Mircea Eliade: *Ordeal by Labyrinth*, University of Chicago Press 1984

—*Symbolism, the Sacred and the Arts*, Crossroad, New York 1985

Joan Evans, ed: *The Flowering of the Middle Ages*, Thames & Hudson 1966

Giorgio T. Faggin: *The Complete Paintings of the Van Eycks*, Weidenfeld & Nicolson 1970

George Ferguson: *Signs and Symbols in Christian Art*, Oxford University Press 1961

John Ferguson: *An Illustrated Encyclopaedia of Mysticism,* Thames & Hudson 1976

Peter Fingesten: *The Eclipse of Symbolism*, University Press of California 1970

John Fletcher & Andrew Benjamin, ed; *Abjection, Melancholia and Love: the Work of Julia Kristeva*, Routledge 1990

S.J. Freedberg: *Painting of the High Renaissance in Rome and Florence*, Harper & Row, New York 1972

Sigmund Freud: *Leonardo da Vinci*, tr Alan Tyson, Penguin 1963

Max J. Friedlander: *From Van Eyck to Bruegel*, Phaidon 1969

—*Hugo van der Goes: Early Netherlandish Painting*, vol. IV, tr Heinz Norden, Sijthoff, Leyden, Netherlands 1967

—*The van Eycks, Petrus Christus: Early Netherlandish Painting*, vol. 1, tr Heinz Norden, Sijthoff, Leyden, Netherlands 1967

Eugène Fromentin: *The Masters of Past Time: Dutch and Flemish Painting from Van Eyck to Rembrandt*, Phaidon 1981

Piero della Francesca

Elinor Gadon: *The Once and Future Goddess*, Aquarian Press 1990
Niny Garavaghlia: *The Complete Paintings of Mantegna*, Weidenfeld & Nicholson 1971
Fred Gettings: *The Hidden Art: A Study of the Occult Symbolism in Art*, Studio Vista 1978
Matila Ghyka: *The Geometry of Art and Life*, Sheed & Ward, New York 1946
Marija Gimbutas: *The Language of the Goddess*, Thames & Hudson 1989
F.M. Godfrey: *A Student's Guide to Italian Paintings 1250-1800*, Alec Tiranti 1965
Rona Goffen: *Giovanni Bellini*, Yale University Press, New Haven 1989
Robert Goldwater & Marco Treves, eds. *Artists on Art*, John Murray 1975
E.H. Gombrich: *Norm and Form: Studies in the Renaissance I*, Phaidon 1985
—*Symbolic Images, Renaissance Studies II,* Phaidon 1985
Cecil Gould: *Leonardo: The Artist and the Non-Artist*, Weidenfeld & Nicholson 1975
—"On the Direction of Light in Italian Renaissance Frescoes and Altarpieces", *Gazette des Beaux-Arts*, 6, XCVII, 1981
John Hale: *Italian Renaissance Painting*, Phaidon 1977
James Hall: *A Dictionary of Subjects and Symbols in Art*, John Murray 1984
F.C.Happold, ed. *Mysticism*, Penguin 1970
M. Esther Harding: *Women's Mysteries,* Rider 1989
Frederick Hartt: *History of Italian Renaissance Art: Painting, Sculpture, Architecture*, Thames & Hudson 1987
—*Sandro Botticelli*, Collins 1954
Anne Hollander: *Seeing Through Clothes,* Viking Press, New York 1980
Michael Jacobs: *A Guide to European Painting*, David & Charles 1980
Charles Johnson: *Memlinc*, Faber, n.d.
P. Jolly: "Rogier van der Weyden's Escorial and Philadelphia *Crucifixions* and their relation to Fra Angelico at San Marco", *Oud Holland*, XCV, 1981, 113-126
Diane Kelder: *Pageant of the Renaissance*, Pall Mall Press 1969
David Kinsley: *The Goddess's Mirror: Visions of the Divine From East and West*, State University of New York Press 1989
Julia Kristeva: *The Kristeva Reader*, ed Toril Moi, Blackwell 1986
—*Desire in Language: A Semiotic Approach to Literature and Art*, ed Leon Roudiez, tr Thomas Gora, Alice Jardine & Leon Roudiez, Blackwell 1982
Weston La Barre: *The Ghost Dance*, Allen & Unwin 1972
Barbara Lane: *The Altar and the Altarpiece: Sacramental Themes in Early Netherlandish Painting*, New York 1984
—"Sacred vs Profane in Early Netherlandish Painting", *Simiolus*, XVIII, 1988
Leonardo da Vinci: *The Drawings of Leonardo da Vinci*, introduction A.E.

Popham, Cape, 1964

—*The Complete Paintings*, introduction by L.D. Ettinger, Weidenfeld & Nicolson 1969

—*Selections from the Notebooks*, Oxford University Press 1952

Michael Levey: *High Renaissance*, Penguin 1975

—*Early Renaissance*, Penguin 1967

Christopher Lloyd: *Fra Angelico*, Phaidon 1979

—*A Picture History of Art*, Phaidon 1979

Emile Male: *The Gothic Image*, Collins 1961

Elaine Marks & Isabelle de Courtivron, eds: *New French Feminisms: an Anthology*, Harvester Wheatsheaf 1981

K.B. MacFarlane: *Hans Memling*, Clarendon Press 1971

G. Marchini: *Filippo Lippi*, Electa Editrice, Milan 1975

James Marrow: "Symbol and Meaning in Northern European Art of the Late Middle Ages and Early Renaissance", *Simiolus*, XVI, 1986

Milliard Meiss: "Light as Form and Symbol in Some Fifteenth Century Paintings", *Art Bulletin*, XXVII, 1945

J.C.J.Metford: *Dictionary of Christian Lore and Legend,* Thames & Hudson 1983

Toril Moi: *Sexual/Textual Politics: Feminist Literary Theory,* Routledge 1988

Edward Mullins: *The Painted Witch: Female Body, Male Art*, Secker & Warburg 1985

Peter & Linda Murray: *The Penguin Dictionary of Art and Artists*, Penguin 1976

Linda Murray: *High Renaissance*, Thames & Hudson 1977

Lynda Nead: *Female Nude: Art, Obscenity and Sexuality*, Routledge 1992

Erich Neumann: *The Great Mother*, Princeton University Press, New Jersey 1972

Shirley Nicholson, ed. *The Goddess Re-awakening: The Goddess Principle Today,* Theosophical Publishing House, New York 1989

Rudolf Otto: *The Idea of the Holy*, Oxford University Press 1958

Erwin Panofsky: *Studies in Iconology*, Harper & Row, New York 1972

—*Early Netherlandish Painting*, Harvard University Press, Mass., 1953

Geoffrey Parrinder: *Mysticism in the World's Religions,* Sheldon Press 1976

Walter Pater: *The Renaissance*, Oxford University Press 1980

Michael Payne: *Reading Theory: An Introduction to Lacan, Derrida, and Kristeva*, Blackwell 1993

Robert Payne: *Leonardo da Vinci*, Robert Hale 1979

Lotte Brand Philip: *The Ghent Altarpiece and the Art of Jan van Eyck*, Princeton University Press 1971

Michael Phillipson: *Painting, Language and Modernity*, Routledge 1978

John Pope-Hennessy: *Fra Angelico*, Phaidon 1974

Mario Praz: *The Romantic Agony,* tr Davidson, Oxford University Press 1933

C. Purtle: *The Marian Paintings of Jan van Eyck*, Princeton University Press, Princeton 1982

Kathleen J. Reiger, ed: *The Spiritual Image in Modern Art*, Theosophical Publishing House, Wheaton, Illinois 1987

Ad Reinhardt: *Art as Art: The Selected Writings of Ad Reinhardt*, University of California Press, Berkeley, 1991

D. Robb: "The Iconography of the Annunciation in the Fourteenth and Fifteenth Centuries", *Art Bulletin*, XVIII, 1936, 480-526

Jeremy Robinson: *Glorification: Religious Abstraction in Renaissance and 20th Century Painting*, Crescent Moon 1994

Patrick Trevor Roper: *The world blunted through sight: An inquiry into the influence of defective vision on art and character*, Thames & Hudson 1970

Robert Rosenblum: *Modern Painting and the Northern Romantic Tradition*, Thames & Hudson 1978

Mark Roskill: *What is Art History?*, Thames & Hudson 1976

John Ruskin: *Works*, ed. E.T.Cook & A.Wedderburn, 39 vols, Allen 1903-12

Elaine Showalter, ed: *The New Feminist Criticism*, Virago 1986

Monica Sjöo & Barbara Mor: *The Great Cosmic Mother*, Harper & Row, San Francisco 1987

Alistair Smith: *Early Netherlandish and German Painting*, National Gallery 1985

J. Spencer: "Spatial Imagery of the Annunciation in Fifteenth-century Florence", *Art Bulletin*, XXXVI, 1955, 273-280

Sidney Spencer: *Mysticism in World Religion*, Penguin 1963

Wolfgang Stechow: *Northern Renaissance Art, 1400-1600, Sources and Documents*, Prentice-Hall, New Jersey 1966

L. Steinberg & S. Edgerton: "How shall this be? Reflections on Filippo Lippi's *Annunciation* in London", *Artibus et Historiae*, VIII, 1987, 25-53

Frank Stella: *Working Space*, Harvard University Press, Cambridge, Mass., 1986

Victor I. Stoichita: *Leonardo da Vinci*, Abbey Library 1978

Peter Streider: *Dürer: Paintings, Prints, Drawings*, F. Muller 1982

Susan Rubin Suleiman, ed: *The Female Body in Western Culture: Contemporary Perspectives*, Harvard University Press, Cambridge, Mass., 1986

Andrei Tarkovsky: *Time Within Time: The Diaries, 1970-1986*, tr Kitty Hunter-Blair, Seagull Books, Calcutta 1991

—*Sculpting in Time: Reflections on the Cinema*, tr. Kitty Hunter-Blair, Faber 1989

Nicholas Usherwood: *The Bible in 20th Century Art*, Pagoda Books 1987

Lionello Venturi: *Renaissance Painting, from Leonardo to Dürer*, Skira/ Macmillan 1979

—*Italian Paintings*, Zwemmer 1950

—*Botticelli*, Phaidon 1964

Marina Warner: *Alone Of All Her Sex: The Myth and Cult of the Virgin Mary*, Picador 1985
—*Monuments and Maidens*, Weidenfeld & Nicholson 1985
Margaret Whinney: *Early Flemish Painters*, Faber 1966
John White: *The Birth and Rebirth of Pictorial Space*, Faber 1957/87
Edward C. Whitmont: *Return of the Goddess*, Routledge 1987
Peter Lamborn Wilson: *Angels*, Thames & Hudson 1980
Mara R. Witzling: *Voicing Our Visions: Writing by Women Artists*, Women's Press 1992
Heinrich Wolfflin: *Classic Art*, Phaidon 1952/80
Marion Woodman: *The Pregnant Virgin: A Process of Psychological Transformation*, Inner City Books, Toronto 1989
Manfred Wudram: *Art of the Renaissance*, Weidenfeld & Nicolson 1985
J.E. Zeigler: "The Medieval Virgin as Object: Art of Anthropology?", *Historical Reflections*, XVI, 1989
Charles Zika: "Hosts, Processions and Pilgrimages: Controlling the Sacred in Fifteenth-Century Germany", *Past and Present*, CXVIII, 1988

# CRESCENT MOON PUBLISHING

web: www.crmoon.com  e-mail: cresmopub@yahoo.co.uk

## ARTS, PAINTING, SCULPTURE

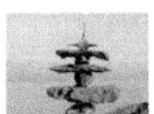
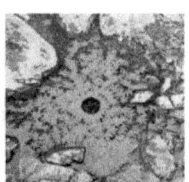

The Art of Andy Goldsworthy
Andy Goldsworthy: Touching Nature
Andy Goldsworthy in Close-Up
Andy Goldsworthy: Pocket Guide
Andy Goldsworthy In America
Land Art: A Complete Guide
The Art of Richard Long
Richard Long: Pocket Guide
Land Art In the UK
Land Art in Close-Up
Land Art In the U.S.A.
Land Art: Pocket Guide

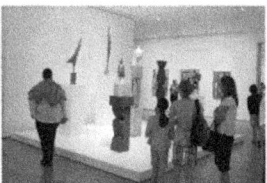
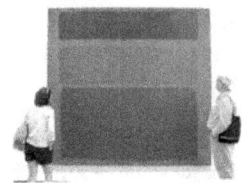

Installation Art in Close-Up
Minimal Art and Artists In the 1960s and After
Colourfield Painting
Land Art DVD, TV documentary
Andy Goldsworthy DVD, TV documentary
The Erotic Object: Sexuality in Sculpture From Prehistory to the Present Day
Sex in Art: Pornography and Pleasure in Painting and Sculpture
Postwar Art
Sacred Gardens: The Garden in Myth, Religion and Art
Glorification: Religious Abstraction in Renaissance and 20th Century Art
Early Netherlandish Painting

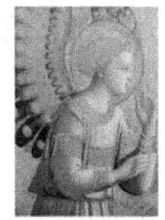

Leonardo da Vinci
Piero della Francesca
Giovanni Bellini
Fra Angelico: Art and Religion in the Renaissance
Mark Rothko: The Art of Transcendence
Frank Stella: American Abstract Artist
Jasper Johns
Brice Marden

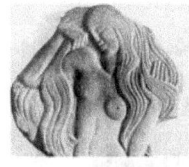
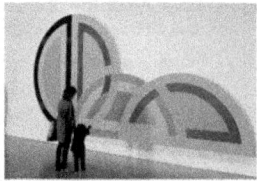

Alison Wilding: The Embrace of Sculpture
Vincent van Gogh: Visionary Landscapes
Eric Gill: Nuptials of God
Constantin Brancusi: Sculpting the Essence of Things
Max Beckmann
Caravaggio

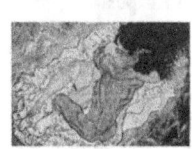
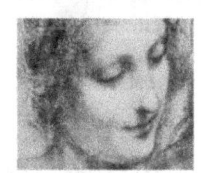

Gustave Moreau
Egon Schiele: Sex and Death In Purple Stockings
Delizioso Fotografico Fervore: Works In Process 1
Sacro Cuore: Works In Process 2
The Light Eternal: J.M.W. Turner
The Madonna Glorified: Karen Arthurs

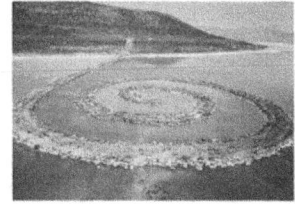

# LITERATURE

J.R.R. Tolkien: The Books, The Films, The Whole Cultural Phenomenon
J.R.R. Tolkien: Pocket Guide
Tolkien's Heroic Quest
The *Earthsea* Books of Ursula Le Guin
Beauties, Beasts and Enchantment: Classic French Fairy Tales
German Popular Stories by the Brothers Grimm
Philip Pullman and *His Dark Materials*
Sexing Hardy: Thomas Hardy and Feminism
Thomas Hardy's *Tess of the d'Urbervilles*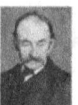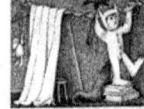
Thomas Hardy's *Jude the Obscure*
Thomas Hardy: The Tragic Novels
Love and Tragedy: Thomas Hardy
The Poetry of Landscape in Hardy
Wessex Revisited: Thomas Hardy and John Cowper Powys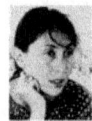
Wolfgang Iser: Essays and Interviews
Petrarch, Dante and the Troubadours
Maurice Sendak and the Art of Children's Book Illustration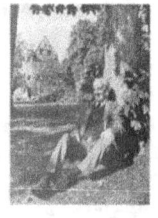
Andrea Dworkin
Cixous, Irigaray, Kristeva: The *Jouissance* of French Feminism
Julia Kristeva: Art, Love, Melancholy, Philosophy, Semiotics and Psychoanalysis
Hélène Cixous I Love You: The *Jouissance* of Writing
Luce Irigaray: Lips, Kissing, and the Politics of Sexual Difference
Peter Redgrove: Here Comes the Flood
Peter Redgrove: Sex-Magic-Poetry-Cornwall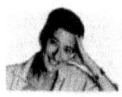
Lawrence Durrell: Between Love and Death, East and West
Love, Culture & Poetry: Lawrence Durrell
Cavafy: Anatomy of a Soul
German Romantic Poetry: Goethe, Novalis, Heine, Hölderlin
Feminism and Shakespeare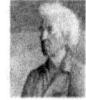
Shakespeare: Love, Poetry & Magic
The Passion of D.H. Lawrence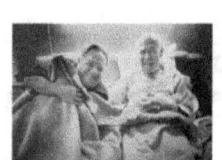
D.H. Lawrence: Symbolic Landscapes
D.H. Lawrence: Infinite Sensual Violence
Rimbaud: Arthur Rimbaud and the Magic of Poetry
The Ecstasies of John Cowper Powys
Sensualism and Mythology: The Wessex Novels of John Cowper Powys
Amorous Life: John Cowper Powys and the Manifestation of Affectivity  (H.W. Fawkner)
Postmodern Powys: New Essays on John Cowper Powys (Joe Boulter)
Rethinking Powys: Critical Essays on John Cowper Powys
Paul Bowles & Bernardo Bertolucci
Rainer Maria Rilke
Joseph Conrad: *Heart of Darkness*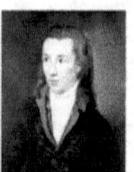
In the Dim Void: Samuel Beckett
Samuel Beckett Goes into the Silence
André Gide: Fiction and Fervour
Jackie Collins and the Blockbuster Novel
Blinded By Her Light: The Love-Poetry of Robert Graves
The Passion of Colours: Travels In Mediterranean Lands
Poetic Forms

POETRY

Ursula Le Guin: Walking In Cornwall
Peter Redgrove: Here Comes The Flood
Peter Redgrove: Sex-Magic-Poetry-Cornwall
Dante: Selections From the Vita Nuova
Petrarch, Dante and the Troubadours
William Shakespeare: Sonnets
William Shakespeare: Complete Poems
Blinded By Her Light: The Love-Poetry of Robert Graves
Emily Dickinson: Selected Poems
Emily Brontë: Poems
Thomas Hardy: Selected Poems
Percy Bysshe Shelley: Poems
John Keats: Selected Poems
Joh n Keats: Poems of 1820
D.H. Lawrence: Selected Poems
Edmund Spenser: Poems
Edmund Spenser: Amoretti
John Donne: Poems
Henry Vaughan: Poems
Sir Thomas Wyatt: Poems
Robert Herrick: Selected Poems
Rilke: Space, Essence and Angels in the Poetry of Rainer Maria Rilke
Rainer Maria Rilke: Selected Poems
Friedrich Hölderlin: Selected Poems
Arseny Tarkovsky: Selected Poems
Arthur Rimbaud: Selected Poems
Arthur Rimbaud: A Season in Hell
Arthur Rimbaud and the Magic of Poetry
Novalis: Hymns To the Night
German Romantic Poetry
Paul Verlaine: Selected Poems
Elizaethan Sonnet Cycles
D.J. Enright: By-Blows
Jeremy Reed: Brigitte's Blue Heart
Jeremy Reed: Claudia Schiffer's Red Shoes
Gorgeous Little Orpheus
Radiance: New Poems
Crescent Moon Book of Nature Poetry
Crescent Moon Book of Love Poetry
Crescent Moon Book of Mystical Poetry
Crescent Moon Book of Elizabethan Love Poetry
Crescent Moon Book of Metaphysical Poetry
Crescent Moon Book of Romantic Poetry
Pagan America: New American Poetry

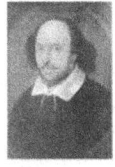
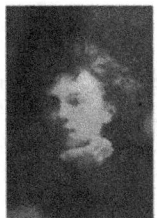
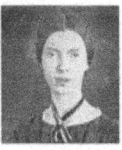
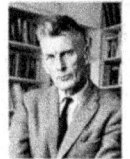
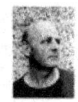
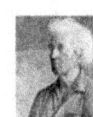
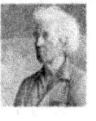
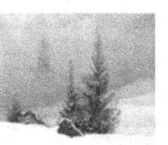
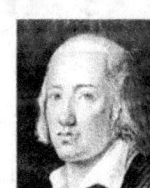
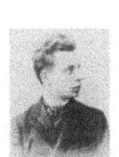
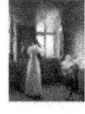
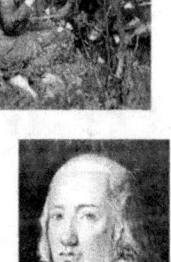

## MEDIA, CINEMA, FEMINISM and CULTURAL STUDIES

J.R.R. Tolkien: The Books, The Films, The Whole Cultural Phenomenon
J.R.R. Tolkien: Pocket Guide
The *Lord of the Rings* Movies: Pocket Guide
The Cinema of Hayao Miyazaki
Hayao Miyazaki: *Princess Mononoke*: Pocket Movie Guide
Hayao Miyazaki: *Spirited Away*: Pocket Movie Guide
Tim Burton : Hallowe'en For Hollywood
Ken Russell
Ken Russell: *Tommy*: Pocket Movie Guide
The Ghost Dance: The Origins of Religion
The Peyote Cult

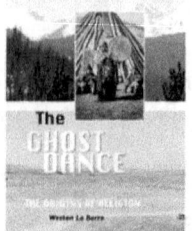
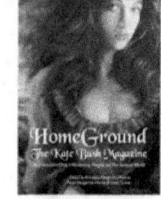

Cixous, Irigaray, Kristeva: The *Jouissance* of French Feminism
Julia Kristeva: Art, Love, Melancholy, Philosophy, Semiotics and Psychoanalysis
Luce Irigaray: Lips, Kissing, and the Politics of Sexual Difference
Hélene Cixous I Love You: The *Jouissance* of Writing
Andrea Dworkin
'Cosmo Woman': The World of Women's Magazines
Women in Pop Music
HomeGround: The Kate Bush Anthology
Discovering the Goddess (Geoffrey Ashe)
The Poetry of Cinema
The Sacred Cinema of Andrei Tarkovsky
Andrei Tarkovsky: Pocket Guide
Andrei Tarkovsky: *Mirror*: Pocket Movie Guide
Andrei Tarkovsky: *The Sacrifice*: Pocket Movie Guide
Walerian Borowczyk: Cinema of Erotic Dreams
Jean-Luc Godard: The Passion of Cinema
Jean-Luc Godard: *Hail Mary*: Pocket Movie Guide
Jean-Luc Godard: *Contempt*: Pocket Movie Guide
Jean-Luc Godard: *Pierrot le Fou*: Pocket Movie Guide
John Hughes and Eighties Cinema
*Ferris Bueller's Day Off*: Pocket Movie Guide
Jean-Luc Godard: Pocket Guide
The Cinema of Richard Linklater
Liv Tyler: Star In Ascendance
*Blade Runner* and the Films of Philip K. Dick
Paul Bowles and Bernardo Bertolucci
Media Hell: Radio, TV and the Press
An Open Letter to the BBC
Detonation Britain: Nuclear War in the UK
Feminism and Shakespeare
Wild Zones: Pornography, Art and Feminism
Sex in Art: Pornography and Pleasure in Painting and Sculpture
Sexing Hardy: Thomas Hardy and Feminism

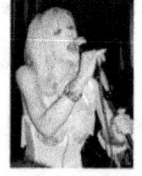
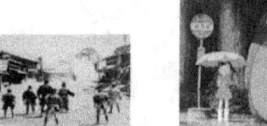
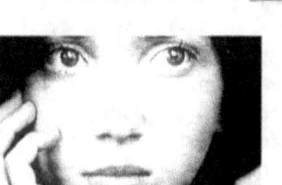

*The Light Eternal* is a model monograph, an exemplary job. The subject matter of the book is beautifully organised and dead on beam. (Lawrence Durrell)
It is amazing for me to see my work treated with such passion and respect. (Andrea Dworkin)

CRESCENT MOON PUBLISHING
P.O. Box 1312, Maidstone, Kent, ME14 5XU, Great Britain. www.crmoon.com

cresmopub@yahoo.co.uk   www.crescentmoon.org.uk

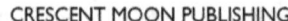